10/19

D1218441

The Mariel Boatlift

THE MARIEL BOATLIFT

A Cuban-American Journey

VICTOR ANDRES TRIAY

University of Florida Press

Gainesville

This book may be available in an electronic edition.

24 23 22 21 20 19   6 5 4 3 2 1

Library of Congress Control Number: 2019931103
ISBN 978-1-68340-092-9

University of Florida Press
2046 NE Waldo Road
Suite 2100
Gainesville, FL 32609
http://upress.ufl.edu

UF PRESS

UNIVERSITY
OF FLORIDA

For my brother, Andy, who has always had the unique ability
to challenge and motivate me at the same time

He commanded and roused a storm wind;
it tossed the waves on high.
They rose up to the heavens, sank to the depths;
their hearts trembled at the danger.
They reeled, staggered like drunkards;
their skill was of no avail.
In their distress they cried to the LORD,
who brought them out of their peril;
He hushed the storm to silence,
the waves of the sea were stilled.
They rejoiced that the sea grew calm,
that God brought them to the harbor they longed for.

Excerpted from Psalm 107: 25–30,
New American Bible, Revised Edition

"Keep, ancient lands, your storied pomp!" cries she
With silent lips. "Give me your tired, your poor,
Your huddled masses yearning to breathe free,
The wretched refuse of your teeming shore.
Send these, the homeless, tempest-tost to me,
I lift my lamp beside the golden door!"

From *The New Colossus*, by Emma Lazarus,
found on plaque at the Statue of Liberty

Contents

Preface

BEFORE STARTING COLLEGE, I can't remember ever having had a friend my own age who was actually raised in Cuba; this despite having been born in Miami, Florida, and raised among a large number of fellow Cuban Americans. For those in my social circle, most of us born in the mid-1960s to parents who had fled Cuba as young adults during the "First Wave" of the Castro-era exodus (1959–1962), the island nation was, in our minds, a mythical place from a remote family past, the place whence our families' culture had originated, the place where many of our parents had grown up together, the former homeland where a seemingly idyllic existence had suddenly been snuffed out by the cruel vagaries of history a half-decade or so before our birth. The adults of our world, in our eyes at least, were survivors who had somehow managed to escape a great cataclysm that had obliterated the land of their birth—and that clearly would have been the land of *our* birth were it not for said cataclysm. Memories of their once-cherished lives in what they considered nothing short of paradise hung over the community as a cloud of nostalgia, alongside traumatic memories of loss, family separation, and foreign exile. The visibility of these communal scars increased in proportion to a person's age. Those of us born in the United States to First Wave families, having quickly "Americanized" and having had a dramatically different life experience than that of our elders, could only live those memories in our imaginations.

I have no recollection—nor, would I assume, do most people my age born in the United States to First Wave families—of the "Second Wave" of Castro-era migration that lasted from late 1965 (more or less around the time many of us were born) until the early 1970s. This exodus occurred during our early childhood, before we ever pondered the world around us or our place in it. Besides the fact that it was a highly structured, relatively quiet, and gradual migration, we were all far too young to have known the meaning of terms such as "Camarioca" or "Freedom Flights." Moreover, anyone my age who came from Cuba during that time did so as an infant or very young child with little to no memory of the island and would have blended in imperceptibly with the rest of us.[1] By the time we reached any level of cultural or historical self-awareness in the early-to-mid-1970s, the Cuban government had welded shut the door on people seeking to leave the island, and the immigration of Cubans to the United States declined precipitously. The rest of our childhoods paralleled those years of minimal-to-near-zero immigration from Cuba.

Entering adolescence, therefore, those in my age group had never genuinely witnessed or been impacted by a sudden mass arrival of Cubans from the island; and perhaps only few of us, myself and my closest friends not included, might have had peers who had spent any of their formative years there. By the late 1970s, in fact, a sense of permanence had grown around the notion that there were two Cubas, one on either side of the Florida Straits, separated by a permanent and impenetrable aquatic wall. Due to the political situation at the time, visits between relatives on opposite sides of the divide were practically unimaginable, and communication between them remained minimal. For most of my peers and me, Cuba—and the Cubans there—may as well not have existed at all, even though in terms of geographic distance, those of us in Miami were closer to Havana than to our own state capital in Tallahassee.

All that changed in 1980, the year I turned fourteen.

During the 1979–1980 academic year I was in the eighth grade and, for that year only, attended a Catholic boys' school then located at the far eastern end of Little Havana, at the doorstep of downtown Miami. A group of us from what were then the western suburbs of Dade (presently Miami-Dade) County, went to and from the school on a public bus along a route that cut straight through the heart of Little Havana. When the Peruvian Embassy crisis (the precursor to the Mariel Boatlift) broke out in April 1980, the Cuban exile community came alive as it had at no other time in my memory. The excitement, especially in Little Havana, was palpable to everyone. Through the bus window I witnessed the hunger strikes, the endless sea of Cuban flags, and the throngs of people participating in passionate patriotic demonstrations near the corner of Southwest Twenty-Seventh Avenue and Southwest Eighth Street; elsewhere, I heard talk about military units being formed for the upcoming war of liberation in Cuba. To an American-born eighth grader with scant knowledge of Cuban affairs, it was all a surreal carnival. Yet, as a Cuban American, as a child from a First Wave family, I knew that I was somehow connected to the extraordinary scene—only I didn't exactly understand how.

Not long after all the excitement began, my mother and I noticed a number of people preparing boats in their driveways and in front of their homes as we drove through a neighborhood just northeast of where we lived. I asked her what they were up to. "They're going to Cuba," she responded in Spanish—almost as if I should have known. Although I have no memory of any further commentary from her, I do recall discerning a certain, undefinable emotion in her tone and feeling as though she had left some things unsaid. At any rate, it seemed incredible to me that Cuba, the mystical land of our parents and grandparents, the Planet Krypton of my imagination that had been obliterated by history sometime around 1960, was still there, still populated, and close enough to reach in the small boats people kept in their yards.

Over the course of the next several months, more than 125,000 Cubans poured into Florida through the Mariel Boatlift. The new refugees, christened *Marielitos* by established exiles (a term soon picked up by non-Cubans), quickly became a permanent fixture in the Miami area. Their numbers were staggering: in May 1980 alone, more Cuban refugees came to the United States via the port of Mariel than in all of 1962, previously the record *year* for Cuban immigration.[2] Yet, except for a few older Mariel refugees I met on a summer job, I really don't remember interacting in any meaningful way with Mariel immigrants my own age during my high school years, which coincided with their first few years in this country. Besides not having had any relatives who came via Mariel (all my relatives who left Cuba had done so by 1961), my peers and I were somewhat secluded in the world of the area's private Catholic high schools.

While attending Miami-Dade Community College (today's Miami-Dade College) after graduating high school in 1984, I finally met and interacted with Cubans my age who'd come over on the Mariel exodus, as well as some who had emigrated after the event. People *my age* who'd been part of a Cuban refugee wave; people *my age* who'd actually lived most of their lives in Cuba; people *my age* who, like those in my parents' and grandparents' generation, could tell harrowing "escape from Cuba" stories. Perhaps most surprising of all, I found myself speaking to them mostly in Spanish, a language I had theretofore reserved exclusively for conversations with members of the older generations.

By 1988, the year I received my bachelor's degree in history from the University of Florida in Gainesville, I had developed an interest in Cuban topics. A few weeks before my summer graduation, I met Emilia, a fellow University of Florida student and the cousin of a Cuban American peer from Miami. In my first extended conversation with her, during a weekend getaway that a group of us took to Crescent Beach near St. Augustine, she revealed to me that she had been born in Cuba and had come to the United States as part of the Mariel exodus. Intrigued, I pestered her for what seemed several hours with detailed questions about her experience. Surprised that I would even be interested in her odyssey, she patiently obliged.[3] Emilia would later express to me that she had been reluctant to tell me that she'd come on the Boatlift—that she was a *Marielita*—as negative stereotypes about Mariel refugees were still prevalent at the time, and she had been stung more than once by people's prejudice after revealing this fact about herself. Almost exactly three years from the day I met her, Emilia and I were married.

The mark left by the Mariel Boatlift went well beyond the one it left on an impressionable Cuban American youth. The event impacted public life in ways no one could have imagined at the outset of the crisis. Immigration policy, the local education establishment, law enforcement, social services, and Cuban exile politics as well as local and state governments were deeply affected by the event. The crisis came to involve a full range of federal entities, including the U.S. Coast Guard, the U.S. Navy, the U.S. National Guard, the U.S. Marine Corps, the Federal Emergency Management Agency, the Department of State, the

Immigration and Naturalization Service, and many more. The exodus from Mariel even influenced that year's presidential contest, in which incumbent Jimmy Carter lost his bid for reelection to Republican candidate Ronald Reagan—a change in administration that would have a profound global impact, especially with regard to the Cold War.

The Mariel Boatlift was also one of several forces propelling the dramatic changes that the Miami area underwent between the late 1970s and mid-1980s. What had been a medium-sized city that was associated mostly with tourism and scarcely received national attention would emerge as a chic, fashionable, vibrant, cosmopolitan, and infinitely complex metropolis recognized by people the world over. The Boatlift also roughly coincided with the emergence of a new generation of Cuban exile leaders who had been young adults at the time of their arrival during the First Wave and who, by middle age, had achieved great personal success and high status in the community. This generation took the cause for a democratic Cuba to unprecedented levels of international prestige and revived activism across a broad spectrum of Cuban exiles. Bolstering their efforts were the testimonies of long-held Cuban political prisoners who had been released during the late 1970s and early 1980s. The published prison memoir of Armando Valladares, *Against All Hope: A Memoir of Life in Castro's Gulag*, created an international sensation. In the late 1980s Valladares was appointed by President Reagan as U.S. ambassador to the United Nations Commission on Human Rights. His book, in English translation, was widely read by the American-born children of Cuban exiles, leaving an indelible mark on them and inspiring many to take an interest in issues related to their parents' homeland.

These changes were accompanied by no small degree of chaos and change at both the national and international level. Five months prior to the Mariel crisis, Iranian extremists had stormed the United States Embassy in Tehran and taken more than fifty American hostages. Less than two months later the Soviet Union invaded Afghanistan. Just as the first boats were arriving in Key West, Florida, from the port of Mariel, President Carter's attempt to rescue the American hostages in Tehran was ending in disaster, marking a low point in U.S. morale. Across the globe in Communist Poland, meanwhile, dissidents were on the verge of launching the Solidarity movement, an effort inspired and aided by the recently elected John Paul II, the Roman Catholic pontiff whose anti-Communist campaign would help bring about the collapse of Marxist regimes across Eastern Europe.

Indeed, without knowing it, Miami and the world were on the threshold of transition in 1980. The hungry, bruised, desperate refugees who stepped off the boats in Key West could not have imagined that their odyssey would be part of that change.

The present work is an oral history of the Mariel Boatlift. Its objective is to tell the stories of Mariel refugees through personal testimonies, collected via recorded interviews, to a general reading audience. It is meant to highlight primarily the stories of those Mariel immigrants who came on the Boatlift to join family in the United States. The selection of interviewees, for the most part, reflects this objective. The work is not meant to provide a literal portrayal or a proportional sampling of the entire Mariel refugee population as broken down by select sociological categories such as race, age, gender, social class, profession, political ideology, sexual orientation, or any other.

It is my sincere hope that a work centered mostly on Mariel refugees who came to join their relatives will make a lasting contribution to the history of the Boatlift—particularly since this group made up, by a large margin, the most numerous segment of the Mariel population.[4] Unfortunately, the mass media's focus on the small percentage of refugees associated with criminal behavior and other social problems helped fuel the grossly inaccurate—yet widely held—notion that the Cubans who arrived in the 1980 exodus were principally drawn from among Cuba's violent felons, dangerous mental patients, delinquents, and other types of so-called "undesirables."[5] In truth, the vast majority of Mariel refugees, whether they left Cuba for family reunification or not, were none of these things. Indeed, all but a small percentage became American citizens, achieved stability, blended into the local culture, became productive members of their communities, and never committed a serious crime. The present work, in addition to relating the fascinating stories of a group of individuals, is intended to give a voice to this historically underemphasized majority of Mariel refugees. That so many of my interviewees did well in the United States should surprise no one, since there was an obvious correlation between having been taken in by family or friends and an ultimately successful adaptation.

The various phases of the exodus are divided into chapters, each beginning with a brief historical narrative succinctly outlining that stage of the event, followed by relevant excerpts from the testimonies. The historical narratives found in the chapter openings, which are based mostly on the wealth of existing secondary sources, are not, by any means, meant to stand collectively as a comprehensive academic study of the Mariel Boatlift. Rather, they are there simply to supply a minimal degree of context and provide some historical guideposts for readers who might be learning about the Boatlift for the first time. Anyone seeking detailed, exhaustive works on the Boatlift that address the multiple aspects of the event can find some listed in the bibliography. Regarding the secondary sources consulted for the present work, I am especially indebted to Mirta Ojito, Alex Larzelere, David Engstrom, Gaston Fernández, Juan M. Clark, José I. Lasaga, and Rose S. Reque, whose highly informative works I consulted most frequently.

Most of the interviewees came to me via personal references provided by my Cuban American network, and a few others could be said to have come through what some social scientists term "snowball sampling," where one interviewee led me to another. I learned of one interviewee in a local newspaper article. Most of the public figures and activists featured were already well known in the community for their efforts during the Boatlift and others were known to me personally.

My search for Mariel interviewees produced only one Afro-Cuban, despite my reaching out to various contacts in a good faith effort to secure more. The narrow window of time I had to conduct the interviews (community college professors are not given semesters off for research), along with limited resources, made a more extensive search impossible.[6] In any event, the single Afro-Cuban voice in the work is not meant to stand in for the experience of the large number of nonwhite Cubans who fled during the Boatlift (estimated to have been between 20 and 40 percent).[7] Nevertheless, this individual's testimony is perhaps the book's most moving and powerful. I had heard bits of his story from an acquaintance, who eventually introduced me to him on a steamy summer morning in Miami outside a large homeless shelter run by the Missionaries of Charity of Mother Teresa. The interviewee and I agreed to meet at the shelter again that afternoon for the interview. For reasons unknown to me, the interviewee did not appear as scheduled. For the next week and a half or so, I waited on several early mornings and late afternoons for him to show up again at the facility. He finally did and told me his powerful and tragic story. Rarely does an interview experience alter how a researcher views the world, but witnessing the selfless work of the Missionaries of Charity first-hand over several days and then listening to this particular interviewee's story did just that. His testimony should act as a reminder to readers that, in addition to the types of success stories related in the book, thousands of Mariel refugees, a large number of them Afro-Cubans with no family or sponsors in the United States, experienced great long-term suffering and injustice. There is no doubt that this segment of the Mariel population merits further research in the future.

The recorded interviews were mostly conducted over several weeks during the summers of 2012, 2014, and 2016. Besides former Mariel refugees, testimonies from local political leaders and activists of the era were included, as were two from Cuban exiles who braved the Florida Straits to retrieve loved ones in Cuba. The interviews were all set in relatively relaxed environments—ranging from private offices and homes to restaurants—and conducted in a conversational format. Only the interviewees' words from these conversations appear in the work, not those of the author/interviewer. It is important to note that in no case do the interviews appear in their entirety; rather, only segments were used and placed in the appropriate chapters.

Although many of the interviews were conducted in English, the majority were done in Spanish and translated into English. Since language used in conversation differs substantially from written language, the words of the interviewees, as they appear in the work, have been edited and rearranged in the interest of flow, structure, sequencing, pacing, and ease of reading. In short, none of the testimonies appearing in the work—whether the interviews were conducted in English or Spanish—are verbatim transcriptions. In numerous cases sentences were rephrased, fused with others, or condensed. False starts were excluded, self-corrections were incorporated, threads of stories separated by tangential or other material were joined together and reconciled, verbal gestures were given written expression, and incomplete sentences were finished. First, second, and third person references and pronouns were corrected or modified when needed, occasional words were added to smooth transitions, superfluous and distracting details were eliminated along with redundancies and unintelligible words, and references to other individuals were sometimes struck (to protect privacy). In the case of interviews conducted in Spanish, the peculiarities and nuances of language rendered certain words, phrases, and expressions untranslatable. In such cases, every effort was made to interpret the true intention and feeling of the interviewee. Colloquialisms and idioms, so often used in conversation by people of a similar language, culture, or subculture, were rewritten when necessary.

Whenever any of these actions were taken, the commitment to retain the true meaning, feeling, and intention of the interviewee remained absolute. All the interviewees (except two, whose later whereabouts were unknown) were given the opportunity to review the parts of their interviews that were used in the book and to offer whatever corrections they found necessary.

The methodology I employed was my own, developed independently for my 2001 book *Bay of Pigs: An Oral History of Brigade 2506*. Although I consulted a few academic oral history guidelines and looked to other oral history books as models, I did not follow any specific practice set forth by any particular academic institution or other group. My independent methodology worked well for the Bay of Pigs book, which was the recipient of the Florida Historical Society's Samuel Proctor Oral History Prize in 2001.

Introduction

ON JANUARY 1, 1959, the Cuban people ushered in the new year with unprecedented celebration. Fulgencio Batista, the nation's dictator who had taken power via a military coup in 1952, had fled the country during the pre-dawn hours, his government toppled by a revolutionary movement composed of an array of pro-democracy organizations. By the end of the struggle, the largest and most important of these organizations was the 26th of July Movement, headed by former student activist and lawyer Fidel Castro. The 26th of July had battled Batista from guerrilla bases in the Sierra Maestra Mountains of eastern Cuba as well as through organized political cells in the cities that, along with the other opposition groups, employed tactics ranging from public protests to unrelenting sabotage. Throughout the conflict the 26th of July had expertly courted the international press, thereby winning admirers and supporters from around the world who became both intrigued and enthralled by the Caribbean island nation's romantic, bearded mountain rebels. Other anti-Batista groups that had played a pivotal role in overthrowing the dictator, less interesting visually, were largely ignored by the international press. When Castro's victory column entered Havana a week after Batista's flight, the young leader—riding atop a tank as though in a modern-day Roman triumph—was exalted as a conquering hero by the domestic and international news media and was cheered wildly by countless thousands packing the capital's streets, balconies, and rooftops. Cubans of all classes were eager for the Revolution to fulfill its promises of peace, prosperity, honest government, and, above all, a return to the democratic Constitution of 1940.

The nation Castro took over was among the most developed in Latin America. Its modern infrastructure was among the best in the region and its middle class the largest.[1] Cuba had also ranked highly in virtually every standard of living indicator, from nutrition, literacy, and health care to automobile ownership, telephone ownership, television ownership, and daily newspaper circulation.[2] The island's greatest deficiency, which everyone believed the democratic Revolution would ameliorate, was its often dysfunctional political life. Despite some previous success with democracy, a more recent history of political "gangsterism," public corruption, and military dictatorship had frustrated many Cubans to the point of political apathy and soured many well-meaning citizens on civic participation.[3] Solving the political problems, it was hoped, would also allow the nation to address its other major challenge: the obvious disparity that existed in living standards between the cities and the countryside. Thus, longing for real democracy, the rule of law, honest government, and solutions to lingering social problems, the Cuban people looked hopefully to the Revolution and its larger-than-life leader.

Disappointment was not long in coming for pro-democracy Cubans. Although Castro filled his first government with well-known, anti-Batista liberals who possessed strong democratic credentials, real power lay with him and his inner circle. Among the Revolution's first moves was to abolish all political parties; the promised free elections, meanwhile, were postponed and then never held. In addition, Revolutionary tribunals were empowered soon after the takeover to convict alleged "war criminals" through show trials carried out with little or no regard for legal procedure and often before fiery crowds demanding "*¡Paredón!*" (the execution wall).[4] The large number of highly publicized firing squad executions (as well as executions that were not quite as heavily publicized) shocked the democratic sensibilities of many in Cuba and brought condemnation from around the Americas. Then, within months, the first signs of Communist infiltration surfaced with the arrival of individuals delivering Marxist instruction within the ranks of the Rebel Army. Soon, to the consternation of many, members of Cuba's Communist Party, which had played virtually no role in Batista's overthrow, began assuming important government positions.

Within months many of the liberals in the government, including the appointed president, Manuel Urrutia, had either broken with Castro or been purged by him. Although Castro would repeatedly deny during this period that he or his Revolution was Communist, it began to become obvious that the liberals had been used merely as a facade to give the leader time to consolidate his authority behind the scenes and to lay the groundwork for ushering Marxist rule into Cuba. By 1960 many of his former democratic allies, including commanders and veterans from the war against Batista, had launched a number of movements to "save" the democratic Revolution from becoming a Communist dictatorship under the young leader.

Any lingering questions as to the Revolution's ideological direction were answered in February 1960, with the arrival of a Soviet scientific exhibition in Havana and a visit from Soviet first deputy premier Anastas Mikoyan. Following the visit Cuba and the Soviet Union established diplomatic relations and forged close economic ties. In the months that followed the Castro regime abolished the free press (much of which had originally been openly supportive of his revolution), confiscated large sectors of the private economy, shut down or took over the island's independent professional organizations, ended the historic autonomy of the University of Havana, crushed the independence of labor organizations, harassed the Catholic Church and its adherents, and brutally suppressed all rival political movements. The regime's diatribes against the United States, as well as its favorable pronouncements regarding Communism, increased in frequency.

As the Revolution's turn to Communist dictatorship unfolded, the democratic opposition to Castro grew. The various and often divided pro-democracy groups began battling Castro's forces in the cities, towns, and countryside across Cuba. The regime, meanwhile, expanded its political police and, in September 1960, created the Committees for the Defense of the Revolution (CDRs), a national block-by-block, building-by-building citizens' vigilance organization designed to root out counterrevolutionary activity at the neighborhood level. A citizens' militia was also created to defend the Revolution against its enemies. Castro's pro-democracy opponents were soon packing the political prisons and increasingly becoming victims of the regime's firing squads.

In January 1961 Cuba and the United States broke off diplomatic relations. The prospect of having a Soviet ally in its backyard was, of course, unacceptable to the Americans. Several months prior to the official break, the U.S. government had started granting political and military support, as well as providing military training, to pro-democracy Cubans battling the regime. Their collaboration culminated in the Bay of Pigs invasion of April 1961, which failed to oust Castro due to the sweeping, last-minute, and politically motivated changes to the military strategy imposed by the Kennedy White House. The invasion's failure allowed Castro to eliminate his remaining opposition and fully consolidate his power. Later that year he formally declared himself a Marxist-Leninist.

Cuban Refugee Waves Prior to 1980

Some scholars divide Castro-era immigration to the United States into distinct "waves." The First Wave brought more than 215,000 Cubans to the United States, mostly on commercial flights, between Batista's 1959 ouster and the Cuban Missile Crisis of October 1962, when commercial flights between the two nations were banned.[5] The largest number of Cuban exiles settled in Miami, Florida, the closest sizable American city to Cuba.

At the very beginning of this period, only a small number of Cubans—made up mostly of Batista associates who feared retribution—felt the need to flee the country.[6] Indeed, in early 1959 few Cubans had reason to fear what was ostensibly a democratic revolution. When it became clear later that year and throughout 1960 that Castro was guiding Cuba toward Communist dictatorship, the number of Cubans choosing United States exile increased exponentially. It would swell after the failure of the 1961 Bay of Pigs invasion. A disproportionate number (although by no means all) of the emigres at this stage were members of Cuba's middle, professional, and upper classes, a large percentage of whom had supported the removal of Batista from power. Because of their educational backgrounds, business skills, and subsequent success in the United States, some have referred to the refugees of the First Wave as the "Golden Exiles."[7]

Before the January 1961 break in diplomatic relations, Cubans seeking to depart for the United States could secure visas with relative ease from U.S. diplomatic facilities on the island. In his *Presidential Decision Making Adrift: The Carter Administration and the Mariel Boatlift*, researcher David W. Engstrom stated that increasingly lenient standards in granting visas "created the impression that the United States had developed a policy of unrestricted immigration from Cuba."[8] Following the January 1961 diplomatic rupture, with Cubans unable to secure exit documents via conventional means, the United States began issuing "visa waivers" for those seeking exile. Around 400,000 waivers had been issued by 1962.[9] Given that these people were fleeing an emerging Communist regime—and because of Cuba's political, geographical, and historical significance to the United States—Cubans could ask for, and usually receive, political asylum upon arrival. Cubans who arrived in the United States during this period were eventually permitted to apply for "indefinite voluntary departure," or parole, which allowed them to remain in the country indefinitely.[10]

During the First Wave, more than 14,000 unaccompanied Cuban minors arrived via a semi-secret program dubbed "Operation Pedro Pan." The effort, which occurred between December 1960 and October 1962, was designed primarily to give desperate parents who could not leave the island a means by which to get their children out of the reach of the emerging Communism in Cuba. It was approved by the U.S. government and coordinated mostly by the anti-Castro underground and the Roman Catholic Church. Those unaccompanied minors with no relatives in the United States to care for them upon arrival (around half), entered the Cuban Children's Program, an effort funded by the U.S. federal government and managed mostly by the Catholic Welfare Bureau of the Diocese of Miami and its director, Father Bryan Walsh. Most of the children would be reunited with their parents (some after several years) in the United States.[11]

In the months preceding the April 1961 Bay of Pigs invasion, the belief that "exile" would be temporary was prevalent among the arriving First Wave emigres. Most believed that the United States simply would not allow a Communist country to exist directly in its hemispheric backyard.[12] Following the failure of the invasion, however, it became evident that the exiles' stay would possibly be a prolonged one. This sense of long-term exile was compounded a year and a half later by the Cuban Missile Crisis of October 1962, the resolution of which included a promise by the United States to the Soviet Union not to intervene in Cuba militarily. For pro-democracy Cubans in exile and on the island, whose primary ally in the battle for a democratic Cuba was the United States, this was a devastating blow and seemed to indicate that Castro might secure his power permanently.[13]

The exiles of the First Wave initially experienced grave economic hardship in the United States, as the Cuban government allowed them to take only a small amount of money and a few changes of clothes with them—everything else had to be turned over to the Cuban state. What they possessed, however, was what Cuban American scholar Miguel González-Pando referred to in *The Cuban Americans* as "human capital." Said González-Pando of the First Wave: "Their educational and professional backgrounds, in fact, placed them near the top echelons of society—in Cuba and in America as well. This wave constituted the island's 'cream of the crop'—those who had studied English at Havana's private schools or had learned it at American summer camps, high schools, and colleges." He also stated that "because Cuban culture was highly Americanized, the members of this particular vintage were not complete strangers to America's way of life: To them, the United States was not terra incognita."[14] The comprehensive Cuban Refugee Program helped the exiles through a wide array of initiatives, ranging from material assistance to health care. Although the greatest percentage of exiles remained in Miami, a large number were induced to settle elsewhere in the United States.

When regular commercial flights between the United States and Cuba were cancelled at the start of the October 1962 Missile Crisis, the First Wave ended. The number of Cubans arriving in the United States thereupon declined, as those who desired to leave the island were, for the most part, left with the options of either escaping by boat across the Florida Straits (a method filled with danger) or receiving a visa from a third country and then applying for a U.S. visa from there (an alternative not within the reach of most Cubans). Consequently, over the next few years, an average of fewer than 10,000 Cubans arrived per year in the United States.[15] Among the arrivals during this period were the members of Brigade 2506, the exile army that had invaded Cuba at the Bay of Pigs in April 1961 and who had been imprisoned in Cuba since after the invasion, as well as members of their families.

The "Second Wave" of Castro-era migration was composed of two events: the Camarioca Boatlift and the Freedom Flights. By the mid-1960s tension in Cuba was on the rise. The Revolution's economic reforms of the early 1960s had largely failed; along with a decrease in agricultural production, the people of the island were reduced to government-imposed rations.[16] Also, the sudden cancellation of commercial flights in October 1962 had left numerous families separated and longing for reunification.[17] Because of these factors, along with others (including increasing government repression), the Cuban government was facing growing internal pressure and looked to emigration as a way to relieve it.

On September 28, 1965, Fidel Castro announced that he would permit Cubans to leave the island beginning on October 10, via the port of Camarioca, on Cuba's northern shore. The prospective emigres' relatives in the United States would be allowed to enter the port on private vessels to retrieve them.[18] Military-age males and certain classes of professionals would be prohibited from emigrating. Upon Castro's announcement, a mad scramble for boats ensued in South Florida, while in Cuba hundreds of thousands filled out applications to leave.[19]

Such an announcement by Castro was not expected by the United States government. Because of Florida's proximity to Cuba, it was entirely possible for Cuban exiles independently to cross the Florida Straits, pick up relatives on the island, and transport them back to the United States. The situation put the administration of President Lyndon B. Johnson in a serious predicament. On the one hand, the U.S. government could not allow its immigration policy to be set arbitrarily in a foreign capital. Furthermore, an unregulated, unsanctioned boatlift carried out on potentially unseaworthy vessels brought myriad legal, political, and humanitarian problems. On the other hand, to turn back refugees escaping Communism would be a major embarrassment for the United States and a blow to its international prestige at a critical time in the Cold War.

In a bold move, the Johnson Administration immediately began formulating plans to replace the proposed boatlift with an orderly, U.S. government–approved airlift of Cubans who wanted to emigrate to the United States.[20] As negotiations with the Cuban government began (through the Swiss Embassy in Havana), the October 10 date Castro had set for the opening of Camarioca drew closer. As it did, Cuban exiles in South Florida continued to procure vessels to sail to Cuba; many did not believe that Castro would agree to Johnson's airlift and wanted to reunify their families while they had the chance. On October 9, a group of boats was prepared to set out for the island.[21]

Over the course of the next few weeks, the exiles retrieved thousands of relatives from Camarioca. U.S. authorities threatened them with fines and arrests. Nevertheless, the Cuban exiles pressed on, the value of reuniting their fractured families far outweighing any penalties the U.S government might impose. In any event, the exiles knew they had little to fear. The government, although issuing "intents to fine" and seizing some larger boats, was nevertheless granting asylum to the Camarioca refugees upon their arrival; in the end, the fines were not collected and the boats were returned.[22] Only when it appeared that an orderly airlift would indeed be permitted were the exiles discouraged from departing for Cuba.[23]

On November 3, just days before the final agreement for an airlift was announced, Castro closed the port of Camarioca. The thousands of Cubans at the port still awaiting transport protested vehemently, and the United States agreed to bring them to Florida on a sealift.[24] In the end Cuban Americans had retrieved nearly five thousand relatives during the Camarioca exodus.[25] Most of the Camarioca refugees were from Cuba's middle class and had relatives already in the United States; however, the boatlift also included a significant number of rural poor and working-class individuals.[26] The orderly airlift agreed upon by the two governments, nicknamed "Freedom Flights" in the United States, was scheduled to begin on December 1.

Castro probably learned some important lessons from the Camarioca experience. First, he saw that he could leverage the emotion of family separation to his advantage; that is, his enemies in Miami would ferry people away from Cuba for him if it meant reunifying with their relatives. Second, he could direct that human flow any way he chose and force the United States to continue its policy of blanket acceptance of Cubans, lest it look hypocritical before the rest of the world. And third, he could use emigration as a safety valve to relieve social pressure in Cuba. These lessons would become valuable to him in 1980.

The orderly migration of Cubans to the United States envisioned by Johnson, the "Freedom Flights," was officially outlined in a "Memorandum of Understanding" agreed upon by the two governments. The accord, brokered through the Swiss Embassy in Cuba, set up an airlift between the Varadero airport (around sixty miles east of Havana) and Miami. It would bring in two flights per day, five days per week, and would transport between 3,000 and 4,000 refugees each month. By the time the Castro regime ended the airlift in the early 1970s, nearly 300,000 new Cubans had arrived in the United States.[27]

Less than a year after the Freedom Flights began, President Johnson signed the Cuban Adjustment Act of 1966. The legislation allowed Cuban refugees in the United States to apply for permanent residency without having to travel to a U.S. Consulate in a third country. Cubans needed only to be admitted to the United States and paroled for two years (later reduced to one year) before being allowed to apply.

After the Freedom Flights ended, Cuban immigration dwindled. Whereas an average of 38,000 Cubans had arrived each year during the airlift, the number plunged to 5,000 per year between 1973 and 1980. Now, as in the years following the First Wave, without a means to leave the country, Cubans fortunate enough to emigrate did so mostly through third countries or by escaping on boats.[28]

With little hope of returning to Cuba, Cuban exiles in different parts of the United States focused on regaining their livelihoods. Although they were initially forced to accept low-paying, low-skilled jobs just to survive, they soon began to prosper. Starting with little or no money, they fell back on their creativity, business acumen, training, ambition, boldness, and connections with companies operating in Latin America.[29] In Miami many began settling and opening businesses in what had become a declining area west of downtown, a neighborhood that would soon emerge as "Little Havana."[30] In the revitalized neighborhood, Cuban businesses and services of every type and variety served fellow exiles and provided employment.[31] The business contacts in Latin America, furthermore, set the stage for Miami later to replace other American cities as the center of commerce and finance with the region.[32] Meanwhile, after initially experiencing several obstacles, numerous professionals had their education credentials validated to practice in their fields in the United States (some doctors and dentists after having operated underground within the Cuban exile community for a period of time). Cubans who had come over while young enough to pursue higher education also soon began filling the area's professional and business ranks and, within a generation, challenged the local non-Cuban establishment.[33] González-Pando classified the years between 1973 and 1980 as the Cuban community's "Economic Miracle Stage."

By the 1970s the Cuban enclave in Miami had burst forth well beyond Little Havana and other areas in or near downtown, and had expanded into Dade County's growing suburban communities as well as into local municipalities such as Hialeah, West Miami, and Coral Gables, bringing with them an array of businesses, professional services, and other institutions. Cuban exiles who had initially settled in other parts of the United States began gravitating to the Miami area, adding to the size of the local community. Many families, especially younger ones, could soon claim middle- and upper middle-class status. A few Cuban American country clubs opened, vaguely modeled (at least in spirit) after the much more grandiose clubs in the old, pre-Castro Cuba. As increasing numbers of exiles became American citizens—after more than a decade of resistance by many, as their hope of returning to a free Cuba was still very much alive—the community also evolved into a nationally significant voting bloc.[34] Its growing political muscle allowed it later to exert great influence on U.S. policy toward Cuba. Cuban Americans would soon be running for office and, in the years after 1980, would eventually dominate the local political scene. In time the community's office holders would include local and state leaders as well as members of the U.S. House of Representatives and U.S. Senate. Two Cuban Americans—one from South Florida and the other from Texas—would seek the Republican nomination for the office of president of the United States in the 2016 election.

Despite the Cuban community's assimilation and relatively rapid socioeconomic advancement, the anti-Castro cause and the hope for a free Cuba (as well as the dream of returning to the island) never died. In the years immediately following the Bay of Pigs invasion, several exiles participated in U.S. government–sponsored covert military operations against Castro. When the United States eventually stopped sponsoring such missions, some exile groups continued the armed struggle by independently launching commando raids and guerrilla infiltrations into Cuba, despite legal action by the U.S. government to stop them. Activism on behalf of the cause, however, had declined overall by the 1970s, as the primary concern of most Cuban American families became achieving economic security and professional and social advancement, rather than working toward a quick return to Cuba. The community was nevertheless supportive of many of those individuals who remained active in the cause, whose focus in the 1970s became increasingly centered on raising awareness of the situation in Cuba and the human rights violations committed by the Castro dictatorship, rather than on armed struggle.

Among the many factors that made militant anti-Castro activism difficult to maintain during this period—besides, of course, the United States' lack of support for the exiles on the one hand and the Soviet Union's full backing of Castro on the other—was the aforementioned low level of communication between Cubans in exile and those on the island. In the years before 1980 the Cuban government had sealed off the island hermetically, to a large degree cutting its people off from the rest of the world. Restrictions on international travel and emigration, along with strict government censorship at every level, reinforced their isolation. Contact with relatives abroad was discouraged and even condemned. Indeed, those in Cuba who had close family among the exiles risked running afoul of the authorities if they communicated with them regularly. In addition, telephone calls between Cuba and the United States, besides being expensive, difficult to place, and of poor quality, were often listened to by agents of State Security (Cuba's version of the KGB), which also opened and read letters from abroad. Travel between the two countries was strictly prohibited. Interaction between the communities and any meaningful exchange of information therefore reached an all-time low. The information-denied Cuban people were nevertheless assured by their government that the *gusanos* ("worms," the term the Cuban regime applied to those who had "abandoned" the Revolution by emigrating) who had left Cuba were suffering unspeakable poverty, discrimination, and social marginalization in the "Yankee Paradise."

Cuba: The Mid-1960s through the Late 1970s

Although it is beyond the scope of the present work to paint a full picture of life in Cuba in the years before 1980 and to provide a detailed discussion of the directions followed by the Castro regime during those years, a broad rendering of some general trends and everyday realities in Revolutionary Cuba follows in order to provide some context for certain aspects of life referred to by the interviewees in subsequent chapters.

By 1961 the Castro regime had fully consolidated its power in Cuba and began adopting all the features of a totalitarian state. On the institutional front, with the help of the Soviet Union, the Revolution's leadership initially attempted to implement a model of political and economic organization and development similar to that of the Soviet Union.[35] Encountering failure, Castro in the mid-1960s set a more radical course by adopting elements of a program that was influenced by Mao's "Great Leap Forward" in China and that had been advanced in Cuba for a few years by Ernesto "Che" Guevara. Among other things, it called for the elimination of material incentives for workers (to be replaced by "moral incentives"), the elimination of money, and "full collectivization of the means of production."[36] It also called for the creation of the "New Man." According to University of Pittsburgh researcher Carmelo Mesa-Lago in *Cuba in the 1970s: Pragmatism and Institutionalization,* the Revolution's New Man was to be "an unselfish, self-sacrificing, frugal, fully-socialized, egalitarian human being."[37] In 1968 radicalization reached its pinnacle under the "Revolutionary Offensive," which Mesa-Lago stated parenthetically was "in some aspects similar to the Chinese Cultural Revolution."[38] That spring the final vestiges of private enterprise on the island were eradicated. The sweep, which involved the confiscation of Cuba's remaining small businesses (including the operations of street peddlers) and ending the activities of skilled workers who had continued to work independently, was carried out within a couple of days.[39] With the exception of some small, quasi-independent farms and some individual vehicle services, the Cuban state became the sole employer and the only provider of goods and services for the people of the island.[40]

The end result of the regime's new initiative was only more failure, exemplified by its high-profile failure to achieve its goal of harvesting 10 million tons of sugar in 1970 as well as the collateral economic damage caused by the single-minded nature of the effort. As a consequence, Cuba was forced into deeper indebtedness to the Soviet Union and became more reliant on assistance from the Communist bloc.[41] Castro was thereupon pressured to "institutionalize" the Communist system in Cuba. Among the numerous changes that occurred in the early 1970s, Castro was, in theory, to give up some of his authority to Cuba's Communist Party.[42] In reality, despite some institutional window-dressing, it seems he gave up little to none and continued to exert complete authority.[43] Other reforms aimed at "institutionalization" included, but were not limited to, adopting a new constitution similar to the Soviet constitution; separating the roles of the army, central administration, and Communist Party; focusing the armed forces on exclusively military matters (i.e., not on production efforts); and folding remaining small private farms into the state.[44]

Throughout these years the Cuban population was kept under control by the authority of a vast institutional structure. Besides the political police apparatus provided by State Security, the previously mentioned Committees for the Defense of the Revolution (CDRs) served as the state's eyes and ears at the neighborhood level, constantly on the lookout for local residents' counterrevolutionary behavior while at home. At workplaces, dossiers kept on employees for evaluating their work performance also measured each worker's "political attitude."[45] Failing to demonstrate enthusiasm for the government and its ideology, refusing to "integrate" into the Revolution by participating in the regime's mass organizations, or ducking unpaid "volunteer" work (often in agricultural fields) could have resulted in harassment, denial of advancement, demotion, or dismissal.

Meanwhile, the education system, besides delivering instruction in academic areas, emphasized Communist formation and indoctrination. Teachers and administrators kept detailed personal dossiers on students measuring their ideological and political development as well as reporting on their participation in the regime's mass organizations. The dossiers, which followed a person into adulthood, also noted the level of their parents' "ideological integration," and whether a child's family practiced a religion—something considered a grave "ideological diversion."[46] Negative notations or deficiencies in any of these areas could have been grounds for limiting a student's academic opportunities or—perhaps even more frightening—earning a student a public shaming at the hands of peers, teachers, and administrators.[47]

Also, beginning around seventh grade, schoolchildren were separated from their families every year and shipped off for a fixed number of days (usually forty-five) to camps in the countryside to complete unpaid agricultural labor. By the 1970s teenagers advancing to a "*preuniversitario*" program (for those seeking to attend university) were often required to attend school full-time away from home at rural facilities, where unpaid agricultural work was part of the daily routine and poor overall living conditions were the norm.[48] Separating the youths from their families served mostly to facilitate a deeper level of political indoctrination. Additionally, only those with an acceptable Revolutionary history (which included a record clean of religious affiliation) could study for certain university careers. In 1971 a Communist Party official declared at the University of Havana that "the right to a university education is a right of revolutionaries only."[49]

Besides actively supporting the Revolution with visible enthusiasm, renouncing all religious beliefs and practices, and expressing only ideas that were officially aligned with those of the regime, it was expected that a good citizen would refrain from demonstrating "deviant" behaviors such as possessing and reading books espousing values that ran counter to those of the state; listening to banned music (at times ranging from José Feliciano to the Beatles); acquiring goods not officially distributed by the government (i.e., engaging in the black market); and being, or even being suspected of being, homosexual. As might be expected, writers and artists were also brought under tight government control. At the Congress of Education and Culture held in April 1971, during the early period of institutionalization, the regime laid down the law on artistic matters. According to Mesa-Lago, the Congress's final declaration "introduced a tougher line on cultural affairs. In the future it would not be enough for writers and artists to proclaim themselves revolutionaries and to abstain from criticizing the regime; they would also have to prove their militancy by producing political works." The declaration itself proclaimed: "Culture like education is not and cannot be apolitical or impartial. Apoliticism is nothing more than a reactionary and shamefaced attitude in the cultural field. Art is a weapon of the Revolution, a weapon against the penetration of the enemy."[50] The declaration went on to condemn foreign writers and artists who had criticized the regime; called for fighting "imperialist cinema, television, and art"; and demanded strict standards in determining which foreign writers and intellectuals would be invited to Cuba—in other words, to deny visits by those who were not in line with the Revolution.[51]

The pressure on the Cuban public to conform to the Revolution's demands was, therefore, substantial. Those brave enough to think and act in a "non-Revolutionary" manner were potentially subject to poor employment prospects, harassment, public shaming, social ostracism, and political prison. In Cuba's brutal political prisons, which held one of the highest per capita political prisoner populations in the world, inducements such as reduced sentences and better treatment were offered to inmates willing to undergo political "rehabilitation"; that is, to renounce one's previous beliefs and to open oneself to being ideologically reeducated in a manner that suited the regime.[52] For young males, the consequences of dissidence were especially punitive. In 1965 the regime created the *Unidades Militares de Ayuda a la Producción* (Military Units to Aid Production, or UMAPs), which used military discipline and forced labor to punish and to correct the behavior of young males (as young as sixteen) who acted in a non-Revolutionary manner or failed to integrate themselves into the Communist system. Those who dressed or wore their hair in an unacceptable manner, had applied to emigrate, were homosexual (a group the government severely repressed and whom it hoped to "reform" in the UMAPs), were deemed to be delinquents, or clung to certain past institutions such as religion, were all candidates for the UMAP camps. Ministers and seminarians were likewise sent, along with a number of writers and artists. In addition to forced labor, torture was reportedly used at the camps against those who refused to comply with the camp authorities' wishes.[53] According to inmates, there were numerous suicides and suicide attempts at these centers. The UMAPs were eventually merged with other youth military work units in the early 1970s as the *Ejercito Juvenil del Trabajo* (Youth Army of Work, or Youth Labor Army).[54]

Being "integrated" ideologically and institutionally, therefore, became not only the official measure of one's value to the Communist society but fundamental to everyday survival. With no outlet for discontent and virtually no chance of emigrating following the Freedom Flights, Cubans across the spectrum had little choice but to adapt and acquiesce to the government's demands. Although there is no doubt that a significant number of Cubans supported Castro and the Revolution during the 1960s and 1970s, the repressive environment created a situation in which a large percentage of the population merely feigned support for the government, a phenomenon called "*doble moral*" on the island. Indeed, being dissatisfied with—or opposed to—the system became a private affair that a person usually shared with no one; at other times it was a deeply held secret expressed only, perhaps, within the confines of a family.

Despite an uninterrupted string of failed economic experiments, radicalism that often bordered on the surreal, and general malaise in Cuba, the regime assured its people that they were building an ideal society. It reminded them of the horrors experienced by the short-sighted bourgeoisie and other enemies of the Revolution who had betrayed the nation by emigrating—even though, in truth, these brethren were prospering in a democratic society just a couple of hundred miles away. The lack of large-scale opposition and the outward passivity of the Cuban people—brought about to a large extent by the Orwellian measures implemented to ensure conformity—may have deluded the regime into believing that virtually the entire population was supportive of it. The events of 1980 would therefore take it completely by surprise.

1

The Road to Mariel

BY THE MID-1970S Castro's relationship with the United States remained confrontational and diplomatic relations between the two nations had not been restored. When Jimmy Carter was elected president of the United States in 1976, however, he brought a fresh approach to dealing with the regime in Havana and hoped to normalize relations. Early on he ended U.S. reconnaissance flights over the island and liberalized travel restrictions.[1] An advocate of human rights, the new president expressed interest in gaining the release of Cuba's political prisoners. Fidel Castro likewise sought a change in the relationship and, among other things, was probably looking for ways to lessen his reliance on—and subservience to—the Soviets.[2] Within months after the election, the two nations reached an accord on fishing rights and, in the summer of 1977, agreed to open "interests sections" in one another's capitals that would operate as quasi embassies. Such moves were supported by the State Department but seen less enthusiastically by the National Security Council (NSC) due to concerns over Cuba's ongoing military interventions in Africa.[3]

To smooth the way toward an ultimate rapprochement, the Castro regime attempted to forge relationships with those members of the Cuban exile community who also sought a change in the status quo. Although the regime had already established ties to highly unrepresentative leftist splinter groups among Cuban Americans, the new links needed to be closer to the exile mainstream in order to blunt (however mildly) the overall community's inevitable opposition to any effort by Washington to normalize relations with Cuba. Thus, in the summer of 1977, Cuban agents reached out to Bernardo Benes, a Cuban American banker in Miami and well-connected Democratic Party activist.[4] Meetings between Benes and Cuban officials were held in foreign cities and, starting in February 1978, Benes and Castro began face-to-face talks centered on, among other topics, the release of political prisoners and the possibility of exiles returning to Cuba to visit relatives. Castro then suggested a public "dialogue" with exiles of the same mindset as Benes and announced in September 1978 that one would soon take place. Benes engaged in his quiet diplomacy with the approval of U.S. officials, whom he kept fully informed of his activities. As before, the State Department was supportive, while the NSC remained more resistant.[5]

Meanwhile, the Castro government and the Carter Administration had begun holding secret talks in May 1978. Cuba was open to allowing some current and former political prisoners leave the island but, much to the chagrin of the NSC, not to withdrawing its troops from Africa. Although agreement was reached on a prisoner release, the subsequent processing of the prisoners by U.S. authorities in Cuba was far slower than anticipated due to the burdensome process imposed by a resistant Justice Department.[6] In October Benes and six other Cuban Americans met with Castro in Havana. They returned with forty-six political prisoners.[7] The Justice Department, under pressure, eventually agreed to expedite the prisoner release process.[8]

In November and December Benes traveled to Havana with the "Committee of 75," the group of Cuba-approved exiles who would engage in Castro's "dialogue." The dictator agreed to release 3,600 political prisoners at the rate of four hundred per month, and allow them to emigrate, as well as to permit exiles to visit their relatives on the island. The prisoner release, however, apparently unbeknownst to the Committee and the public, had already been agreed to in the secret talks between the Cuban and United States governments.[9] The Cuban exile community, although pleased by the release of political prisoners, remained mostly opposed to dialogue with Castro, believing that such talks would implicitly legitimize the regime and thereby strengthen it. The dialogue's participants were denounced by many in the community as *dialogueros* and tools of Cuba's intelligence services. Visiting the island also divided people in the community, since this was likewise seen as legitimizing the regime as well as enriching it financially.

By early 1979 Castro had reason to feel optimistic. His interventions in Africa had been generally successful, and he had been appointed chairman of the Non-Aligned Movement, a prestigious post for him. Moreover, he had made two regional allies: Nicaragua, which was now under Sandinista rule, and Grenada, under Maurice Bishop.[10] Having recruited a handful of people from the exile community to engage in a dialogue, he had seemingly created division among his principal enemy abroad; not only could this be construed as a political coup, but it would result in a windfall of cash provided by exiles returning to visit their relatives. No one could have predicted how Castro's fortunes would change before the year was out.

The exile visits set the stage for what became one of the most destabilizing moments in Cuba since the early 1960s. Whereas some exiles had managed to visit the island in 1978, the Cuban government, wishing to maximize the cash flowing into the island, permitted more than 100,000 emigres to visit their families in 1979. It even opened special "dollar stores" where the visitors could purchase goods for their relatives (at inflated prices).[11] Items ranging from radios to kitchen appliances were sold at these stores.[12] Moreover, each visiting exile was required to purchase overpriced travel amenities, many of which they were unlikely to use.[13] By the end of 1979 the regime had earned a staggering $100 million in desperately needed hard currency from the visits.[14]

But the visits also yielded something no one had anticipated. The exiles, having earned a good standard of living abroad, brought with them stories of their lives in the United States. The Cuban people, who for years had had only limited contact with the outside world, sat in living rooms across the island staring at pictures of the emigres' homes, automobiles, and businesses. They listened, no doubt rapt, to stories of vacations, overflowing grocery shelves, and all the amenities available in a free country. And it wasn't only family members who interacted with the visitors, but an endless stream of neighbors and friends who were electrified by their presence; soon, all the talk in Cuba was about the "worms" who had returned as "butterflies."

After years of being told by the government that the exiles were living marginalized, impoverished lives abroad, many Cubans were now learning the truth.[15] It was also, undoubtedly, the first time many had been in proximity to such "wealth" since nearly half the country's population had been born after the Revolution and had known only material scarcity. As if to confirm their prosperity, the visitors freely spent thousands of dollars purchasing appliances and other impossible-to-acquire items for their relatives at the stores opened by the government. While some visitors no doubt exaggerated tales of their success and engaged in petty boasting, the message was nevertheless clear: elsewhere in the world, hard work pays off and enhances your standard of living, as it had once done in Cuba. Of course, Cubans who had never believed in Communism and still remembered the pre-Communist era were not at all shocked by the apparent prosperity enjoyed by the emigres—rather, what they now heard merely validated their beliefs.

It would be a mistake, however, to assume that the only nerve touched during the visits was a material one, for many Cubans also saw what life in a free country meant beyond just the procurement of consumer goods. In the world beyond the isolated island, they saw that people were free to travel abroad, choose their jobs and careers, open businesses, elect their governments, practice the religion of their choice, express their opinions freely, and live without constantly being monitored. Their exposure to the exiles, therefore, not only stimulated Cubans' material appetites but, much more important, brought to the surface a profound desire for individual freedom. Indeed, in one of the earliest surveys of Mariel refugees, political motivations—such as "life was intolerable under a Communist regime," "you felt continuously under surveillance," and "I don't like that kind of system" far outstripped economic motives for emigrating.[16]

Young people who had lived their entire lives under Communism were probably jolted more than anyone by the "window to the world" that the returning exiles had provided, as frustration, disillusionment, and restlessness had been evident in them long before the visits. Alex Larzelere, a former Coast Guard officer and one-time research fellow at National Defense University, stated in his work *Castro's Ploy—America's Dilemma: The 1980 Cuban Boatlift* that Cuba's young people were "very much aware of the unfulfilled promises of the Castro government, conscription, volunteer labor, rationing, and the sacrifices they were asked to make for the sake of the revolution." He further stated that they "found themselves in a situation of limited opportunities for social mobility. The only way young people could succeed under the Castro regime was to conform. But in conforming, their drive and ambitions were stifled."[17] Indeed, according to Carmelo Mesa-Lago, in the decade before the Boatlift, the Cuban government had faced real problems with much of the island's youth—problems that became manifest in a soaring school dropout rate, an increase in juvenile delinquency, and a rise in what the Communist authorities regarded as rebellious behaviors and attitudes. Among other measures to deal with these issues, the regime had launched an effort to ratchet up membership in the Young Communist League and, as noted in the introduction, created the Youth Labor Army in the early 1970s. Furthermore, to crack down on juvenile delinquency, the age of "legal liability" was reduced from eighteen to sixteen. According to Mesa-Lago, "In addition, tough sanctions (up to life) were introduced for crimes against the national economy, abnormal sexual behavior, and other offenses."[18] It would be reasonable to assume that the hopelessness evident in many young Cubans can explain, at least in part, the desire so many of them had to leave Cuba, especially after getting a glimpse of what life was like just across the Florida Straits.

In any event, given that the exiles who ventured to Cuba did so because of diplomatic "talks" between Cuba and the United States, a renewed hope for emigration opportunities blossomed. During the visits many separated families vowed to act immediately if events in fact led to Cubans once again being permitted to leave the island. Many who had no family in the United States were likewise hopeful that a means to leave the country might soon present itself. It would not take long.

By the end of 1979, despite the inflow of cash from the visits, Castro's fortunes overall had taken a turn for the worse. When the Soviet Union invaded Afghanistan, Castro's leadership position in the Non-Aligned Movement became precarious, especially after his government voted against a United Nations resolution condemning the action (Afghanistan was a founding member of the Non-Aligned Movement).[19] More immediately, blight had destroyed much of the island's tobacco crop, and the global price of sugar, Cuba's primary export, had declined. In late December Castro stated that Cuba was "sailing in a sea of difficulties."[20] The Cuban people, who for twenty years had been promised a bright future under the Revolution if they worked hard, made collective sacrifices, and accepted limits on their individual freedom, were now being asked to endure even greater privation. Their situation was no doubt harder to bear after the exile visits, as Cubans could now compare their lot to that of their countrymen across the Florida Straits. For many, that promised land now seemed to beckon more loudly than ever before.

By late 1979 and early 1980 the situation in Cuba was reaching a breaking point. For the first time in years, outward acts of political rebellion occurred. Anti-government leaflets began to circulate and anti-Castro graffiti appeared; there were incidents of fires set by saboteurs.[21] Crime and vandalism were on the rise.[22] More subtle forms of protest such as job absenteeism and lower worker productivity—predictable under the circumstances—became major problems for the government.[23] The regime reacted aggressively by arresting thousands of citizens, some for actual infractions and many under Cuba's *Ley de Peligrosidad* ("Dangerousness" Law), which allowed the government to arrest anyone who it felt posed a "potential" danger.[24] Meanwhile, the surveillance operations of the Committees for the Defense of the Revolution were stepped up and work supervisors were given enhanced power over worker discipline.[25]

The number of Cubans attempting to flee the country and make it to the United States by boat spiked during this period; some of the vessels used were built secretly and others were acquired by theft. The desperation to get out of Cuba was also made evident by the number of boat hijackings that began to occur, in which captains were coerced by escapees to sail to Florida. For ordinary people to employ such means to procure vessels was not surprising, as the government had made it virtually illegal for citizens to have boats of their own. Equally unsettling for the regime was the fact that large numbers of Cubans began seeking asylum at Latin American embassies in Havana. Earlier treaties and past practice had allowed citizens of Latin American nations to seek asylum in one another's embassies if they felt their lives were imperiled or if they feared incarceration for political reasons.[26] The Peruvian and Venezuelan embassies in Havana, because of their location and the layout of their facilities, became the main sanctuaries for asylum seekers. Since embassies were guarded by Cuban military personnel, those seeking refuge there sometimes used vehicles to gain access forcibly.[27]

The Cuban government was angered by the nations that had been granting its citizens asylum in their embassies. It was also furious that the United States had welcomed the recent rash of escapees, including the boat hijackers, as political refugees. The regime wanted, instead, for the United States to issue entry documents to Cubans who wanted to emigrate.[28] Doing so would relieve the pressure building on the island and spare Cuba the embarrassment of so many ordinary citizens risking their lives to escape what Castro touted around the world as a model society. It was politically impossible, however, for the Carter Administration to give in to the Cuban government's demands, because the latter still refused to pull its troops from Africa as the United States had requested. Also, because of recent tensions with the Soviet Union, the Carter Administration felt it needed to assume a firmer foreign policy stance with regard to Communism.[29] Appearing to accommodate America's historic enemies or giving the impression of being bullied by them could have been disastrous in an election year. In the end the United States agreed to issue only a limited number of visas. Therefore by early 1980 the Cuban government was facing internal pressure that seemed likely only to increase and, as it had done in 1965, began searching for a way to relieve this.

Well before April 1980 there were clear signs that the Castro regime might unleash a Camarioca-style boatlift to relieve the pressure building inside Cuba. In January 1980 the CIA reported, "The Castro regime may again resort to large-scale emigration to reduce discontent caused by Cuba's deteriorating economic condition."[30] The head of the U.S. Interests Section in Havana, Wayne Smith, was warned directly by Cuba's vice president about another Camarioca if the United States continued to welcome illegal departures while keeping avenues to legal emigration closed.[31] Smith's alerts to Washington went unheeded. Cuban exiles had also informed officials about the possibility of another boatlift, and even the head of the Cuban Interests Section in Washington, D.C., had warned about such a possibility.[32] In March Castro himself stated, "We are not going to be taking measures against those who plan to illegally leave the country while they [the United States] encourage the illegal departure from the country. We were forced to take measures in this regard once. We have also warned them of this. We once had to open the Camarioca port."[33]

With things along the southern U.S. border teetering toward crisis, it took only the action of a small group of asylum seekers—and Fidel Castro's reaction to them—to touch off a chain of events that resulted in one of the most dramatic migration episodes of the post–World War II era. On April 1 six Cubans commandeered a bus that one of them drove for a living and, in an elaborately planned scheme, crashed it through the gates of the Peruvian Embassy. Cuban guards, ever vigilant for gate crashers, opened fire. Two escapees were wounded, but none was killed. One of the guards, however, died when struck by a stray bullet.[34] Though the bus did not make it all the way through, it was far enough onto embassy property for those inside to be granted asylum.

The Castro regime was enraged and demanded that Peru turn over the asylees, a request the Peruvians refused. Apoplectic, Castro decided to teach them a lesson and to send a message to other Latin American embassies. On Friday, April 4, he ordered the removal of all guards from the Peruvian Embassy, destroyed the guard houses protecting it, and hauled away the boulders placed there to prevent unauthorized vehicles from entering.[35] The government then announced that it would no longer protect the facility, stating: "We cannot protect embassies that do not cooperate in their own protection."[36] The embassy was now open for any asylum seeker who wanted to enter. The regime hoped that perhaps several dozen Cuban malcontents would converge on the facility—enough people, enough of a mess, to pressure the Peruvians and others into rethinking their asylum practices.[37]

The first groups of Cubans entered the Peruvian Embassy grounds within a short time. Others watched furtively from nearby to see if it was all some sort of hoax. Soon, a steady stream began to go in; by midnight, nearly three hundred people had entered.[38] The next day the government announced that those who had arrived at the embassy after the guards were removed would be free to leave Cuba so long as Peru or another country accepted them.[39] By Sunday, April 6, it became a stampede of thousands. When Castro finally cut off access—thirty-eight hours after the guards' removal—10,865 Cubans of all conceivable backgrounds (including Communist Party members) had crossed into the embassy grounds seeking asylum.[40]

News media from around the world took great interest in the situation in Havana and transmitted shocking images of the nearly eleven thousand Cubans seeking asylum at the Peruvian Embassy. Given the dimensions of the embassy grounds (approximately the size of a football field), overcrowding became chronic.[41] Some took up residence on the building's balconies and tiled roof, while a fortunate few crowded tree branches. Before long dehydration, sunstroke, and gastroenteritis set in; the stench of human waste hung in the air and disease threatened.[42] The Peruvians, while unwilling to cast out the asylum seekers, had no means to supply them with food, water, medical assistance, and sanitation. The Cuban government, the only entity capable of offering such relief, agreed to distribute food in small boxes but did so in amounts that would feed only a fraction of the people there. Among its intentions, no doubt, was to stimulate disorder and discord among the starving asylees in order to show the international news media that they were essentially "dangerous" people.[43] Meanwhile, Cuba refused offers of humanitarian aid from outside organizations, including the International Red Cross.[44]

The Castro government, humiliated by the spectacle of so many people desperately wanting to leave Cuba, reacted to the situation at the embassy by launching a campaign against those who had taken refuge there: the asylum seekers were derided as *escoria* (scum), drug users, social parasites, anti-socials, delinquents, and, the ultimate target of the regime, homosexuals.[45] Meanwhile, pro-regime mobs were sent to surround the embassy and shout insults at those inside; despite their deteriorating condition, the asylees fired back with spirited chants of "*Libertad! Libertad!*" and sang the national anthem. At one point, a furious Castro reportedly told Jamaican leader Michael Manly, "I am going to turn this shit against the United States."[46]

Cuban exiles in Miami had not been sitting by idly as the drama in Havana unfolded. While the community had never lost its passion for the Cuba cause, activism had declined somewhat over the years, as mentioned earlier. The Peruvian Embassy crisis revived the community's passion as if by an electrical charge, unleashing a wave of patriotic emotion. Many believed that the moment for which they had so patiently waited—the collapse of the Communist regime—was imminent. Rallies were held in support of those in the embassy; in Little Havana, two blocks were occupied by a throng of demonstrators who held vigils and participated in public hunger strikes to show their solidarity with the "Havana 10,000." In New York City Cuban exiles gathered near Cuba's United Nations mission and "waved Cuban, American and a few Peruvian flags and carried placards demanding 'human rights for the 10,000.'"[47] Exiles also launched fund-raising drives as well as food and clothing collections for the "Havana 10,000." They raised tens of thousands of dollars and tons of food and clothes in only a couple of days.[48] A flotilla was organized to try to deliver the goods.[49] Some activists began organizing militarily, believing that a war of liberation was just around the corner. A sense of purpose, a spirit of unity, of the kind unseen in years, swept across Miami's Cuban community.[50]

On April 7 Fidel Castro went personally to the Peruvian Embassy and told the asylum seekers that they would be permitted to emigrate if foreign nations granted them visas.[51] In an apparent attempt to end the media frenzy, the government then distributed safe-conduct passes for the asylees to go home, promising to contact them as soon as they were cleared to leave the country. Only a few thousand accepted the offer, the rest wary of Castro's promises and fearful of retribution from government mobs if they left the embassy. A few thousand more departed after April 11, when passports and exit documents were offered in addition.[52] For those who left, their fears of violence were confirmed as government thugs lay in wait to assault them outside the embassy grounds, at the places where the buses they were provided dropped them off, and outside their homes.[53]

The United States at first chose to view the crisis in Havana as a problem to be resolved among Latin American nations, especially those of the Andean Pact, which met during the second week of April to seek a solution.[54] As for American assistance, President Carter agreed to provide $4,250,000 to help resettle the Peruvian Embassy asylees and to accept 3,500 of them—around one-third—into the United States.[55] Other nations agreed to accept lesser numbers.

In mid-April, as Peru prepared to transport the first group of one thousand asylees to Lima, Cuban state media began complaining about the distance between the two capitals and suggested they be processed somewhere closer to Cuba.[56] Although the regime was clearly implying that they should all be taken to the United States, Costa Rica stepped up and offered to process them on its territory before resettling them in the countries that had agreed to accept them. The Cuban government had no choice but to accept the offer. On April 16 the first group landed in San José, Costa Rica's capital, shouting, "¡Libertad!" and kissing the ground. The arrivals spoke publicly of the treatment they had experienced in Cuba and about being assaulted by a government mob at the airport.[57] They showed their new cuts and bruises. Media reports also revealed that these people were not what the Castro propaganda machine had depicted, but rather mostly average working-class Cubans, the sort the Revolution was supposed to have championed.[58] On April 18, with Castro facing further embarrassment, the Cuban government cancelled the Costa Rica airlift. By that time only 678 refugees had been transported. The Cuban government then announced that the embassy asylees would have to fly directly to the countries that had agreed to take them.[59] In any case, the regime had another plan up its sleeve.

As alluded to earlier, Fidel Castro had apparently had a Camarioca-style boatlift in mind for some time and, at some point during the tumultuous days of April 1980, likely saw that the Peruvian Embassy crisis was the sort of pretext he needed. Napoleon Vilabóa, a member of the Committee of 75, was in Havana at the time and reportedly concocted the details of a scheme to transport the Peruvian Embassy refugees to the United States. Specifically, Cubans abroad could be invited to sail to Cuba on private vessels to take the embassy asylees to Florida, in exchange for also letting them take their relatives from the island. In effect, Castro could solve the problem posed by the asylees and, as in 1965, open an emigration safety valve to relieve the pressure plaguing his government. Vilabóa met with Cuban officials and with Castro himself to discuss his idea, assuring them that the exiles would respond positively to such an offer.[60] In her highly acclaimed memoir about the Mariel Boatlift, *Finding Mañana: A Memoir of a Cuban Exodus,* Pulitzer Prize–winning journalist Mirta Ojito summed up Vilabóa's thinking: "He was sure that Cubans from South Florida would be willing to come to the island to transport the thousands of embassy refugees back to the United States, but only if—and this was a crucial if—the government permitted them to retrieve their own relatives as well."[61]

Back in Miami a few days later, Vilabóa received the go-ahead from Cuban agents. The point of departure would be the port of Mariel, around twenty-five miles west of Havana along Cuba's northern coast.[62] On April 17 Vilabóa went on Spanish language radio in Miami to announce the proposed sealift.[63] The exiles hesitated, as the Costa Rica airlift was still in operation at this point. There was also, naturally, a degree of skepticism. The next day, however, the Costa Rica airlift was called off and Cuban Americans soon began receiving word from Cuba that the story was indeed true.[64] Anyone who wanted to leave Cuba for the United States would be permitted to do so via the port of Mariel (except, as in 1965, certain professionals and those of military age), so long as a boat came for them. Miami exploded.

Meanwhile in Cuba, the Castro regime was celebrating its 1961 victory at the Bay of Pigs and called for an enormous march across Havana on April 19. Predictably, the demonstration, christened the "March of the Fighting People," was redirected against the 1,500 to 2,000 asylees still at the Peruvian Embassy.[65] The government had reportedly suspended the issuance of safe conduct passes in order that there would still be asylum seekers at the embassy to torment during the march.[66] The Revolutionary spectacle, according to the *New York Times*, consisted of hundreds of thousands of chanting marchers brandishing "posters and effigies of worms of every description, worms carrying suitcases, worms being flushed down toilets, gangster worms, worms wearing too much makeup. Jimmy Carter, shown variously protecting or welcoming worms or being kicked in the seat of the pants by Cuba, was also a popular target."[67] Perhaps emblematic of the reality that lay behind the thin veneer of political loyalty in Cuba, some of the demonstrators broke away from the march, hopped the fence, and joined the asylum seekers.

Cuban Americans who planned to retrieve their relatives at Mariel immediately began securing and preparing boats. Some owned their own vessels, and those who did not quickly purchased them, sometimes on the spot.[68] Others sought out captains-for-hire along the Miami River and in the Florida Keys. Some of the relatives who hired captains went to Cuba with them, while others simply supplied the captains they hired with lists of relatives to give to the Cuban authorities and then waited in Key West or in Miami for their return. It was also common for two or more families to pool together money, hire a captain, and send him to Cuba with a list from each. Boat stores, meanwhile, did a brisk business selling all types of marine supplies.[69] Everyone knew this boatlift could be even bigger than Camarioca, as the exile community was much larger and had a great deal more money than in 1965.[70] The exiles made telephone calls and sent telegrams to relatives in Cuba, letting them know that they were on their way to get them; that finally, after so many years, they would soon be together.

On April 21 the first boats returned from the port of Mariel. The more than forty refugees they carried included relatives who had been retrieved by family members and individuals from the Peruvian Embassy group.[71] Within a few days, more than one thousand vessels set sail for Cuba.[72] Meanwhile, officials in Washington, D.C., apparently had not prioritized what was happening along Florida's southern shores. Few, in fact, had taken the previous warnings about a boatlift very seriously. An interagency meeting held by the Bureau of Refugee Programs a few weeks before had concluded that despite the warnings, there was no threat of a new boatlift from Cuba.[73] The White House, in any event, was distracted by seemingly larger issues. The failed U.S. effort to rescue the American hostages in Tehran occurred almost simultaneously with the start of the Mariel Boatlift; the Soviet invasion of Afghanistan, only a few months old, was likewise absorbing the administration's attention, as were soaring oil prices and political fires in other parts of the world.[74] The Bureau of Refugee Programs was facing crises involving Cambodians, Vietnamese, Afghans, and Somalis.[75] In short, Cuba was not the first thing on the minds of administration officials. Unfortunately for Carter, by the time events in Florida reached a crisis level it took a monumental effort to gain control over them. Little could anyone have predicted how the Boatlift would impact the nation; nor could the Carter White House have foreseen that it would adversely impact the president's re-election that year.

This chapter presents the experiences of five people who were among the thousands of asylum seekers in the Peruvian Embassy. The interviewees discuss their lives in Cuba prior to the Boatlift as well as their ordeal at the embassy. Included among the testimonies is that of a young writer who, although never going into the embassy himself, witnessed the events there first-hand and would later leave Cuba via the port of Mariel.

Ronald Díaz

Ronald Díaz was born in 1957 and grew up in the city of Santa Clara. His father worked for Cuba's railways and his mother was a telegraph operator.

My mother, whose family had previously owned businesses and stores in Cuba, was never with the Revolution. My father, though, was in favor of the government and opposed to my leaving for the United States until the last moment before I departed. He'd said that I wouldn't study there, that I wouldn't have any opportunities. In Cuba, they convince you that the United States is a bad country. My father also never wanted my mother and me to leave because he had a brother who was on the Party's Central Committee in Havana. We had a chance to go in 1967, when my mother's relatives left, but we didn't go because he was opposed to it.

I always felt resentful in Cuba. From the time you entered primary school, they tried to indoctrinate you politically. They'd put you out in the sun to sing the national anthem; they'd have you chant, "We shall be like Che!" and all that. But I was a rebel inside and never liked the system; they didn't permit freedom of religion or freedom of expression, and I knew there wasn't a future there. I remember seeing, in the 1960s, how all those peasants in the Escambray Mountains, whose lands had been confiscated, were fighting Castro and how they were executed and called bandits. One begins to notice that it's all just a lie, that anyone who stood against their government was called a mercenary, a worm, and a traitor. From the time I was young, I would tell myself, "I have to get out of here."

It was when I finished primary school that my cousins and aunts and uncles left the country. They'd write to us and send us pictures from New York and Niagara Falls. The desire to leave grew inside me during those years. When I finished secondary school, I received a scholarship to study in Havana, but I didn't finish my studies and was drafted into the military. I did three years in a unit (*Ejército Juvenil del Trabajo*) that cut sugar cane and did other work. I experienced a lot of hunger there and escaped many times.

None of my relatives went to Cuba during the visits of the late 1970s, but there were people close to my family who did. We went to see them and saw how they came from the United States with everything; they had freedom, freedom to travel, freedom to do everything. The people saw how the exiles came back with money and how they'd go to the stores and buy things that you couldn't. The visits had a major impact and they influenced the youth psychologically, as well as the rest of the people. But something was already coming because people in Cuba were suffering repression—when you prohibit things is when people most want them, and in Cuba everything was prohibited, even the Beatles' records. At one point you start asking yourself, "Why do they prohibit me from leaving? Why do they prohibit me from listening to something?" Then you think to yourself, "There must be something good out there."

I learned about the Peruvian Embassy through the Voice of America. In Cuba, they wouldn't tell you anything that was going on, only that a group of delinquents had gone into the embassy on a bus and that they had killed a guard. The Voice of America told us how there were people going inside; how there were three thousand, how there were five thousand. That Saturday night, I saw a friend of mine in town and said to him, "Look, there are so many people at the Peruvian Embassy. They're going to close it any minute; we have to take advantage of this and go there." So we went to Havana on a bus.

The embassy was already closed off by the time we got there, but we jumped the fence through the back. By then, the grounds were full; there were around ten thousand people inside there. There were women, children, elderly people, everything. For food, they would distribute around eight hundred little boxes for ten thousand people; there was just a little piece of yucca or sweet potato with rice inside. They distributed such a small number so that they could film the people when they fought over them; that way, they could depict everyone in the embassy as the scum of society, as delinquents from the street. When I went home later with my safe conduct pass, I saw scenes on television that I never saw inside the embassy; they showed people with knives and things like that, monstrous things. They never showed the children, the elderly, or the women; in truth, there were all sorts of people in there, even policemen.

There were mobs outside the embassy and they held rallies on the main avenue. The government brought in students and people from the CDRs to scream at us, "Down with the worms! Out with the delinquents and scum! We don't want them!" The people inside shouted back, "¡Libertad! ¡Libertad!"

I was in there for a week. At one point, they started giving safe conduct passes. When you left, they'd put you on a bus that took you to places in Havana where organized mobs hit you with rocks and sticks. I got on one of the buses, but I had the luck to have gotten off before it got to one of those places.

I arrived at the train station in Havana that night and, luckily, the

Havana to Santiago train was departing. Since my father worked for the train system, I knew some of the workers. They hid me and I got back to Santa Clara at dawn the next day.

Andrés Reynaldo

Andrés Reynaldo was born in 1953 in Calabazar de Sagua, a small town near Cuba's northern coast in Las Villas Province. When he was two years old his family moved to the Old Havana neighborhood of the Cuban capital. His father, who was born poor in the countryside, had studied at rural schools established by the Batista government and later, while working in the sugar industry, received an accounting degree through a correspondence program at the University of Havana. When the Castro Revolution took over in 1959, the elder Reynaldo was employed as an accountant for the Cuban Sugar Company. Andrés was five years of age.

My family was middle class before the Revolution and lived in an apartment on Obispo Street in Old Havana. We lived a good middle-class life in a peaceful area. For my first two years of schooling, I attended a small neighborhood private school called Ramírez de Mendoza.

My father and uncles never believed in the Revolution. I have one uncle, one of my father's brothers, who worked as a tax auditor. When Fidel Castro entered Havana on the morning of January 8, 1959, he went to the airport and left the country on the next flight. He said that Fidel was a delinquent and that these people were the worst thing that could happen to the country. My relatives weren't Batista supporters, but felt that these new people were the worst thing that could happen to the country.

When they nationalized the American companies in Cuba, my father went to work for the National Institute for Agrarian Reform. At that time, it was a super-ministry controlled by Communists like Che Guevara and Carlos Rafael Rodríguez. My father had a good position there and they asked him to be in the militia. My father said no, and because of that he was "marked." My father never served in the militia, was never part of a CDR, and was never part of the Communist Party. So, he never held an important post at work despite being a very capable individual. He always worked second to the head of a department. There were times when his bosses would tell him, "Listen, integrate and you can join the Party," but he never did it. He was not openly an opponent, but he was someone they didn't trust.

When they closed the private schools in 1961, my former private school had its name changed and it became the primary school for the whole neighborhood. Obispo Street itself was like Cuba's Wall Street and that's where we lived; but within two blocks in either direction it was a port neighborhood and a rough area. Anyhow, the Revolutionary atmosphere at the new school was extreme. Instruction went from, "Danny is a boy and María is a girl," to "'F' is for 'Fidel' and 'C' is for 'Camilo' and for 'Che.'" There was a time when certain teachers would bring us in individually to ask us questions about our parents in private. "Is your father a Revolutionary?" they would ask, or, "What does your father say about Fidel?" I was six, seven, eight years old at the time.

Curiously, during this period the people of Old Havana were a bit different from the rest of Havana, in the sense that Old Havana was a place forgotten by the government until the 1970s. Now that I'm older, I think that was of great advantage to those of us who lived there. This was why: first, when they started cleaning out the professors at the universities and secondary schools—many of them had said they were leaving the country—they were sent as "punishment" to schools in Old Havana. So in primary and secondary school I had university professors teaching me. One of them would teach history out of the textbook for fifteen minutes and then, suddenly, close the book and give a different history lesson. She never said that one version was better than the other, but she would give a different history class. Besides that, our proximity to the port gave us access to a great deal of information from the outside world. As children, we'd go do business with foreign sailors—Moroccans, Greeks, and others. We'd buy gum from them; two or three packs for three or four pesos, and we would then sell each piece for two pesos. All that exposed us to something different; we saw people dressed differently, we'd get magazines from them, and now and then information filtered in though them.

Still, my generation lived a certain illusion with the system. In the first place, we were ignorant of the past. At fifteen or sixteen, one doesn't know much about the past; one lives in the present and absorbs whatever is present. For us, it was a present with a great deal of propaganda, with a great ethical call from the Revolution to fight in Latin America. Later, when I was at the university stage—and I would say this was a phenomenon that happened to many of us—I started to take an interest in the past and to draw contrasts with the present. One starts to develop a greater consciousness. I started talking to my grandparents. My maternal grandfather, for twenty years, had carried around an enormous wooden chest of sorts and sold clothes in the countryside. When he was around fifty years of age, in 1956 or 1957, he set up a store in Calabazar de Sagua, about the size of a living room, from where he sold clothes with his brother. He was able to save money and purchase a nice home. When the small businesses were confiscated in 1968, they took it away from him, saying he was part of the bourgeoisie. He was a man who'd worked more in his life than the entire Central Committee. So, you start noticing things, the levels of injustice, and that transforms you little by little. A process of disillusion starts to set in at the university, and you start to pretend to be in agreement with the system, only because if you didn't at least pretend to be in agreement they'd throw you out. But it was a slow process for that generation, because one still had links to the Revolution.

In 1978 my first book of poetry won an official prize that was given to young writers. That event furthered the process of disillusionment and alienation for me. As soon as I won the prize, State Security came to meet with me and said, "From now on, you'll have an official to report on you. This is Comrade Alexei, and he'll come and talk to you now and then." I realized right away that as soon as you distinguished yourself, you were brought under the control of State Security.

At around that time, 1978–1979, friends of mine who'd left Cuba in the 1960s came to visit. They were all young women and had been classmates of mine at the beginning of secondary school. When a group of us sat down and talked, I realized that Cuba was a place I needed to leave. Reading something in a magazine isn't the same as what someone your age and with your same background tells you.

Meanwhile, my book was going to be translated in Poland. I planned with these same friends that I would get out of the airplane at the first stop along the way there—it could have been in Gander, Canada, or Barajas Airport in Madrid, or Stockholm. The plan was to stay there, call them, and then they'd find a way to get me out and bring me to the United States. But then, in the middle of all this, the Peruvian Embassy incident came about.

I remember I was with a group of friends on the porch of a restaurant where we'd get together to drink tea and talk. For days before that, we'd been hearing through the Voice of America that there were groups of people who had entered the Venezuelan Embassy. Suddenly, someone came in with a copy of *Granma*.[76] The newspaper contained a note saying that the guards had been removed from the Peruvian Embassy, which was practically an invitation for people to go in.

When the first broadcast of Voice of America that night reported that there were eight hundred people in the embassy, Havana awoke; people set off en masse to the embassy. My friends and I discussed whether or not this was a trap. One of them said, "I'm going over there," and he went into the embassy. Later, another friend also went in. I had gone to the embassy's perimeter to accompany each of them. The first time, at around seven o'clock at night, there was a multitude there; there was a great commotion, with people jumping the fence in a great state of euphoria. The second friend decided to go in at around nine o'clock that night. By then, there were police cars outside that had been abandoned by policemen who'd gone in. A bus carrying tourists was stopped there as well, with the tourists on board asking, "What happened?" because their driver had gone in. It was uncontrollable.

Carlos Cabrera

Carlos Cabrera was born in Havana in 1949. From a young age he suffered from poliomyelitis and required the use of a cane. One of his uncles, Felo Bergaza, was an internationally renowned piano player and entertainer. The only child in his family, Cabrera spent time living in East Berlin as an adolescent in the 1960s when his mother served as a consul at Cuba's embassy there. As an adult, he worked at different jobs before leaving Cuba through the port of Mariel.

I was denied permission to leave Cuba five times. I had no way of leaving until the event at the Peruvian Embassy. When that occurred, several people called to tell me about it. First, I had a cousin who used to give English classes at the university to high-ranking officials in the government. The day of the embassy incident, he was calling me at home but couldn't get hold of me. It seems a colonel had gone by the university saying he had a message from *El Comandante* [Fidel Castro] and that he wanted a meeting with the government people my cousin was teaching, which was a group of around eight to ten people. My cousin stayed for the meeting and heard the colonel say, "Fidel ordered the embassies to be opened, to see who goes in." That was after the bus went into the Peruvian Embassy. The colonel was apparently upset at Fidel's capriciousness.

When I got home that night, I found out that a friend of my wife had already gone into the embassy with her daughter and husband. She had called my wife to tell her that there were eight to ten thousand people in there; since people would go in and out she was able to call her. She said to her, "Come over here; everything is OK. Nothing is going to happen to you." My wife told me about the phone call when I got home and she also told me that my cousin, the English teacher, had been calling constantly. When I finally reached him, he told me, "Fidel has removed the guard from the embassy." I told my wife we had to go, but she didn't want to, and so a discussion ensued. I finally said, "Let's go." I went to get the man who lived across the street, who was married to one of my mother's cousins, and said to him, "Listen, two things. First, if you want your son to come with me, I'm going into the Peruvian Embassy. Second, I want you to drive me there in my car." He said, "OK." And then he told his son, "Go with Carlos."

Four of us went: me, my wife, the cousin's son, and my daughter. We got there late, at eight or nine o'clock at night. I saw people from the Ministry of the Interior out front dressed as civilians. I knew a lot of people from the Ministry because the National Institute of Sports and

Recreation had earlier built them a squash court and I had been given a release from my job and sent over to teach them about the game and how to play. I would play with them and got to know some of them. So, I told my wife, "This has gotten bad. If we can't get in, we'll have to leave." I climbed the fence first so that I could help my wife and daughter over after I was in. When I did so, people outside the grounds, the police, grabbed my cane and started hitting my leg. I found myself hanging on the fence, one leg outside of it and the rest of my body inside. I knew a lot of people in Havana, so I heard voices inside the embassy crying out, "Carlos, wait, I'll help you!" One of them came and helped me over. After landing inside, I looked around and saw that my wife and daughter weren't there and that I had lost my cane. I climbed the fence again to jump back outside to look for my family. While I was on top of the fence, I started fighting with a man outside who had started pulling me and trying to take a Rolex watch I had on. I started hitting him. At that moment, my wife appeared, inside, and said, "Hey, hey, we're here!" There was a man who'd seen them while they were still outside and asked if they wanted to come in. They said yes, and he told them, "Look, there's a hole over here." He lifted the fence and they went in. Meanwhile, I had been hanging on the fence.

Most of the ex-political prisoners were at the front of the embassy grounds near Fifth Avenue, near the flag, and I went over with them [his wife and daughter had moved to the building's roof]. Outside, on Fifth Avenue, on the grass island in the middle of the street, there were three lines of policemen; every twenty feet, they had an armed officer.

One day, a taxi tried to come in and they opened fire on it; one of the shots broke through a window and hit a child inside the embassy building. It didn't kill him, but he suffered a major injury.

I later sat with two young men, and every time someone from the government came by that I knew, I'd tell them, "That's such and such," and I'd tell them the person's rank—remember, I spent two or two-and-a-half years around people from the Ministry of the Interior [playing squash]. One of those people suddenly started calling to me from the outside; he was dressed as a waiter, but he was really a lieutenant colonel in counterintelligence. Calling out to me could have cost him his life. He asked me why I didn't tell him I was leaving; but how was I going to tell those people that I was going to leave the country? He asked about my wife and daughter, and I said, "They're up there [on the roof]." Then he lifted his hand and a truck came in and delivered more than seven hundred little food boxes. There were 10,800-plus people in the embassy—later there were 10,300-plus; then 9,000-plus—but they gave us only seven hundred boxes, maybe a thousand. Many people didn't eat. The political prisoners at the front knew that women and children were in the buildings, so they made sure the food boxes went to them.

After eight days, we found out that the government was giving safe conduct passes. If you left there with a safe conduct pass, they put you on a bus and dropped you off at places where people would beat you. Anyhow, I told my wife, "Let's go." She said, "Let's wait two more days." I said, "Let's go," because they weren't giving us a means to exit the country. We had spent the eight days eating nothing, just drinking water, and we had each lost sixteen pounds. When we left the embassy, they made passports for us and took our photographs. When the guy I knew from the Ministry saw me leaving, he told the bus driver to drop us off wherever we wished so we wouldn't be dropped off with the rest of the group. In any case, when the bus driver closed the door, he said to me, "You can get out wherever you want because you're a friend of mine." I didn't remember the man, but after eight days of tension I just said, "Hey, how wonderful, how are you?" He left me at a place from where we walked to a cousin's house.

Michellee Cabrera León

Michellee Cabrera León is the daughter of Carlos Cabrera. She was seven years of age at the time of the Peruvian Embassy crisis.

I turned seven inside the Peruvian Embassy. I remember having heard discussions in my household about leaving Cuba. My father had wanted to leave, but my mother was afraid. At the time, I was an only child and my mother was very overprotective of me.

One night, I remember my parents were talking and arguing. Then, before I knew it, we were standing before a fence. My father is handicapped and uses a cane to walk, and I remember he started climbing over the fence to go in first. There were a lot of people there, a lot of screaming, and when my mother and I started to climb the fence, somebody told us, "There's a hole here," so we went in through the hole. My mom then went over to try to help my father over; there was a guy on the other side of the fence trying to pull something from him to steal it, and he had gotten stuck. We were finally able to bring him over.

I remember there were a lot of people at the embassy and I remember them walking in a circle around me because there were things such as bottles being thrown at us from the outside, where there was a big commotion. Then, before I knew it, we were separated—my mother and I were on a roof of the building and I didn't see my father until we got out. My mother told me he was in another section.

We were at the embassy for around eight days. While we were there, they would give us small boxes of food—inside them there was rice and scrambled egg. My mother would give me half in the morning and the other half in the late afternoon. She didn't eat for a whole week so that I could have all of it. Whenever I'd finish eating, she would save the box so that I could use the bathroom in it. She would also tie a shirt or something at the edge of the roof and I would sit under it because it was April and sunny all day. We went out, I think, twice; I know we went once, to hose off with the people who wanted to bathe. I remember, maybe once, they took the kids into a room with a big sink and my mom washed me there.

I also remember meeting a girl there who had a little toy, and on the day of my birthday she gave it to me. When I was asleep that night, someone stole it.

We left [with safe conduct passes] and went home. We couldn't go out and we couldn't talk to people, for whatever reason. I had friends who came to my house to play but, not knowing what was happening, I couldn't go to their houses.

Manuel Nieves

Manuel Nieves was a native of Havana and grew up in the Old Havana neighborhood. From a working-class family, he was four years old when the Castro government took power. He married in 1972 and had a daughter while still in Cuba. He later had a son in the United States. He departed for the United States a few days after leaving the Peruvian Embassy.

I was never integrated into the Revolution and never joined the CDR or volunteered to go to Angola or anything like that. There was great repression in Cuba and no freedom; you had no right to elect people to represent you and they forced you to do volunteer labor. Those were the kinds of things I was against. No one ever had to tell me, "This system is bad." That's something no one had to point out; a person is born knowing that people deserve freedom, and that people have the right to express freely—without offending or disrespecting anyone—their ideas and arguments.

The government took things away from my generation little by little, things that future generations never got to know. And then, in 1968, they finished taking over everything. The next generation didn't know what it was to go to the market or to have a business. My daughter didn't know what an apple was; I knew what apples were, and I knew Christmas Eve, Christmas, and Three Kings Day, but my daughter didn't. She only knew the 26th of July because that's when they gave out little toys.

I never finished my studies. In Cuba, one must have "*doble moral*" in order to study. One can't even choose a career. They tell you, "Sure, you want to be an engineer, but we need doctors to send to Venezuela, Angola, Algeria." And you have to go. Plus, if you didn't do volunteer work, you had no right to anything.

I got married in 1972, at seventeen, and started working as a diesel mechanic at my father's workplace. Those were very difficult, turbulent years for me. I was called to do military service before my daughter was born and was placed into a special unit to listen to the enemy's conversations. We were told, "From now on, you will speak English twenty-four hours a day, and you'll have English instructors. You are not allowed to speak Spanish." Our job would be to listen to conversations at the Guantánamo Naval Base and the U.S. Coast Guard. So, the first day in the classroom was all in English. Then, that first night, we had a meeting where an officer asked us, "Who here plans to leave this country someday?" I raised my hand. The officer told me, "You can't be here. If I could, I'd execute you. You need to leave."

So I was transferred to a construction unit in the military and was eventually sent to a unit in Camacho, in a swamp on Cuba's southern coast, to build a shooting range. I spent a lot of time without seeing my daughter or my wife; the only one I was able to see was my father. The place where I was sent was in the middle of a cane field and we slept in a structure that had a dirt floor, no walls, and a palm-thatched roof. At midday four of us would receive a bottle of a Russian cherry marmalade and two eggs; at night they served us rice with a big spoon. I had problems there. On the first day I was walking in the mud with rubber boots that were too big for me. I stepped, lifted my foot, and the boot stayed behind; but I had to keep walking or they'd hit me with a bayonet. That afternoon, they held an inspection. An officer, a first-lieutenant, asked me, "Where's your boot?" I said, "I lost it."

I got out of the service in 1978. Between then and 1980, I made two attempts to leave Cuba on a raft. The rafts broke both times and we had to destroy them and go back. Then, in 1980, I asked for my vacation in April; in previous years, I had taken it in August. During that vacation time, a friend of mine came to get me and said, "Nieves, I read in *Granma* that Fidel has removed the guards from the Peruvian Embassy." A group of our friends was already there; we were all against Communism. So my friend and I went to the embassy. When we went in, there was no one there since it was only ten o'clock in the morning. Soon, more people started to arrive. Those of us who knew one another from the neighborhood—thirty-plus of us—all stayed in one place and didn't move.

Later on, my mother took my wife and daughter to the embassy. My mother walked past the people outside, who were hitting her, while carrying two bags of food. When she got to the gate with my family, I grabbed my daughter, brought her over, and told her mother, "She's going to stay here with me." Her mother then followed her over the fence. My mother had brought a cake because it was my daughter's birthday. We sang Happy Birthday to her there in the embassy.

They later gave permission for people to leave the embassy grounds so they could use some bathrooms that were outside. My wife wanted to go, but I said, "I don't like it. It's a trap; they'll get us out there and we won't be allowed to come back in." She said, "Yes, yes, people are going in and out." So I listened to her. We never made it to the bathrooms. As soon as we got to the sidewalk, a commotion erupted. I grabbed my daughter and put her up over the gate again; then I jumped in and then got her mother over. But my wife and I hadn't been able to go over at the same spot over which I'd passed my daughter, so, when we got in, we couldn't find her. What a frightening experience! A couple found her and shouted, "Look, your daughter! Your daughter is here!" What joy when I found her!

Later, when the food ran out, they started giving out small bags of milk. I got one, but couldn't get it to my wife and daughter because by the time I got to them it had broken. Since our daughter had nothing to eat, she and my wife went home with safe conduct passes. After they left, I was standing by the gate—by then, there were far fewer people in the embassy—and three cars stopped out front. A group of men got out—two of them in long-sleeved *guayabera* shirts and the rest in short-sleeved ones. One of them was Ramiro Valdes [Minister of the Interior], who I recognized by his goatee. He came to within a few feet of me at the gate. He said to a group of us, "I would execute all of you!" We all hit the ground in response.

When my wife had gone to get my daughter her pass to leave the embassy, they wouldn't give it to her because she was a minor and I had to sign. I heard my name called over the loudspeaker and I went over and signed. So I went out too. When you left the embassy, they'd put you on a bus and drop you off at a place where there was a mob that would throw rocks, sticks, eggs, and everything else at you. People would run. When I got out, I didn't run, I walked. I was lucky not to get hit by something.

I got home that night, and the next day I told Pancho, the head of the CDR, "Look, Pancho, you know my situation. I am going neither to hide nor run. You could decide to do with me as you wish." He said, "No. no. You won't have a problem. When your exit permit comes, you can go." They did no *acto de repudio* against me or anything, because I never had a *doble moral*.

Jacqueline Capo

Born in 1972, Jacqueline Capo is the daughter of Manuel Nieves. She left Cuba at eight years of age.

My grandmother on my mother's side was very Catholic, so I grew up Catholic and we went to church at the beautiful Iglesia de las Mercedes in Havana. When we'd go to Mass, police armed with rifles were always outside the church to see who was going in and out. Even though I was young, I would think, "Why are there people with guns outside when I'm going to worship God?" I couldn't be baptized in Cuba because, at the time I was born, they were really hard on the people that did, but I was baptized less than a year after I came to the United States. In school, I remember we had to wear the red neckerchief of the *Pioneros*. I used to hate wearing it; you had to recite all that stuff about Che Guevara and I used to just mumble it. Maybe it was from listening to my family, but I always remember thinking there was something more.

I knew my dad wanted to leave the country, but I guess when you're that age—I was only seven when everything happened—you don't really think, "I'm going to go somewhere else and it's going to be totally different." But I knew my father was against all that, the system there. His mother would tell me, "Talk to him, talk to him, settle him down and tell him to take it easy." So, I would say, "Dad, take it easy, take care of yourself." Even though I was young, I was always aware that people have to do whatever they need to do.

The day before I turned eight, my grandfather on my dad's side came to my mom's house—my parents were sort of separated, they'd later get back together—and he told her that my dad had gone into the embassy. My father's mother, my mother, and I then went to the embassy on a bus. They took practically all the food that was for my birthday party to give it to him. When we got there, my dad was at the fence. He talked to me and said, "Get closer, so I could give you a kiss," and I went and kissed him. Then he lifted me up and brought me in. He said to my mother, "She's already in, so if you want to come with us, fine." I guess she freaked and that's when she jumped. It had never crossed our minds to stay.

There were a lot of people inside the embassy; they were all on top of each other and I remember there were people in the trees. While we were there, a guy had a seizure and was foaming at the mouth. That made an impression on me. But I was fine, just going with the flow; I was with both my parents. I remember that everyone in the embassy was helping each other; whoever was in there, at the end of the day, wanted to leave and that's why they were all there. And everyone protected each other because we all had a common enemy, which was Fidel. I remember the people outside were throwing bottles at us to try to hurt us, but we knew they didn't really want to be there. While we were there, we slept on the ground, like we were camping. Anyhow, I celebrated my birthday there at the embassy, and they sang Happy Birthday to me and we ate cake.

My mom and I eventually left the embassy. She had to sign a paper. A policeman escorted her home to make sure nobody would hurt her in front of her house. They dropped us off, and no one said anything. She didn't know if we would ever be able to go to the United States because in order for you to get your job back, you had to say that you didn't want to leave the country. She was also afraid that I wouldn't be able to go back to school. Anyhow, I remember going back to school like normal. My mom went back to work, and my dad left the country.

My dad started writing letters from the United States saying how much he missed me, how he wanted me to have a future. The person that finally convinced my mom to go to the United States was my grandfather. He asked her how she was going to let me grow up without a father, and he told her about the opportunities she was going to give me in the United States. My father had already signed a paper saying he wanted me to leave, so she went and presented the papers saying that we wanted to leave the country.

2

The Odyssey Begins

THE MARIEL BOATLIFT caught the United States government as well as state, county, and local government in Florida utterly unprepared. When the first boats began arriving on April 21, federal authorities in South Florida processed the arriving refugees in the same manner they always had for Cuban escapees.[1] Then, on April 23, the State Department issued a public reminder that it was unlawful to transport undocumented aliens to the United States. It warned of fines, boat seizures, and prison for those doing so.[2] It was hoped that the announcement would discourage Cuban Americans from setting out to Cuba. That assumption, of course, only laid bare the administration's misapprehension of the crisis: softly worded threats were not going to stop Cuban Americans from reuniting with family members now that Castro seemed disposed to release them. One Cuban American was quoted during the Boatlift as saying, "I want to see them arrest me for going to get my parents."[3]

The following day, as the Carter Administration was launching its failed military effort to rescue the American hostages in Tehran, over three hundred boats were already anchored at Mariel.[4] Two days later, on April 26, with the Iranian rescue fiasco still on the front burner, the administration held the first high-level meeting about the Cuba situation, chaired by Vice President Walter Mondale. Those at the meeting considered different approaches to stopping the exodus. It quickly became clear, however, that options were limited. To force back boats carrying people fleeing Communism was unacceptable, as the United States had condemned such actions by other nations in the aftermath of the Vietnam War just a few years earlier. Such an approach would also result in the administration losing whatever cooperation it might otherwise receive from Cuban Americans in stopping the exodus.[5] And it would lose any support it might garner from the community in the November elections.[6] Moreover, using force on the high seas was potentially life-threatening to those involved.[7] In addition, it would reverse the historic U.S. policy of welcoming Cubans.

Of course, stopping boats from departing in the first place would likewise have been unworkable, given the determination of Cuban Americans to retrieve their relatives and the limited logistical capability at that moment of the Coast Guard and Navy (which were now also tasked with whatever rescue operations the Boatlift might require). It was also potentially illegal, as it would restrict the right of American citizens to travel; that is, it was perfectly legal for Americans to depart the country on private boats.[8] Besides issuing pleas, fines, and a series of confusing and sometimes contradictory warnings, the administration could do little more than require the boats carrying refugees to land in Key West so that new arrivals could be screened and processed there.[9] It would likewise provide for the safety of the boats returning from Cuba.[10]

The Carter Administration also attempted to stem the flow of boats sailing to Mariel by reaching out directly to Cuban Americans. On April 26 Deputy Secretary of State Warren Christopher met with a group of Cuban American leaders at the State Department and urged them to use their influence to stop members of their community from sailing to Cuba. He suggested that if they did so, Castro might be convinced to pursue a more orderly migration, such as the Costa Rica air bridge. For their part, the Cubans wanted the United States to send ships and airplanes to help ferry over those among their countrymen who wanted to depart the island. With the administration again misreading the emotional climate in Miami, the meeting failed, and some of the Cuban Americans walked out in indignation.[11]

Things on the island, meanwhile, were intensifying. On May 1 a crowd of roughly one million people gathered in Havana's Plaza of the Revolution to listen to Fidel Castro's May Day address. In it the leader denounced those who requested to leave Cuba through foreign embassies as "thugs, delinquents, and lumpens." He famously announced to the crowd, "He who has no revolutionary genes, he who has no revolutionary blood, he who does not have a mind that [can] adapt to the idea of a revolution, he who does not have a heart that can adapt to the effort of heroism required by a revolution: We do not want them; we do not need them." On those picking up refugees at Mariel, Castro sarcastically stated, "They are doing an excellent sanitation job for us."[12]

The following day around eight hundred ex-political prisoners and their families (along with several visa applicants) gathered outside the U.S. Interests Section in Havana. Almost two years had passed since Cuba and the United States had reached the agreement that would allow current and former political prisoners to emigrate, and they were calling because they had received word that their processing would begin in early May. Their eagerness to leave Cuba was understandable, since those who had been classified as current political prisoners rather than "ex-political prisoners" had been given first priority, thereby extending the wait of the latter. After being assured that processing would commence soon, the ex-prisoners and their families began to disperse. As they did so, buses suddenly appeared and men carrying an array of hand weapons alighted from them. Other armed groups quickly converged from other streets. The armed bands violently attacked the former prisoners and their families. It was believed that some of the victims may have been killed. Amid the chaos, more than 450 people, many of them badly injured, sought sanctuary inside the Interests Section. Granted entrance, the majority would stay there through much of the summer. On May 17 a Cuban government–organized, million-person march denounced the United States and those exiled inside the Interests Section.[13] Similar though smaller demonstrations were held in different cities throughout Cuba on that day.[14]

On May 5, only days after the violent clash, President Carter addressed the League of Women Voters in Washington, D.C. By that time around 14,000 Mariel refugees had already landed in Key West.[15] At the end of a response he gave to a question about the Boatlift, the president memorably stated, "We'll continue to provide an open heart and open arms to refugees seeking freedom from Communist domination and from economic deprivation, brought about primarily by Fidel Castro and his government." Although the administration later said that the president's words had been misunderstood, his use of "open heart and open arms" indicated to many that he had approved of the Boatlift. Administration officials, who for days had been trying to find ways to stop the exodus, scrambled to explain that the president had *not,* in fact, given his blessing to the Boatlift. Adding to the confusion, Carter's use of the word "refugee" seemed to grant the arrivals an immigration status—one with important legal implications—that had not been conferred.[16] The message, unintended as it may have been, had nevertheless been sent. Over the next two weeks the number of Cubans arriving in Key West soared to over 43,000.[17] The day after the "open hearts, open arms" speech, Carter declared a state of emergency in Florida and approved $10 million in emergency funds.[18]

As the confusion spread, the United States continued to pursue international efforts to end the Boatlift. It preferred a multilateral solution, since it wanted to avoid adding to the discussions the issues that Cuba sought to address bilaterally, such as ending the U.S. economic embargo on Cuba, the U.S. Naval Base at Guantánamo, and U.S. surveillance flights.[19] On May 8 and 9 a conference was held in San José, Costa Rica, that included the United States and several European and Latin American nations as well as some international organizations. Unfortunately, most countries offered only limited assistance. Great Britain and Costa Rica alone agreed to stand with the United States and attempt to reach out to Cuba to propose a more orderly migration. Cuba flatly rejected the overture.[20] Further diplomatic efforts during the summer of 1980 ended just as unsuccessfully.

Among the early concerns for the Carter Administration, the American people, and, increasingly, Cuban Americans, was the alarming discovery that Castro was using the Mariel exodus to send not only the Peruvian Embassy asylees and the relatives and friends of exiles to the United States but also an array of other Cubans, including those whom it deemed "undesirable" or "anti-social." Stories soon began to circulate of boat captains forced to take "strangers" to the United States aboard their vessels—strangers who allegedly included common prisoners, mental patients, and delinquents—as a condition for retrieving friends and family members.

After failing in its initial efforts to stop the Boatlift and under mounting pressure from Congress and the public, the beleaguered administration formulated a new policy.[21] For any policy to be effective, however, it needed both to address the goal of family reunification and to ensure that the United States controlled the migrant flow. Thus on May 14 President Carter announced a five-point plan. First, the United States would launch an orderly airlift and sea lift of "screened and qualified" Cubans to the United States. The groups given priority would be the Cubans currently besieged in the U.S. Interests Section; political prisoners who had been promised entry in 1978; the asylees from the Peruvian Embassy; and "close members of Cuban American families" (a registration center would be opened in Miami immediately to identify such people).[22] U.S. boats currently at the port of Mariel would be encouraged to return without refugees aboard, and threats of fines and criminal prosecution for bringing in any further refugees would be reiterated. Any criminals who had arrived on the Boatlift to that point would be subject to exclusion proceedings. In addition, support from the United Nations and other international organizations would be sought.[23] The United States would also strengthen the Navy and Coast Guard in the Florida Straits and begin strictly enforcing U.S. law.

Unlike in 1965, this time Cuba rejected the United States' proposal for an orderly migration process. The plan was criticized in *Granma*, which also printed insulting political cartoons lampooning President Carter.[24] With more than a thousand boats from the United States still anchored at Mariel, Castro's refusal to negotiate an orderly exodus, and the administration's reluctance to interdict and force the return of vessels carrying refugees, the plan's prospects for success initially seemed dim indeed. The extent of the challenge was made even more apparent when captains returning from Cuba with boatloads of refugees after May 14 reported that they were prohibited from leaving Mariel—some at gunpoint—without taking those identified by Cuban authorities.[25] Others claimed they had been threatened with fines.[26]

In any event, by midsummer the number of boats sailing for Cuba had waned. The increasing U.S. Coast Guard and Naval presence in the Florida Straits and more effective law enforcement eventually proved successful and resulted in a higher number of fines and boat seizures for those returning from Mariel.[27] Perhaps more important, Cuban Americans had largely soured on the Boatlift, as Castro forced them not only to take a large number of "strangers" as the price for retrieving their relatives but also to overload their boats to life-threatening levels. Cuban Americans had originally expected that the Mariel Boatlift would resemble Camarioca, when they were, in fact, permitted to retrieve their relatives and friends—and only their relatives and friends. Feeling as though they had been duped, many lost interest.[28] Although May would bring in a record-shattering 86,488 refugees to the United States, the number of boats departing for Cuba declined deeply between June and the time Castro arbitrarily ended the Boatlift in September. In fact, more than 75 percent of all Mariel refugees entered the United States between the start of the Boatlift on April 21 and the end of May. By the end of June, more than 92 percent of the total had entered.[29]

Cuba: A Harrowing Farewell

As mentioned earlier, when the decision to open the port of Mariel was announced, telephone calls and telegrams between relatives in Cuba and the United States soared into countless thousands. *U.S. News and World Report* reported: "Long lines of people formed each morning at the telephone-company building in downtown Havana, waiting to call friends and relatives in the U.S. who could arrange passage."[30] Exiles in the United States instructed their family members to be ready to depart, and passed along information about the boats they had procured and when they were expected to arrive. Those on the island, feeling anxious as well as hopeful, tended to keep the news to themselves to avoid possible persecution.

The Cuban government made shrewd political use of the Boatlift by trying to cast all those leaving via Mariel in the same light as it did those who had sought asylum at the Peruvian Embassy: as *escoria* (scum), traitors, parasites, social dregs, thugs, loafers, criminals, drug users, deviants, etc. In doing so, the regime could both morally stigmatize those individuals and blame Cuba's economic problems on them, thereby framing their departure as a social cleansing.[31] The vitriolic rhetoric was embodied in aggressive physical action: for the duration of the Boatlift, the government unleashed its supporters in the CDRs and elsewhere to organize *actos de repudio* (acts of "repudiation" or public disdain) against those leaving. The incessant *actos de repudio* across Cuba produced a surreal atmosphere for months and resulted in thousands of innocent people being publicly terrorized, humiliated, and beaten by Revolutionary mobs. Some of the victims reportedly died in the process.[32] For the thousands of Cubans who knew that family or friends would be coming to retrieve them, the time between learning that they would be picked up and the day government officials came to their door was, therefore, a trying one.

When an *acto de repudio* was organized in a town or neighborhood, it was common for the CDRs to pull employees from work, children from school, and neighbors from their homes to take part. The pressure to participate in the acts was so great that many joined not only because it was required of them but out of fear that their own loyalty would become suspect and that the violence would be turned against them. One nervous woman in a Havana mob whispered to a reporter during an *acto de repudio*, "You have to understand . . . some of us are living with double personalities." She further stated, "I am a member of the CDR but I do not approve of this."[33] It was ironic, if not predictable, that the crowds often included people who knew that they, too, would soon be leaving via Mariel. They joined the *actos de repudio* (though usually in a subdued manner), because it was practically required by their workplaces or schools to do so, and because they needed to be free of suspicion, lest they too be harassed, beaten, or, even worse, somehow barred from leaving.[34]

Among the most common *actos de repudio* organized by the CDRs were those directed against the homes of people who were leaving. Families who were discovered to be among those registered to emigrate often had their residences surrounded by mobs that would, perhaps for hours, engage in acts such as chanting vulgar and demeaning slogans, banging on pots and pans, throwing rocks and eggs, smashing windows, spray-painting insults and spreading feces on exterior walls and doors, erecting effigies, and hanging signs deriding those inside the homes as traitors. Gas and electricity to the homes were sometimes cut off. The most extreme *actos* seem to have been reserved for those who had previously been active Revolutionaries, as their decision to emigrate was viewed as the worst form of treason.[35]

When the moment finally came for an individual or a family to depart for the port, it was common for the neighborhood CDR to organize a special farewell—replete with chanting, beatings, and rock and egg throwing—as the emigrants exited their homes and tried to board waiting vehicles. The victims had no choice but to endure the violence, a situation often made all the more horrific by the presence of lifelong neighbors, workmates, school friends, and even relatives taking part in the aggression.

Besides homes, an *acto de repudio* could occur almost anywhere. Those standing in line at immigration offices were attacked.[36] Sometimes would-be emigrants' workmates launched *actos de repudio* against them when they went to request a *baja* (release) from their places of employment (one of the requirements for those exiting the country). One man, interviewed for this book and whose story is related later this chapter, had an *acto de repudio* organized against him by the staff at the hospital where his wife had just given birth. In some cases mobs chased people down in public and dragged them down city blocks or the lengths of small-town main streets.[37] Some individuals were forced to wear signs identifying them as "worms," as they were jeered by mobs.[38] One eyewitness recalled an incident in her region:

At a university outside Ciego de Ávila, it was discovered that a professor was leaving the country. His father was a Communist and he himself had studied in the Soviet Union and was a Communist Party member. When he went to get his workplace discharge, which indicated that he was leaving the country, a mob made up of students, university staff, and fellow professors set on him and shoved him several kilometers in the direction of the town, kicking him, beating him, and throwing rocks at him the whole time. He passed out, unconscious, at the edge of town near a drainage ditch where he was left for dead.[39]

Teachers often pointed out children in their classes whose families were among those leaving, thereby inciting their classmates to harass them.[40] In some cases Revolutionaries who had learned that a child—especially a teenager—was due to leave Cuba with his or her family, offered the child the opportunity to be "rescued" from his or her traitorous parents. Stories of Revolutionary teens defying their parents—that is, "heroically" choosing the Revolution over their families and remaining in Cuba—circulated throughout the island.[41] One refugee from a small city in Camagüey, an eighth grader at the time of the Boatlift, remembered such an experience while her family was quietly waiting for a relative to arrive at Mariel:

> I had a math teacher, a Revolutionary and a really scary guy, who called me in one day and said, "I've heard rumors that you're leaving the country." Terrified, I lied to him. "No, that's not true. I'm not leaving," I said. He stared at me intensely. He knew I wasn't telling the truth. He said, "You know, if you refuse to join your parents, you can stay here in Cuba. There are good Revolutionary families who can adopt you." I just shook my head, mumbling, "No, it's not true. We're not leaving." I was so scared.[42]

It is important to note that not all Cubans who chose to leave the island were directly victimized by mob violence. Many somehow escaped persecution. Also, as one might expect, it was not uncommon for local CDR leaders, teachers, school administrators, workmates, and supervisors not to participate in the aggression and instead, when possible, to protect lifelong friends, colleagues, and neighbors.

Normally, on the day word arrived that a family or an individual had been cleared for departure, an official—often a policeman or soldier—would arrive at the party's front door to inform them. The refugees were then given a short time to prepare for departure. The departing individuals were reportedly required to present their discharge papers from military service (in the case of adult males), signed releases from their workplaces (in the case of employed adults), and their national identity cards to immigration officials.[43] Leaving home was sometimes a violent experience, given the special CRD farewells detailed earlier.

Anti-Socials and Undesirables

The largest group of the more than 125,000 Mariel refugees comprised people who sought to join relatives in the United States. Thousands of others were among those who had earlier sought asylum at the Peruvian Embassy, ex-political prisoners and their families, and other political non-conformists. A large number of the emigrants were simply people who requested permission to leave and received it. Also, as noted, the Cuban government forcibly mixed into the refugee population those it defined as "undesirables" and "anti-socials," classifications that included petty criminals, the mentally ill, alcoholics, vagrants, prostitutes, Jehovah's Witnesses and members of other religious sects, homosexuals, and others.[44] Numerous teenagers labeled as "troublemakers" by their local CDR were also compelled to depart, unaccompanied by a parent or guardian.[45] It is important to point out that many of the so-called "criminals" sent on the Boatlift were people guilty of things such as dealing in the black market for food and other basic necessities, having previously attempted to leave Cuba, or guilty of avoiding military service—offenses that, for the most part, would not have made these people criminals in democratic countries.[46] Also, it goes without saying that many who were considered as "anti-socials" or "undesirables" would only have been so by the standards of the island's Marxist regime.

In their article "Marielitos Ten Years Later: The Scarface Legacy," B. E. Aguirre, Rogelio Sáenz, and Brian Sinclair James described the process for registering and certifying so-called anti-socials and undesirables during the Boatlift:

> A special certification was created, the so-called *cartas de escoria* (dreg's letters). Government officials insisted that would-be emigrants publicly confess their criminality and degeneracy. These confessions were duly signed and recorded by the authorities,

and, afterward, the confessed "deviants" received official letters stating and corroborating their moral blemishes.[47]

Besides being identified and rounded up by a CDR or other government entity and pressured to leave Cuba, anyone who wanted voluntarily to confess to being an undesirable or anti-social in order to emigrate could have walked into one of the special immigration offices the regime set up around Cuba and done so.[48] By the same token, Cubans who wanted to leave the country, but who had neither family requesting them at Mariel nor ways to fit truthfully into the government's category of undesirable or anti-social, could have lied to an immigration officer or CDR leader, or bribed that person, in order to receive an official certification as such.[49]

The regime also went into Cuba's common (i.e., non-political) prisons and induced certain inmates currently serving time to exit the country via Mariel.[50] Sometimes they were persuaded by threats to extend their sentences.[51] Again, while some inmates may have been serving time for serious felonies, many others were serving time for offenses that would not have been considered serious crimes in other societies. Nearly six hundred people suffering from mental illness were likewise selected to be placed into the mix of refugees.[52]

Castro's motives in sending undesirables and anti-socials to the United States via the Mariel Boatlift has been a subject of speculation. Some reasons, however, seem clear. From the start of the Peruvian Embassy crisis, the Cuban state portrayed those expressing a desire to leave the island as scum, parasites, degenerates, social dregs, and the like; what Castro, using a Marxist term, referred to in his speeches as "lumpen" (from "lumpenproletariat.")[53] As such, the regime wanted to present evidence for the charge; hence, its compulsion to mix into the refugee population a certain number of people matching the description and then to inflate the number via the methods described.

Depicting the emigres of the Mariel period as undesirables also served the government in mitigating the international humiliation caused by the spectacle of so many working-class citizens taking such desperate measures to flee Communist Cuba. And it was done to embarrass the Cuban exile community. Until that time, Cubans who had fled the Communist island, the "Golden Exiles," had been praised for the success they had achieved in the United States and elsewhere. As such, the exile community, Castro's greatest enemy, had won great respect. By exporting to the United States people ready-labeled as anti-socials and criminals and then mixing in enough of them to give credence to the charge—and ensuring that the American news media focused on them—the regime hoped to tarnish the reputation previous exiles had earned.[54]

In addition, the regime sought to retaliate against the U.S. government. As Juan M. Clark, José I. Lasaga, and Rose S. Reque stated in the special report *The 1980 Mariel Exodus: An Assessment and Prospect*, it appeared that Castro "was trying to 'punish' the United States for failing to curtail the escapee flow through boat hijackings . . . that had proliferated in 1979 and 1980." By controlling the flow of people, Castro also hoped to gain leverage with the United States on other issues.[55]

Exporting such a large number of people, undesirable and otherwise, served the interests of Cuba's leaders in other ways. First, by ridding themselves of those who were dissatisfied with the system, the regime would lessen the potential for anti-government activities. According to Clark, Lasaga, and Reque, the regime's actions "discouraged the more dangerous temptation to plot or engage in subversive actions against the government in the hope of legally fleeing that totalitarian system."[56] Moreover, instantly reducing Cuba's population by such a degree—125,000 people, or around 1 percent of the population—would free up scarce housing and jobs, thereby relieving economic pressure and potential trouble.[57]

Although there were, indisputably, some dangerous people among the Mariel refugees, their percentage of the overall Mariel population was minimal. Despite the Cuban government's depictions of the emigrants and the U.S. media sensationalism that followed, INS numbers showed that fewer than 2 percent of the Mariel refugees could have been considered serious criminals.[58] Others have determined the number to have been lower, and some believe it was somewhat higher. Given the inexact nature of determining someone's past in Cuba, the precise number may never be known. One thing, however, is clear:

despite the presence of some truly threatening people (some of whom would be guilty of serious crimes in the United States, including a few high-profile murders), the Mariel population overall was *not*, by any means, largely made up of murderers, thieves, rapists, mental patients, etc., as many so steadfastly believed.

In any event, on the day a family or individual was cleared to leave Cuba and had produced the required paperwork, the official who had come for them would usually report the departure to the local CDR. At that point (often after an *acto de repudio*), the refugees were sent to report to the Círculo Social Gerardo Abreu Fontán, a social club on Havana's shoreline, for additional processing. The refugees, especially those from places other than Havana, were usually taken there in government-provided cars or buses from their hometowns. After having endured so much tension for what could have been days or weeks, the refugees felt they were approaching safe haven as they departed for the Abreu Fontán.

For many, in fact, their nightmare had only just begun.

This chapter traces the odyssey of several Mariel refugees from the time they learned they were leaving Cuba through their arrival at the Abreu Fontán.

Raúl Inda

Raúl Inda was born in 1946 in Ciego de Ávila, Camagüey Province. He was among the thousands of Cuban youths who possessed visa waivers in the early 1960s to depart Cuba via Operation Pedro Pan but was unable to do so because of the 1962 cancellation of flights. In 1965 he was sent to a UMAP camp. In the UMAP, besides being subjected to forced labor, he regularly witnessed acts of torture committed against the youthful inmates as well as deaths. In later years he managed to conceal his record and attended medical school. Though his past was discovered toward the end of his studies, he was allowed to finish his medical education.

I was married just before finishing medical school. Since I was already "marked," I was sent to a remote town to practice. It had a small rural hospital of just over twenty beds. I spent six months there, almost as a punishment. Later, I was sent to the sugar mill town of Pina—whose doctor had gotten into trouble—and my situation improved. After two years, I went to Havana to specialize in neurology.

As I was completing the neurology program in Havana, the Mariel Boatlift broke out. Those of us who didn't sympathize with the system had heard about the boats arriving at the port. Anyhow, I was with a patient when I received the call from home in Ciego de Ávila. It was my then wife, who was nine months pregnant. She told me, "Such-and-such is *there*. And you're on the list." I knew what she was telling me: that her relative who'd left Cuba in the 1960s was getting us at Mariel. I said, "OK, I'm going home right away." I had to go back to Ciego de Ávila to get my papers together and go to the immigration office there.

When I got to Ciego de Ávila, I found out that my family was indeed on the list and that immigration had said that I could leave even though I was a doctor. We took all our papers to the immigration office the next day. The following day, they put us into three Fords that belonged to the government—a Ford was a luxury in Cuba, like a Cadillac—and left for Havana. In addition to my wife, my six-year-old son, and me, we had my wife's family with us, which was quite large.

Along the way, my wife's water broke when we stopped to have lunch at a town called Jagüey Grande. We went to see a doctor there and he confirmed that she was in labor. He advised us to go back to Ciego de Ávila, but we were closer to Havana. So we went on to Havana and made it to the maternity hospital. By the time we got there, my wife was dilated eight centimeters. Of course, I had been prepared to deliver the child myself in the car.

They let me into the delivery room and I witnessed my son's birth. Then the hospital's administrator, who'd seen that we had arrived in a Ford, called me over and took me into the room where the on-duty doctors stayed. He lashed out, "Are you leaving the country?" Try to imagine my situation. I had my wife and baby there, in their hands, and here I was practically under guard and likewise in their hands. I didn't know what they were thinking or what their intentions were;

I didn't know what repressive action they could take if I said yes. I had to play for time, so I said, "No, no, the one leaving is my mother-in-law. We're just going to see her off." It was all I could think of at the moment to save the situation. I left.

I soon received word from Mariel that our boat was going to depart. Now I knew there was no time to play around and I asked for a discharge from hospital. I was denied.

So I took the child. I wrapped him in my mother-in-law's shawl, picked him up, and told my wife, "We're leaving." She said, "What?" I said, "We're *leaving*." I couldn't say anything further.

We had to walk down two flights of stairs to get out of the hospital, and by the time we did so around thirty to forty hospital employees were gathered to carry out an *acto de repudio* against us. Word had apparently gotten around the hospital. They shouted, "Ungrateful scum! Worms!" and whatever else they could think of. We had to walk through there to get to the taxi I had waiting outside. As we were making our way out, someone directed me toward a small office belonging to the hospital administrator. A man from the Party, who was more decent than the administrator and more educated, told me, "Come in here, please." Inside the office, he asked, "What's going on here?" The administrator, the same one with whom I had earlier had an encounter, said, "This individual wants to go *to hell*."

I'd taken enough by then, so I stood up, with my child in my arms, and said, "Not to hell, to the United States!" I almost lost control of myself. Can you imagine hitting someone with a newborn child in your arms? They held me back and my wife took the baby. As we were leaving the office, a woman there told me in a low voice, "*You* take the child," and kept walking. It seems the mob was waiting outside in order to assail me; but, as long as I was holding the child, they wouldn't touch me. So, I took the child myself. We made it outside and went into the taxi. The mob started hitting the taxi as we got in.

We went to the home of some relatives of mine in the Santos Suárez neighborhood of Havana so that we could buy milk and diapers for the baby, who was only a few hours old. We also had to rest. We later called a different taxi because the first driver had said, "I can't take you to the Abreu Fontán." His hands were trembling on the steering wheel. After a couple of hours recuperating in Santos Suaréz, we took a different taxi to the Abreu Fontán.

Gustavo and Bertha Ulloa

Gustavo and Bertha Ulloa were born in 1941 and 1936, respectively, and raised in Sancti Spíritus, Las Villas Province. They were married in 1966. Bertha's father was a businessman prior to the Revolution, representing Cerveza Cristal Tropical and Coca Cola in Sancti Spíritus. Gustavo's father was also a local businessman and worked for the Batista government in a bureaucratic capacity. Their families' businesses were confiscated by the Castro government and both were harassed harshly by Revolutionaries in the early days of Castro's rule. Gustavo eventually graduated from university and worked as a government accountant in Cuba. In spite of religious repression under Communism, Gustavo and Bertha remained practicing Catholics.

[Gustavo]: I had it marked on my dossier that I was religious. Twice they called me at work and told me, "Listen, you should stop going to church. You'll see—we'll make you a big boss. We'll give you a car." I said, "You're not going to take my religion from me. I do enough, given that you people have taken everything away from me. I'm not grateful to you for anything." Later, at the time they reorganized the provinces, I had a high position in finance and they called me and told me the same thing: that they wanted me to integrate into the Revolution. I said no again. Then they told me I couldn't continue in my position and I said, "OK." So they demoted me and lowered my salary.

[Bertha]: Mariel started the following year. In Sancti Spíritus we had no news of anything. What we knew we heard through the Voice of America. During that time my brother, may he rest in peace, called to tell us that he had a boat ready to bring everyone in the family who wanted to leave Cuba. Gustavo asked his parents if they wanted to leave, but they said no. My mother told one of my aunts, a widow, and she also said no.

[Gustavo]: My father said, "Gustavo, when you're established there and can help us, then we'll go. We don't want to be a burden to you and your brother-in-law." Plus, my father had cancer.

[Bertha]: And Gustavo's parents died there. He never saw them again.

One of my nephews came on the boat to pick us up—not my brother's son, but the son of one of our sisters. He arrived on a shrimp boat my brother had chartered called the *Long Horn*, and he turned twenty-one on May 10, the day he left for Cuba.

[Gustavo]: The president of the CDR came to tell us that we had someone waiting at Mariel. Then the people from the CDR came to seal the house and we went to stay at Bertha's aunt's house. I went to the immigration office in town to find out at what time we were leaving on the bus they were providing, but I had to go surreptitiously because the mob was looking for me to attack me. The man at immigration asked, "Are you Gustavo Ulloa?" I said yes. Then he asked me about my wife and mother-in-law and said, "They can leave, but you can't." I said that if we couldn't all leave then none of us was going. Since our house had already been sealed, I told the man to tell the CDR to give the key back to me and they did. At that point, we really began to suffer. We were practically in hiding. They even had to come from the church to give us communion at the house.

[Bertha]: My brother in Florida had a friend in Cuba who was the sister of a high-ranking military official in Sancti Spíritus. My brother called and asked her to speak to her brother. Thanks to that and a doctor friend of ours who lived next door to another high-ranking official, we got out.

[Gustavo]: That doctor friend lived next to a military officer whose father had had a business before the Revolution that sold white *criollo* cheese. It so happened that my father used to buy cheese from him. While Castro's war was going on [against Batista, years earlier] this man's son was with the Revolution and they [the Batista authorities] were searching for him to kill him. So my father told this man, "Listen, they're looking for your son to kill him. I'm telling you this as a father." This man hid his son and they didn't kill him. And now, this son was a high-ranking military officer and lived next door to our doctor friend. The officer told our friend, "Look, I owe my life to this guy's father. Tell him to go back to immigration and I'll give him a letter for them to let him leave."

[Bertha]: My nephew had departed for Cuba on May 10. We didn't leave Cuba until June 3. The reason it took so long was simply that my husband worked in matters of the economy and those were considered state secrets. Later, when he got to the United States, he was questioned a great deal.

The night before it seemed we were going to receive permission to leave, the mobs went to our house. They were there from around 6:00 p.m. until after midnight. They banged on the large bronze door knockers and pushed on the doors, but my father years earlier had reinforced them. We took my mother to her room, which was well back from the street, so that she wouldn't see what was going on. The people outside were shouting insults at us, but the leaders didn't let them throw eggs and garbage because the provincial Party office was next door. So they just banged on the doors and shouted insults over and over, calling us "worms," and "scum" and everything else. We were terrified. I didn't want my mother to see any of it. She would ask what was going on and I would tell her not to worry. We were praying.

[Gustavo]: When they finally went to the house to let us know everything was set for us to go, my wife called to me and said, "Hey, there is a soldier here." They told us it wasn't because we were under arrest, but because the soldier was going to accompany us to Havana. We were told to take money for the expenses we'd have there. So we went to Havana with the soldier and a driver. Later, at the port, they took all our money.

After around six hours of driving, we got to Havana in the afternoon. They took us to an old club in Havana called the Abreu Fontán, but it wasn't called that before the Revolution.

Marino Mederos Sr. and Marino Mederos Jr.

Marino Mederos Sr. was originally from Camajuaní, Las Villas Province. In 1952, at the age of thirteen, he moved to Havana and later worked at a boarding house near the university for several years. He then joined the army and served in the years before Castro's seizure of power. Afterward, he worked at various jobs. His son, Marino Jr., was born in Havana in 1970.

[Marino Sr.]: My wife's sister and her husband went to Cuba during the visits of the late 1970s. While they were there, people would ask the husband what life was like in the United States. He'd tell them, "Well, anyone can live over there if he's a hard worker. He can solve his own problems and live really well." During their second visit, they told me it was possible that there would soon be a second Camarioca. I told them definitely to send for us if the opportunity arose. Later, when they were departing from the airport, they called and told me that it didn't matter whether or not there would be an opening, that they were going to try to get us out via Spain.

I was in my hometown in Las Villas getting my paperwork together to leave through Spain when the Peruvian Embassy incident broke out. It was still going on when I got back to Havana. A few days later, the exodus from Mariel began. My brother-in-law called to tell us that they were there, at Mariel, and to stay put. They told us that the authorities were going to alert us at any moment. We stayed at home waiting for twenty-five days.

[Marino Jr.]: I was only ten years old, but I remember that when the incident at the Peruvian Embassy occurred things on the street got violent. After my uncle called to tell us he was at Mariel, State Security came to the house and said to my mother, "We heard it was possible that you were leaving. Will you do so if someone comes for you?" My mother said yes. From that moment on, things changed for us. First, there was the *acto de repudio*.

[Marino Sr.]: Most of our neighbors took part in the *acto de repudio*. I had a car, and I had previously helped out a lot of them, taking them to the doctor and all sorts of other places. I had even lent money to some of them so they could buy medicine and other things. Yet they were all there, taking part in the *acto de repudio*. They called me "traitor," and "worm," and "scum." The kids from our building who used to play with my son depicted him as a mouse on the building's mural.

[Marino Jr.]: There was a mural at the entrance to our building and they drew a picture of me there wearing jeans—of course, there were no jeans in Cuba—and the jeans were torn at the knees as if we were beggars. They also depicted me as a mouse leaving the country and going into a garbage can. Those were my friends who did that to me, the kids I played with on a daily basis. And the people who carried out the *acto de repudio* were our neighbors, people we had known for years, people my father had done a lot of favors for. To me, as a little kid, that made a big impression. After the *acto de repudio*, we peeked through a little corner of the window and saw the people outside giving speeches at a podium, talking about the Revolution and about us being traitors. That was a big shock. We couldn't even go out on the balcony because they'd egg us and throw rocks at us.

In our building there were two apartments per floor. Our apartment door faced the stairwell that looked up, and the other apartment faced the one that looked down. One night, someone threw an automobile tire against our door. One of my uncles was over and he went out to see who had done it. We never found out, but we knew it was the kids. Our front door was also covered with eggs, and so was our balcony.

When I got to school, my fifth grade teacher stopped the class— and I remember this like it happened yesterday—and said to the kids: "This is my student. He is leaving for whatever reason and that is not his fault. His parents are the ones taking him. Whoever touches a hair on his head will have problems." She was a very strong teacher and the kids didn't mess with her. So I didn't have any problems at school—the problem was when we would leave the school. My father had to walk us home because otherwise people would throw eggs at us.

[Marino Sr.]: After twenty-five days, my brother-in-law called and told me, "Our boat is leaving. They had told us that they would bring you here at any moment."

[Marino Jr.]: What happened was that my uncle and a few other families had chartered a large boat in Florida to go pick up all their relatives. When they got there, they were waiting for twenty-five days. They didn't bring enough food for so many days, and so they had to leave the port to eat at restaurants, which were charging very high prices. Then their money ran out, and they had to go back—that's why so many people left without their relatives. Still, in order for them to be allowed to leave, they had to load their boat with people. The boat was designed to carry two hundred people, but the authorities packed in around six hundred. After they left, we had to wait several days longer.

Finally, on May 18, at four o'clock in the morning, military officials came to pick us up at home to go to the port. Since my father had a car, they told him to drive it himself to the Abreu Fontán so that he could turn it over to the government when he got there.

[Marino Sr.]: When the officials got to the house, they told me, "You have ten minutes to get ready." I said, "That's nine-and-a-half more minutes than I need." We were already dressed and waiting. Then they called the people from the CDR, who came over to see what was going on. When they got there, they told my mother, who lived with us, and a niece who was a student and was also at the house, that they could go with us. But my mother didn't go because she still had children in Cuba.

When the time came to leave, we were asked to pick up a man with his wife and daughter on Galiano Street. Since there were three or four soldiers in each car going around picking people up, not everyone fit in their car. Anyhow, the woman backed out at the last minute and the husband came alone. We didn't know them.

[Marino Jr.]: From there we went to the Abreu Fontán.

Lourdes Campbell

Lourdes Campbell was born in 1964 and grew up in the town of Morón, Camagüey Province. She was among the many children and adolescents in the Mariel exodus who had been born and raised at a time when the Castro Revolution was in full swing.

I recall growing up with a constant feeling of fear, living as we did in a small town under a Communist regime. You did and/or said everything with extreme caution. I have vivid memories of having to sneak in through the back of the church to go to Sunday school. Growing up, I learned from my parents that we lived in a society that once upon a time had been beautiful and wonderful. I used to visit our neighbor and sit quietly while she ironed so that I could listen to her animated stories about her ancestors from Spain. Her parents had owned grocery stores in Cuba before the Revolution and she would tell me all about the abundantly stocked shelves and the *chorizos* and hams hanging from the ceiling. For me, it was like hearing about Cinderella; she may as well have been telling me a fairy tale. Of course, the old days of abundance and carefree living had to be spoken of quietly.

My first contact with that fairy tale was when my aunt and cousin came to Cuba for a couple of weeks during the visits of the late 1970s. My aunt had left Cuba in the early 1960s, and my cousin was born in the United States. The whole neighborhood was captivated with them, feeling as though they had fallen from a rainbow. My aunt brought a suitcase full of new and fresh smelling clothes. The government constantly broadcast that the Cubans in exile were starving and discriminated against, even though no one believed a word of it. Personally, my aunt's visit was a confirmation that it was all a bunch of lies. I remember a famous line that went, *"Nos vamos a la Yuma para comer jamón planchado"* ["We're going to the United States to eat sliced ham"]. It was known, but never acknowledged, that the United States was a paradise where everyone wanted to go.

When the incident at the Peruvian Embassy came about, I remember being scared because you never knew what might happen. But my parents told me, "No, no, it's a good thing." They explained to me that it might lead to the possibility of leaving the island. At my young and crucial age, this news was shocking; even though going to the United States was like a dream come true, I was daunted by the fact that I would be leaving behind people I knew and loved. I was plagued with the question of whether or not I would ever see my relatives again. But one thing was certain: I was not to speak a word of this to a single soul.

I was in tenth grade when the Boatlift started and in a boarding high school—the type you were sent to if you had the grades they required for university study. If you didn't have the grades to get into one of those schools, you had to attend a technical school. The Communist indoctrination at the boarding school was relentless. By sending us there, they also secluded us from our parents and all outside information. We had no television nor any connection to the outside world. In addition to the "free" education we received there, we had the added bonus of working the fields in a very unsafe and risky environment. I recall several classmates getting seriously injured. The school was in the middle of nowhere and we spent most nights with no electricity, which may have been a blessing in disguise since the lack of proper lighting prevented us from seeing the maggots squirming on our food trays. We were only allowed to visit home every other weekend, provided we had completed our school assignments and reached our field work quotas.

The day I left my town forever fell on one of those visits home. I was enjoying myself at my grandmother's house, quietly reading a book on her bed, not realizing this would be the calm before the storm. My grandmother suddenly raced into the room all out of breath and said, "You have to go home. Immigration is at your house and you're leaving in two hours." My thoughts raced, my heart nearly stopped, and my whole body went numb. "Is this true?" I asked myself, "Is today the day I'm leaving?" As soon as I felt my legs again, I ran home as fast as I could.

My aunt in the United States had made arrangements for us to be picked up by one of the boats going to the port of Mariel. We ended up being among the many families who were separated during this process. We were told that of our family of six, only two people could depart. My parents made the decision that my father would go and that he would take me, as the oldest of their four children. They were hopeful that my mom and siblings would be able to join us in the United States later.

The immigration agents informed us that we couldn't pack anything, as all possessions belonged to the government. We were allowed to take only one change of clothes and the clothes on our backs. But we were lucky because we didn't have to endure an *acto de repudio*. I believe it was only because things happened so rapidly. When word got out, people came quickly to say goodbye. The feeling was so surreal. I was leaving behind my mom, my sisters who were five and thirteen, my brother who was seven, my grandparents, and the only life I'd ever known.

A cab took my father and me to the city of Camagüey. I vividly remember the image I had from the back seat, looking at my life fading into the distance. The thought of possibly never seeing my family again is branded in my heart as one of the most painful experiences I've ever lived through.

When we arrived in Camagüey, we were transferred to a bus that took us to Havana. Along the way we went through different towns where people were not as kind as my neighbors had been; they threw eggs at us and shouted insults and obscenities. It was becoming clear to me that we were suddenly being viewed as traitors and the scum of society. Everyone on the bus was paralyzed with fear. My father kept telling me to stay still and to be quiet. The unsettling feeling I had was foreign to me. I felt like a tree that had been abruptly pulled from the ground, vulnerable and no longer rooted.

Andrés Reynaldo

I always thought that the Peruvian Embassy was a trap and that if I went in they wouldn't let me leave Cuba. But as soon as they opened Mariel, I called my friends in the United States and told them—if they could—to send a boat for me. They paid a thousand dollars for a tug-boat called the *Valencia* to come for me.

I left on May 17, so I spent almost a month witnessing things in Cuba—every day, at all hours, and in all places. For example, the only Western Union office in Cuba was at the corner of my block. Many of the people leaving Cuba had to go there to send messages to the United States. In front of it, there was a bar where hundreds of militants from the Communist Youth would gather to deliver blows to whoever was going in to send a telegram, or coming out from having sent one. And it wasn't only blows. There were moments in which they would throw potatoes at people with razor blades stuck inside them. In the countryside, they say it was worse; the *actos de repudio* there were deadly because they could hack you to death with machetes. Also, in the rural towns they'd park buses in local parks and force everyone they considered to be a delinquent, gay, or intellectually disabled into them.

It was the closest thing there could have been in Cuba to the Cultural Revolution in China. But there was one aspect of it that wasn't even a characteristic of Communist countries. That is, in Communist countries, the police would come out and beat you and take you prisoner—but they wouldn't organize a mob to come after you, this method they employed in Cuba of involving the people, of taking children out of school to take them to *actos de repudio*.

When you left through Mariel, if you were male you had to present the following documents: your discharge from military service, a discharge from your job, and your identification card. The only document I had that was in the clear was my military discharge. The identification card said who you were—and, if it said you were a doctor, a university graduate, all that, they weren't going to authorize you to leave the country. I was a writer and I had won a prize, so I thought I probably wouldn't be allowed to leave if I presented my identification card. Therefore I went to a police station and said I had lost it. When you lost your identification card in Cuba, no one could immediately give you a new one with all the required seals and things since making one was a thorough police process. So they'd give you a yellow paper, with your photograph on it, explaining that "the citizen" was waiting for a new identification card—but it said nothing about you. So that's what I had. My work release I falsified; I wrote that I was the guy who cleaned the floors, that I was "scum," that from a Revolutionary perspective, people like me had to leave the country. Then I signed it. But instead of signing the name of my boss—who was a man I was fond of—I signed as if the head of the department was Jorge Luis Borges, the famous writer.

I worked at a center of the Ministry of Culture where artists produced lithography and where they stored important works of lithography. I was a poet, and worked there mostly as an editor. My boss knew I was leaving and, during my last days in Cuba, I told him I was taking a vacation at home. So I was at home waiting. Then, around May 14, I received a call from the boat captain at the Hotel Tritón, who said, "Are you Mr. Reynaldo?[59] I have your name here on a list of people I'm going to request. Don't move from your home because they're going to get you at any moment." On the 17th, in the afternoon, the police came to pick me up. They talked to the president of the CDR and told him, "We're here to get Andrés Reynaldo. I'll give you half an hour to prepare the *acto de repudio*." But the man from the CDR said, "No, I'm not going to carry out an *acto de repudio*. I saw that man grow up here with my children." And they never did the *acto de repudio*; on the contrary, they gave me a farewell as if I were going away to study in the Soviet Union.

I was taken by a policeman on a motorcycle with a sidecar. I sat behind the policeman and we picked up someone else who sat in the sidecar. From there, we went to the Abreu Fontán.

José García

José García was born in 1966 in Sancti Spíritus, Las Villas Province. His parents' families had been well-to-do landowners and business-people prior to the Revolution. Shortly after his birth, one set of grand-parents left Cuba via the Freedom Flights and settled in New York City. His other grandparents, who were born in Spain and had immi-grated to Cuba in the 1920s, returned to Spain in the 1970s. As a child in Communist Cuba, García carried the burden of being from a fam-ily considered to have been part of the pre-Revolutionary bourgeoisie. In late 1979, his father, as the son of Spaniards, was able to acquire Spanish citizenship and received visas for Spain. As he was waiting to make arrangements for the family's departure, the Mariel Boatlift was announced.

While we were waiting to go to Spain, we heard about what was hap-pening at the Peruvian Embassy. It was all very strange; there was an eerie feeling that permeated the atmosphere. People were asking, "Did you hear what happened?" Other people said, "Oh, people are just talk-ing. I don't think anyone would dare do that." Then we started hear-ing rumors about people who had disappeared from town and about people who had gotten into buses or into cars and had gone to Havana. All of a sudden, over 10,000 people had gone into the embassy. It was weird. First you had people coming from the U.S. to visit, and now all of a sudden this was going on at the Peruvian Embassy. You felt like something was changing, like something was about to happen. When we found out they were letting people leave Cuba through Mariel, my mother called my grandmother in New York. My grandmother told her that my uncle had already departed for Mariel three days earlier.

My uncle was a salesperson for Goya Foods and he had been in a store in Manhattan when my grandmother called to tell him what was going on in Cuba. He borrowed five thousand dollars from the guy who managed the store and went straight home. Another guy we knew, a close family friend, was also going to Mariel and my uncle sent word for him to wait so they could go to Key West together. I think that same night they flew from Newark to Miami and, within hours, were in Key West. They hired a captain there, a pretty shady guy who'd been in Vietnam, and I'm not sure how much they paid him but it may have been a thousand dollars per person. My uncle and three other Cubans got on that boat and went to Cuba.

About a week later, my uncle called from the Hotel Tritón and told my mother he was there.[60] It was an amazing moment, something we had dreamed of for years. I've never won the lottery, but I would think it's probably the same sensation. Yet, at the same time, it was kind of strange. All of a sudden, I thought, "Oh, my God, I'm going to leave this place. This is where I grew up, where I have my friends." My parents, meanwhile, were nervous wrecks.

We were waiting for a month for immigration to come and get us to go to Mariel; meanwhile, my uncle was waiting at the port. As time passed, many people found out that we were going. One day the son of the local CDR leader came to my house and said to me, "My mother wants to talk to you. We would like to have a brief meeting with you and it's important that you come over." For a kid to get that call is pretty nerve-racking; this was a lady who had a lot of power. When I went over, they said to me, "We've heard rumors that your family might be leaving Cuba because people have been coming to your house and walking away with stuff. We know that your parents have never been with the Revolution, but we know that you're happy with it." I must have done a really good job disguising everything. Then they said, "When the time comes for you to leave, you can come and stay with us. We'll take care of you. If you stay, you can keep your house—that's your family's house and no one else can keep it." Then they started citing examples of other kids in town who had done that. "You know that such-and-such girl?" they said, "Her parents left a week ago, but she was heroic—she stayed behind!" I just sat there thinking to myself, "Is this lady out of her mind? Does she really think I'm going to leave my family?" I just said to her, "Oh, OK, sure, no problem, thank you." Then I gave her a hug and walked away. I got home and wondered if I should tell my father, but someone had already told him and he was upset. My mother was pretty upset about it too, but she had to tell him, "Just cool it. Calm down, because you can destroy the whole thing."

The *actos de repudio* were going on at that time and they were pretty scary. I had nightmares for days thinking that could happen to us. One day at school, they said we were going to someone's home to "demonstrate our gratitude to the Revolution." You had to go because if they took attendance and you weren't present you had to explain yourself. During the *acto*, people were throwing eggs and shouting all sorts of things. That was when I said to myself, "What they're doing to these people is uncivilized. How could they be doing this to this poor family that everyone in town knows?" It made me really think that I wanted to get out of there, that I didn't want to be part of this country. And I was there knowing that my uncle was waiting for us at Mariel. As you can imagine, I was thinking, "If somebody here turns around and says, 'Oh, he's leaving too,' they could just as easily turn on me."

One day a tall, lanky man in a military uniform came to the house. He asked if we were the García family. We said yes. He said, "You have received permission to leave the country." I took off to get my dad, who was at the other end of town. On the way back home, he stopped and called some people with whom he had made plans for us to stay before we left so we wouldn't have to suffer through an *acto de repudio*.

We went to the outskirts of town to wait for the cars that were going to take us to Havana. There were around fifty others there getting ready to leave; among them were some schoolmates who I never thought would have left Cuba. Suddenly, a motorcycle showed up with two militiamen. They called my father's name and said, "We have orders for you to come with us so we could ask you a few questions."

My father told us to go on ahead, that he would somehow meet up with us later. They took him. At that point, my mother broke down; I broke down, too; and my sister was going crazy asking what was going on. Half an hour later, we saw the same militiamen coming back with my father. He had been questioned because he had a Spanish passport and they wanted to know what that was all about. They also wanted to know about the house. We had a very nice house on prime real estate right in the center of town. Anyhow, they let him go but said they would come get him if they had other questions. So after that, you can imagine what it was like every time we ran into an official who wanted to see our documents.

From Sancti Spíritus, we went straight to the Abreu Fontán in Havana.

Manuel Vega

Born in 1949, Manuel Vega was from a small town in Havana Province. His parents were upper middle-class cattle farmers whose land was confiscated early in the Revolution. At the age of sixteen, Manuel, who would not integrate himself to the Revolution and possessed documents to exit Cuba, was sent to UMAP camps (described in the introduction) for three years. He later received a university degree and worked as a mechanical engineer in the sugar industry.

My brother was one of the first to go to Cuba when they allowed the visits of the late 1970s. He had left Cuba back in 1966, three days before he turned fifteen, shortly after I had been sent to the UMAP. My father had wanted to get him out of the country before he reached military age and paid 25,000 pesos to get him out through Spain. My brother went to Spain by himself and, while he was there, received the assistance of the Catholic Church. Forty-five days after arriving, he moved to San José, California, where our aunt lived.

When he visited us in Cuba, I had already graduated from the university and was working as the head of a machine center. During the visit, he asked me, "Brother, why don't you leave Cuba?" I said, "Because if I present papers saying that I want to leave the country, they'll eliminate me from everything. Plus, the chances of leaving are zero." If there was a real chance of leaving Cuba, I would have taken the risk. But there were no guarantees. He wanted to know if our parents could leave, and I told him, "Our folks can leave whenever they want, but the one here who cannot present papers to leave the country is me, because they'll destroy me." I had already been in the UMAP and I didn't want to go through something like that again.

Until the visits, no one in Cuba knew anything about the outside world. The visits were the first informational opening in twenty years. The people saw how the visitors—some of whom had left the country only a few years earlier—were able to return and take things to their families that no one in Cuba had. A saying developed: "A minute of business pays more than eighty years of work." People compared their lot to the visitors and asked, "How is it possible that I've spent twenty-one years here and these people who left five years ago have a car and food—and even dress differently." Some of the visitors showed off, but 80 percent of them told the truth about life in the United States.

The visits also helped provoke the Peruvian Embassy crisis. When it broke out, I was forced to go to an *acto de repudio* because of my job. At workplaces in Cuba, they'd say, "Get on this truck. We're going for a ride." On the way, they'd give you food, rum, and other things you couldn't normally acquire. Anyhow, they drove us past the embassy and the people shouted silly things like "*¡Pin pon fuera! ¡Abajo la gusanera!*"[61] The government always found words—*gusano, escoria,* etc.—to disqualify all of those who were not with them. They'd repeat it over and over until it became popular. They're masters of propaganda. But I would say that 90 percent of the people who went to the *acto* were like me: forced by their workplaces to go. No one goes to those things willingly, but if at work they tell you that you have to go, you can't just say no without proper justification; you can't just say, "I'm not going."

I had left the Ministry of Sugar in mid-1979 because I knew that, being part of it, I would never be able to leave Cuba. I had asked for a transfer to the National Institute for Agrarian Reform, where there was an agricultural technology school that gave classes to people from various countries. There were Angolans, Congolese, Ethiopians, and others there who were learning from Cubans things like how to repair tractors and agricultural equipment. Anyhow, in 1979, a friend there had offered me a position as vice principal of the school and I accepted it. When I presented my resignation at the Ministry of Sugar as a mechanical engineer, I had to go through a judicial process in order to transfer. I won my case.

Once I was at the school, I started looking for a way to leave the country since I no longer had the pressure that came from being with the Ministry of Sugar. My brother went to Cuba for a second time in March and he again suggested that I start to prepare things in order to leave the country. I said that the only way I would dare leave with him is if the government authorized me to do so and if he came to Jibacoa Beach on a boat to get me, our parents, my wife, and my children.

Incredibly, that's what happened—only instead of Jibacoa, it was Mariel.

We had no communication with the outside world, but we thought my brother would come to Mariel because there were families in the United States coming over and receiving authorization to retrieve their relatives. But since I wasn't absolutely certain he was coming, I had to keep going to work. I found out on Tuesday, April 22—through a person in my town who had spoken to someone in the United States—that my brother was going to Mariel. My wife and I worked until Thursday and took Friday off, since that would give us Friday, Saturday, and Sunday for them to come pick us up at home to go to the port. If we weren't picked up, we figured we'd go back to work on Monday.

My family in the United States had gotten together and purchased a twenty-two-foot boat, and my brother took a friend to Mariel with him who knew how to pilot boats in the Gulf. They got there on April 23, and requested us. The authorities picked us up at home on Saturday, April 26. When they came, they sent a single patrolman since the chief of police in our town didn't think I would leave the country—because of my position, people thought I was a Revolutionary. The chief said, "We're here to get your parents. Your brother is in Mariel. He claimed you as well, but we just sent one patrolman because we know you're not going to leave." I said, "You're wrong. Send for another patrolman because I'm leaving as well." He never imagined that I would leave—at that time I even had a state car, a 1955 Buick, which was considered a luxury. But he behaved well with us. They never carried out an *acto de repudio* against us in my town. My father had been a powerful man there who'd always helped the townspeople and he was good to everyone. As soon as we left—and we learned this from people who stayed behind and later came to the United States—people shouted at the police, "The father of the town has left."

We left for Havana with the two patrolmen: my father, my mother, my wife, my nine-year-old daughter, my eight-month-old son, and me. We saw no one until we arrived at the Abreu Fontán.

Emilio Izquierdo

Emilio Izquierdo was from Bahía Honda, Pinar del Río Province. Before the Revolution his family had owned a truck stop that sold a wide variety of products. In the early 1960s his father, whose business had been confiscated by the government, was sent to political prison for aiding anti-Castro rebels. A practicing Roman Catholic, Emilio was sent to a UMAP camp (described in the introduction) in 1965 at the age of eighteen. He was there for more than two years. He later worked at different office jobs until his 1980 departure from Cuba.

In 1979 cousins I hadn't seen since I was fourteen came to visit Cuba. One of them told me, "You guys may not realize it, but you live in miserable conditions. We're going to do everything possible to get you out of here."

After the visits, the events at the embassies started in Havana, with people crashing through gates and things like that. The city was a boiling pot getting ready to explode, and it finally culminated in the incident at the Peruvian Embassy. I was in Havana at around that time doing the paperwork to get my family out of Cuba; my father was an ex-political prisoner and the United States and other governments had been making arrangements for them and their families to be able to leave the island.

I went back to Bahía Honda because my wife's sister was having a troubled pregnancy. Things got complicated for her, so I returned to

Havana to take her to the gynecological hospital there. When we drove past Mariel, I saw the bay covered with so many boats that you could barely see the water. I told my wife I was going to stop and take a look. When I did, some special forces emerged from the mangroves. They pointed their guns at me and said, "Get back in the car! Get out of here!"

I eventually went back home and back to work. Then one night at midnight, I received a call from relatives in Miami saying they were trying to secure boats for us. When I got a message days later saying there was a boat waiting for us at Mariel, I told my wife to get everything ready to leave.

The government people in my town knew I was leaving before I did and my house started being watched on April 29. By then I had been required to resign my job and the pressure on me was increasing; remember, I had already been applying to leave the country through my father's political prisoner status. Then Castro called the "March of the Fighting People" across the island for Saturday, May 17. On that day, they gathered the schoolchildren, teachers, and public functionaries in my town and sent them to the homes of anyone who had boats waiting for them at Mariel or who were making arrangements to leave the island. The police came to the house to "protect us." When we asked what was going on, they told us they were conducting the "March of the Fighting People." They said, "The people are irritated with all of you for rejecting the Revolution . . . all of you have betrayed the Commander in Chief and the Revolution." I thought, "They've taken everything away from us! They've imprisoned us! How can I be betraying anyone? I've never been part of them!" The mob threw eggs at us, and did the same to all the homes of the people who were leaving.

Later that day the authorities came to get us for the trip to Mariel. They put my father, my uncle, and me into the open bed of a Czech truck; they put my mother, my wife, and my two daughters into a four-door Russian jeep and took them out of town by a different route. Before we departed, they lined up the townspeople along the sidewalks. As we left town on the open truck, they hurled eggs and all sorts of dirty things at us. It was disgusting. Then, as we drove along the road that led to the river—it was a rocky road filled with loose stones—we came under a barrage of rocks thrown by the crowd. My uncle's skull was fractured and he arrived at our first destination, the town of San Cristóbal, all bruised and covered in blood.

At San Cristóbal we were taken to the local offices of the Ministry of the Interior and thrown into an outdoor holding area designed for prisoners. We stayed there from the night of May 17, to around 3:00 p.m. on May 18, when we were all put on board one of the buses that had been picking people up in Guane, Pinar del Río, and other towns in the western part of the island. Everyone on the bus was going to Mariel. The trip to Havana was horrible. My uncle was surrounded by thousands of flies that had been attracted by the blood that covered him.

Isis Gottlieb

Isis Gottlieb, the only child in her family, was from Velasco, near the city of Holguin, Oriente Province. She was born in 1974 and was five years of age at the time of the Mariel Boatlift. Before the Revolution her paternal grandfather had been an agricultural inspector for the government. Her father, who became a high school physics teacher, was seven years of age when Castro took power in Cuba. Her mother was five.

I remember my father saying he'd always wanted to come to the United States. My grandfather once told me that he and my grandmother had considered sending him and my uncle during the Pedro Pan flights of the early 1960s, but that my grandmother did not want to do it. There was a big fight in the family about it, but my grandmother had said, "Absolutely not. Either we're all going together or nobody goes." So, of course, they stayed. My father would always give my grandmother a hard time about that.

I would say that by 1970, most of my relatives were in the United States. My dad had two or three aunts in Miami. My mother's mother was from a really big family and six of her sisters lived in Chicago. Their children also lived there. I remember my great-grandmother in Chicago would always write really pretty cards to me and put packs of gum in them. I loved that Juicy Fruit gum! I remember getting to my last stick and how horrible that would be. I never wanted it to go away. Once, I put my last piece under my pillow, hoping it would be there the next day. It got into my hair and my mom had to cut it really short. My relatives would also send me outfits once in a while. They were so pretty. I thought, "Wow. They have so many pretty things in the United States."

I don't remember too much about the Boatlift prior to the actual day we left Cuba. I do remember the songs people would sing against those who were leaving, and a lot of people talking and whispering. Everything was a mystery. Anyhow, the day before we left, my mother told me, "We're leaving for the United States." But she told me we were going to go there for a visit. So as far as I knew, we were all going on vacation. I wanted to bring a suitcase along, but they told me, "No, you can't bring anything. There's not enough room on the boat." I thought, "OK, great, I'm going to be given pretty dresses when I get there." I remember hiding all my stuff under my bed, including my violin and a little doll I had, to make sure no one took it while I was gone.

We left Cuba on May 20 or so. The ones who left with my family were my father's parents and my father's brother with his wife and child. I remember it was an ordeal to find a car to take us to Havana and that my grandfather had to stand in a very long line to be able to talk to someone there. Finally, this person came in a car and picked up all eight of us. I had to go on my parents' laps; my cousin, who was my same age, had to sit on his parents' laps. We would pull over on the open road to sleep; it was hot, too. We were stopped at a checkpoint once, and I remember everyone getting really nervous. But we were fine.

After a few days we got to Havana and were told to go to the Abreu Fontán. A mob was throwing rocks at us while we were standing in line to go in. Some people would drive by in cars and throw rocks as well. They were all shouting, "Traitors!" and "Worms!" and "Imperialist Yankees!" My father was holding me and trying to protect me. By that time, I was saying, "Wow. It's really hard to leave Cuba. I don't think I want to come back!"

Miriam Vilariño

Born in 1965, Miriam Vilariño was raised in a small town near Bay-
amo in Oriente Province. She was one of five sisters who ranged be-
tween the ages of four and eighteen at the time of the Mariel Boatlift.
Her grandfather, an immigrant from Galicia in Spain, had been a
farmer and cattle rancher in Cuba before the Revolution. As young
men, her father and uncles had initially supported Castro's war against
Batista and had joined the effort. They quickly concluded, however,
that Castro was a man who was not mentally and emotionally well.
In 1960, therefore, they joined the fight against him and were subse-
quently captured and arrested.

My father applied to leave Cuba as an ex-political prisoner and received permission to go to Venezuela. We were in the process of taking
our medical exams to go there when Mariel broke out.

While my father was in Havana having the final medical check done
on my third sister, Carmen, the authorities came to our house to tell
him that he either had to leave the country through Mariel or that he
could never leave. We contacted him in Havana and he came home to
Oriente right away. When they told him that he had to leave through
Mariel, he told them that he'd leave even if it had to be on a *yagua* [the
part of a palm branch that lies flush on the trunk and attaches the rest
of the branch to the tree]. So we turned over our home and all our
possessions.

They ordered us to report immediately to the Las Mangas prison in
the city of Bayamo. We did so, and from there they put us on a bus to
Havana. When the bus came to its first stop at a self-service restaurant
in Camagüey, we got off to eat. A few minutes later, the driver, who
knew my father was with five young girls, came running over to where
we were standing in line and told us, "Run! An *acto de repudio* is coming! Get back on the bus!" While we were boarding again—my parents
were carrying the two youngest and the driver had grabbed another
two of us—the mob surrounded the bus. They shouted and threw eggs
at us. It was alarming. The driver told us to close the windows and

not to say or do anything because he had seen that they were slicing people's hands with knives. We were terrified.

Later, our bus got a flat tire. Another bus stopped and its driver asked our driver if he could help. When the other driver said that he was transporting common prisoners, our driver told him to go on because his bus was filled with children. I remember one of the prisoners on the other bus stuck his head out the window. He had enormous eyes that bulged out and he was tattooed all over. Our driver told certain family men in our group that there was a possibility that those prisoners were being taken out of the country through the port of Mariel.

When we finally got to Havana, we were thrown into the Abreu Fontán like dogs.

Braulio Saenz

Braulio Saenz was from Havana. His father was a prominent veterinarian before the Revolution and became the technical director of the pathobiology station in Santiago de las Vegas. His mother was doctor of natural sciences and a teacher at the Rosalía Abreu Foundation Technical-Industrial School. Saenz received a doctorate in science from the University of Havana shortly before the Castro takeover (the University had been closed by Batista during Castro's war but, according to Saenz, was reopened briefly for graduate dissertation defenses). He worked as a scientist during the 1960s and 1970s and, because of his profession, was denied permission to leave the country on different occasions. In 1979 Saenz was fired from his job after he and his wife applied to go to the United States, via the Red Cross, to visit his ailing mother-in-law. He left Cuba in 1980 through Mariel with his wife and two daughters.

During the exile visits of the late 1970s the people looked through a window to the world and saw what they didn't have—like is happening now except that now it is much worse. But that was materialism, and that wasn't my point of view. My incentive was freedom. What I wanted was freedom. The most horrible thing in the world is to feel like a slave.

I lived in Rancho Boyeros, near the international airport. There was a market on a nearby corner and one day I went in to buy something. When I came outside again, I saw a large, air-conditioned bus filled with tourists on their way back to the airport. I was on the sidewalk and it passed just three or four meters from me. A pane of glass separated me from the passengers. I thought, "How incredible. Inside that glass there is freedom. These people came to Cuba for a little while and now they're leaving. Outside the glass, I can't even leave because I have no freedom of action in my own life." That's crushing. Freedom was what interested me—to be able to decide what one wants to do is everything, without freedom there is nothing. Realizing I was a slave was a difficult experience for me.

After I was fired from my last job [for having applied to go abroad to visit his mother-in-law in the United States] I was unemployed for a year. I went to Santiago de las Vegas and saw the municipal official there. I gave him my identity card and told him that I was Dr. Saenz and that I had been out of work for a year and that I had a wife and two children and I couldn't be unemployed in a system in which unemployment doesn't exist. He sent me to a secondary school in another town to work as an English teacher. The school later made me the chairman of the English department and I accepted. Then they offered to make me head of the language institute and I said no.

I was working at that school when the Mariel Boatlift started. My wife spoke to her brother, who was a U.S. military officer, and he chartered a shrimp boat to come for us.

One day after class one of my teachers had a problem with the regional secretary of the Party. She called me and I went with her, as head of the department, to the regional secretary to defend her. I solved her problem and went home. It was my last professional act. When I got home that day, I was very tired, not just from work but from the pressure of dealing with the teacher's issue. My wife said to me, "Supper is ready. Are you going to eat?" We had a pretty home with a porch that ran along the front and side. I said, "No. Give me ten minutes. I'm going to sit on the porch to cool off and then I'm going to take a shower.

Then, I'll eat." As soon as I sat down, a policeman stopped before us. He said, "You have ten minutes to get out of the house." I asked him, "For what reason?" He said, "You've been claimed at Mariel and you need to leave." We already knew that things worked like that. We were told to go to the Fontán. The policeman left.

I changed out of my work clothes and my wife threw away the supper she had cooked. We left the house walking. We lived two blocks from the main street, Rancho Boyeros Avenue. When we got there, I told my wife, "Stay here with the girls. Don't do anything to attract attention. I'm going to get a taxi." I walked two blocks down the Avenue, where the taxis gathered that went to Santiago de las Vegas. I got into one, sat, and told the driver, "Look, my wife and two daughters are up ahead. Please stop to pick them up." When he stopped, an *acto de repudio* was starting to form around them. I opened the door for them and they got in. When we left, the driver asked, "Where are we going?" I said, "The Fontán." He said, "That's not on my route." I had gotten paid that day, and I took out a twenty-peso bill. "Is this on your route?" I asked him. He said, "Yes, that's on my route." They never had time to carry out the *acto de repudio*; they were getting organized and screaming and calling people over, but we had gotten into the car and took off in time.

Inside the car, I told the driver, "Do not leave me a block away from the Fontán. Leave me at the entrance where there is a guard post. Leave me next to a soldier." I requested that because they would beat people up there, too. The man behaved very well and parked the car next to the post. I got off with my wife and daughters and told the guard, "We've been called here to leave the country."

Andrés Pazos

Andrés Pazos was born in Havana in 1946 and was thirteen when Fidel Castro came to power. His parents, immigrants from Spain, owned a bodega that was expropriated by the government in 1968. Pazos attended the University of Havana and became a certified public accountant. He later worked as an accountant in a government enterprise that distributed material for light industry in Cuba.

I had it in mind to leave Cuba from the time I got married. When Adolfo Suárez, the first president of Spain after Franco died, improved relations with Cuba he instructed Spain's embassy in Havana to make a list of all the Spaniards on the island who wished to be repatriated to Spain with their families. My father was number three on the list. When they'd called to ask if he wished to be repatriated, we all said yes. So, they put us on the list and we began waiting for authorization from Cuba to leave. While we were waiting, the Mariel Boatlift broke out.

My wife had family in the United States and we called them right away and asked them to send a boat for us. "We'll pay you back later," we told them, "but you have to get us out of here." They chartered a shrimp boat to come pick us up.

One night, State Security came to our house to get us. They carried out an inspection and asked us to turn over the house keys and car keys. My mother had died during the two-year period during which we were trying to leave, so departing Cuba that day were my father, my wife, and me. People were in front of the house screaming in a *repudio* meeting as we boarded the little bus they'd sent to transport us; it was a rather small *acto de repudio* because we had lived there for a long time and my parents were very kind people. It was mostly just a group from the CDR that was there; in fact, a lot of the people I saw screaming elsewhere didn't go scream at us. The bus—which in addition to the driver carried a militiaman and a State Security agent—picked up other people in the neighborhood until it was full. It took us to the *Círculo Militar y Naval*, which they called the Abreu Fontán.

Cuban refugees aboard a vessel arriving in Key West, Florida, from the port of Mariel in Cuba. Photo by Dale M. McDonald. Courtesy of the State Archives of Florida, https://www.floridamemory.com/items/show/98688.

The *El Dorado* arrives in Key West, Florida, during the Mariel exodus. Photo by Dale M. McDonald. Courtesy of the State Archives of Florida, https://www.floridamemory.com/items/show/98693.

For many refugees, finally arriving in the United States was an emotional experience. Photo by Dale M. McDonald. Courtesy of the State Archives of Florida, https://www.floridamemory.com/items/show/98690.

The U.S. Coast Guard patrolled the Florida Straits during the Mariel Boat-lift. Photo by Dale M. McDonald. Courtesy of the State Archives of Florida, https://www.floridamemory.com/items/show/98707.

Most of the boats departing for the port of Mariel in Cuba did so from docks in Key West, Florida. Photo by Dale M. McDonald. Courtesy of the State Archives of Florida, https://www.floridamemory.com/items/show/98710.

Cuban Americans in Key West searching for loved ones on boats coming in from Mariel. Photo by Dale M. McDonald. Courtesy of the State Archives of Florida, https://www.floridamemory.com/items/show/98721.

Cuban authorities deliberately overloaded vessels departing Mariel to hazardous levels. Photo by Dale M. McDonald. Courtesy of the State Archives of Florida, https://www.floridamemory.com/items/show/100760.

The Florida Marine Patrol was one of the entities that helped manage the Mariel crisis. Courtesy of the State Archives of Florida, https://www.floridamemory.com/items/show/117277.

Cuban refugees received food, clothing, medical care, clean cots, shower facilities, and other emergency assistance at the seaplane hangar at Trumbo Point in Key West. Photo by Dale M. McDonald. Courtesy of the State Archives of Florida, https://www.floridamemory.com/items/show/98697.

Refugee boats arriving in Key West, Florida, from the port of Mariel. Photo by Dale M. McDonald. Courtesy of the State Archives of Florida, https://www.floridamemory.com/items/show/98732.

Cuban refugees arriving from Mariel recall the kind treatment they received from the many U.S. military personnel who were called in to Key West to assist with the Mariel crisis. Photo by Dale M. McDonald. Courtesy of the State Archives of Florida, https://www.florida memory.com/items/show/98689.

The author's wife, Emilia Ferrer-Triay, an artist, was thirteen when she departed Cuba on the Mariel Boatlift. On her journey across the Florida Straits, the boat carrying her sank; she and the other passengers were rescued at sea by the U.S. Coast Guard. Thirty-four years later, moved by the plight of Cubans who continued risking their lives to escape the Communist island and inspired by the memory of her own experience, she created this ink collage titled *Fidel Castro's Masterpiece: The Death of Freedom.*

3

Herded into the Abreu Fontán and the "Mosquito"

SHORTLY AFTER THE FOUNDING of the Cuban Republic in the early twentieth century, Cuba's military elite established for itself a private recreational club called the *Círculo Militar y Naval*. The institution would later include segments of Cuban society, such as professionals, who were not members of the military. After several years at different locations in the Cuban capital, the *Círculo* opened a modern facility along the Marianao shoreline in the 1950s, close to more elite clubs such as the Havana Yacht Club, the Biltmore Yacht Club, and the Miramar Yacht Club.

When Fidel Castro brought an end to the era of private clubs in Cuba, the *Círculo* was expropriated by the Revolution, along with the others. It was later converted into a recreational facility for a workers' organization and renamed the *Círculo Social Gerardo Abreu Fontán*, after a revolutionary killed by the Batista government. The club soon fell into disrepair. Mirta Ojito remembered, "Before the revolution it had been a playground for the rich; since the revolution it had belonged to the workers—and it showed. Pre-1959 it must have been a grand building, with its tiled floors, high ceilings, and carved stucco columns framing perfect views of the ocean. When we arrived there, it was in disarray: peeling paint, broken windows, and untended gardens."[1] It was to this club, referred to simply as the "Abreu Fontán" or "the Fontán," that nearly all those leaving on the Boatlift were required to report, and it was the first of two stops before reaching the port of Mariel.

From the time they arrived at the Abreu Fontán to the time the boats carrying them to the United States were at sea, Mariel emigrants were completely at the mercy of Cuban authorities. Given that the institutional machinery that concentrated, processed, and released the emigrants was a twenty-four-hour operation that functioned over the course of months, individual experiences at this stage varied somewhat. Nevertheless, some overall patterns were clearly discernible from the interviews conducted for the present work as well as from information provided by other sources.

Cubans departing through Mariel quickly learned that the physical and verbal attacks launched against them would not end upon departing their homes. The Cuban government, unyielding in its effort to make the emigration process as degrading, painful, and frightening as possible, ensured that Revolutionary enmity would rain down on those leaving the country to the very last moment it could exert its influence. Arrival at the Abreu Fontán exemplified this reality, as many of the refugees—men, women, and children alike—were met near the entrance by a mob composed of egg-throwing, rock-hurling loyalists who also delivered blows, shouted insults, and chanted slogans as the emigrants made their way past.[2] One person reported having had potatoes thrown at him and his family.[3]

After running the gauntlet of harassment and entering the Abreu Fontán, the emigrants found terror of the Revolution's mobs replaced by terror of the Revolution's bureaucracy. They were forced to sit and wait—in some cases for long hours and sometimes for as long as a week—to be called for processing by the officials stationed there. They waited on the grass, on the baseball field, on the sand, and in exterior hallways, never quite certain of why they were there or how long it would be until they were allowed to go to the port of Mariel. Cubans who had lived under the Castro government had long grown accustomed to waiting in line for basic items such as food, clothing, and toilet paper; rarely had they waited in line for something that would so immediately and permanently change their lives.

During the Mariel exodus the Abreu Fontán often became overcrowded with refugees. As they waited to be called for processing, the jam-packed emigrants were allowed to purchase overpriced sandwiches, yogurt, soda, and other items.[4] The availability of such foodstuffs, however, was inadequate to feed the multitude concentrated at the facility.[5] While a guard could occasionally be bribed to secure extra milk or other items, hunger nevertheless prevailed.[6] Adding to the overall misery, the toilet facilities were reportedly filthy.[7]

When finally called, the refugees were directed to a series of long tables where officials interrogated and processed them.[8] The system was designed, in part, as a final filter to deny exit to those deemed ineligible to leave Cuba—even if they had previously gained clearance to do so. Reasons for final denial could include possessing skills deemed indispensable to the Revolution, being someone in whose education the Revolution had invested heavily, or being of (or close to) military age. The interrogations proved to be one of the points at which numerous families experienced the worst horror of the Mariel experience: family separation. In many cases certain family members were permitted to leave the country, while other members were not.[9] Those denied the right to emigrate were thereupon thrust back into Cuban society, where their lives could become a living torment as they were now officially marked as traitors and enemies of the state for having wanted to leave the country.

When a group of refugees was finally called to be taken from the Abreu Fontán to Mariel, they were transported on government-provided buses. Some experienced additional *actos de repudio* at this juncture.[10] Mirta Ojito recalled: "Shortly after, we were seated in a bus with no windows—intentionally removed to expose us to the fury of the protesters outside. As we left Fontán, we crouched down in our seats, uncertain of what to expect. Those who did not were pelted with tomatoes and eggs thrown by the mob. Some people cried, while others cursed under their breath. An old lady prayed."[11]

The next stop, much to the angst of those departing, was not the port of Mariel but a desolate, seaside camp a couple of miles from it called El Mosquito. The facility made the overcrowded, dilapidated, germ-infested Abreu Fontán seem as though it were still in its late 1950s glory. Upon arrival at El Mosquito the refugees were forced to queue up, sometimes for hours, outside a small building at the camp's entrance. They reportedly had to walk through a metal detector before they were finally called into the structure.[12] Once inside, they were interviewed individually by government officials and forced to turn over all their documents and most of their possessions—including cash, jewelry, personal valuables, keepsakes, and even the telephone numbers of friends and relatives in the United States.[13] The immigrant cliché "I came to this country with only the clothes on my back" was quite literally true during the Mariel Boatlift. The next stop in the building was a space behind a small curtain where the refugees were strip-searched to ensure they were not smuggling out any hidden items.[14]

The inspection finished, the refugees stepped out of the building at the opposite end and entered a stark, frightening camp, complete with barbed wire fences, attack dogs, and armed guards. As in many prison camps, spotlights were set up to scan the facility during the nighttime hours.[15] Across barren Mosquito, separate compounds were established for the different categories of refugees. Although accounts vary on this point, these categories reportedly included those whose families abroad had claimed them; those who had been in the Peruvian Embassy; political prisoners and their families; and the so-called undesirables or anti-socials, who included inmates from Cuba's common prisons (individuals from the prisons and hospitals were reportedly taken from their institutions directly to El Mosquito).[16] The latter compound was more heavily guarded than the others and separated from them by some distance. More than a few refugees would arrive in the United States sporting fresh wounds and dog bites from their stay at El Mosquito.

Each compound at El Mosquito consisted of large open-sided tents of green canvas, containing rows of military bunks. As the number of refugees increased, sleeping space became scarce; many adults slept on the floor or outdoors, especially men, who ceded their bunks to women and children.[17] The authorities at El Mosquito provided the refugees scant food, amounting to little more than small cups of yogurt, tiny portions of unsalted hard rice with green-colored (and often burned) bits of egg, and small biscuits. Many were sickened by the limited, grim fare. Procuring the dreadful cuisine was itself an odyssey, as the refugees were forced to wait in long queues where guards kept them in line with physical aggression, streams of verbal insults, and the menacing presence of attack dogs. Drinking water, meanwhile, was exposed to the scorching sun all day long.[18]

Amid the oppressive heat, soaking rains, squalor, unforgiving mosquitoes, aggression of the guards, horrid stench, and dangerously unsanitary conditions, the refugees listened closely for the names of their boats to be called over loudspeakers. Anxiety reigned with regard to being called, as they had been informed that if they did not respond to the call right away, they would not be able to leave the country.[19] Or they would have to wait longer until another boat became available.[20] Since the boats' names were called all day and night, accidentally nodding off could impact the future of an entire family. Adding to the stress, many of the boats had English language names, which were being announced on muffled loudspeakers by non-English-speaking Cubans; as such, even the keenest listener might miss the critical call.[21]

When a group was finally called—which, as at the Fontán, could occur within a few hours or after several days—the refugees were once again herded onto a bus. This time it was a short trip to the port of Mariel. Unbathed, bedraggled, beaten, drained, dehydrated, and malnourished, the shell-shocked refugees, devoid of virtually all material possessions, were one step closer to freedom. Most could not imagine that the final leg of their odyssey could be the most precarious of all.

This chapter includes testimonies detailing the refugees' arrival and stay at the Abreu Fontán and the Mosquito. Included among the various stories are those of families separated at this stage.

There were more than a thousand people at the Abreu Fontán when we got there. We were given small mattresses to sleep on, since the boats weren't yet leaving. After waiting a number of hours, they called me over a microphone. I went over, and they told me that since I was a doctor, I couldn't leave without a discharge from the Ministry of Public Health.

I was of the opinion that we, the nuclear family, should not be divided. We told my mother-in-law to go on ahead to the United States with the rest of her family. If we sent her, we figured she could claim us later. So my mother-in-law left and my wife, my six-year-old son, the baby, and I turned back.

We went back home to Ciego de Ávila. After a couple of days there, a mob carried out an *acto de repudio* against us. They gathered across the street to throw eggs, rocks, tomatoes, and everything else at the house. Since I had never been a member of the CDR or anything, most of the insults were directed against my wife because she, in order to keep up appearances, had been in the Federation of Cuban Women and was part of the CDR. They'd shout, "Traitor! Worm! Bootlick!" and all those things they would say. The next day I boarded up the circulation vents that ran high up on the walls.

Then they carried out another more violent *acto de repudio*. This time they were pushing on the doors as if to burst in. I grabbed a machete and stood in the living room just in case someone came through. I lost control at one point and was about to go outside—I'm not a valiant guy or a tough guy or anything, but there are moments when one has just had enough. But then my six-year-old son grabbed my leg and cried, "Daddy, don't go outside," and I didn't go. If I had gone out, the mob would have killed me; that was their intention. So we put up some bars behind the door and moved furniture behind it for reinforcement.

Eight months later, my wife and children were able to get visas to leave through Costa Rica. I stayed behind by myself.

Anonymous

This interviewee chose to remain anonymous. She was the daughter and granddaughter of sugar cane planters in a small provincial town and had attended Catholic boarding schools before the Revolution. After the Castro government expropriated the family farm, her father became an anti-government guerrilla and was arrested in the early 1960s. He was released after several years. The interviewee eventually married, settled in Havana, became a housewife, and had three children. She and her husband had applied to emigrate from Cuba more than once before 1980, but were unsuccessful.

We found out about the Mariel Boatlift through a telephone call from my husband's sister, who told us, "Listen, we're going there on a boat to get all of you." That was on April 25, 1980. That same day, she and my mother-in-law—they had both come to the United States before—chartered a boat and paid five hundred dollars per head. We started jumping up and down, saying, "We're all leaving! How wonderful!" My daughter was seven, one son was fourteen, and my other boy was almost sixteen.

An olive-green jeep showed up in front of the house. Some military men got out and told us, "You're all leaving." When they boarded us on the jeep, they lined up the entire block to carry out an *acto de repudio*. They chanted at us, but you could tell they were forced to do it because we got along well with all of them. My seven-year-old daughter didn't even know what was going on, didn't know that they were carrying out an *acto de repudio*; since they were clapping, she just said to them, "Goodbye, goodbye!"

When we got to the Abreu Fontán, they interviewed us and put the final stamp on our identity cards. With that stamp, you were marked: at that moment, you lost your job and you lost your home; they put a seal on your house and they could carry out all the *actos de repudio* they wanted against you. It was there, at the Abreu Fontán, where they told us, "The one who is sixteen cannot leave. All of you can depart except the sixteen-year-old." It was, supposedly, because he was about to turn military age; he was still fifteen but was getting ready to turn sixteen. It was as though a jar of cold water had been poured on us. What do we do now?

My husband knew that he couldn't return to his job with that stamp on his papers; he knew they wouldn't give him another job, either. He said, "It's going to be very difficult to support a family without a job." Then he said, "Listen, I'll stay with him [the older son] and see how I could arrange his release from military service." He knew there were ways to arrange it, like claiming illness or doing like the people who lined up and said they were homosexuals and got out as such. But none of that would work for the boy because he was raised with a moral base, in the sense of never deceiving, of never feigning things, of never lying. He didn't know how to get into a line and pretend to be a homosexual.

My husband told me to get the other children out of Cuba because the younger one, at fourteen, was coming up on military age and it would then be much more difficult for all of us to leave. Plus, we were decided upon gaining our freedom and not to continue living in that country with so much oppression. My daughter started crying.

My daughter, my younger son, and I were put on a bus right away and taken to the Mosquito—that was on April 25 or 26. We didn't get out of the Mosquito until May 9. Since we were among the first to arrive there, they were still in the process of putting up the tents. So we spent the first day on the *diente de perro* [jagged, exposed rocks]; there were no bathrooms, there was nothing. Little by little, they set up the tents—which had no walls, just a roof—and put some small cots into them.

The whole place was full of guards. The military personnel told everyone, "If you don't hear your names when they're announced, you'll stay here forever. You have to be attentive." They did it that way so that people couldn't sleep. So my fourteen-year-old son had to spend all day listening for our names while he stood in the hot sun on the *diente de perro*. His feet got very swollen. Meanwhile, I was taking care of my seven-year-old daughter on a cot I was able to get in the tent—I had to stay on it, because if I left it even for a moment someone else would have taken it and she wouldn't have had a place to sleep.

Every day they gave us hard, undercooked rice and a burnt scrambled egg. That was our only food. At one point, my son got sick and they had to take him to the infirmary—which was in a different tent—to lay him on a cot. He vomited so much that his eyes had red spots on them.

At the beginning, you could see this was about family reunification because you saw family groups there. But then they started to release people from the prisons. When they got to the Mosquito, I had to take care that they wouldn't violate my daughter. It was frightful. Then the authorities started to bring in attack dogs to control the prisoners. The guards grew so obstinate that they would set the dogs on those who were there for family reunification the same as they would on the delinquents.

[She relates the fate of her husband and older son when they left the Abreu Fontán, after the latter was denied permission to leave Cuba]: When my husband and son went out of the Abreu Fontán to get the bus to go back home, they had to run because a mob went after them with rocks and sticks. My husband shouted, "Run! Run! Run!" They grabbed on to the bus as it went past and freed themselves from the beating. When they got home, they saw that the authorities still hadn't put the seal on the house. So they went to the CDR, who were friends of ours, and they gave my husband the key back. From then on, he and my son had to take care not to be killed.

My son had been among the top students in his class and had been nominated to attend the prestigious Lenin School—the nomination was because of his grades, not his political activity. Anyhow, his school gathered in front of our house and carried out an *acto de repudio*. They threw eggs and rocks at the house. My husband had to reinforce the door and windows with wooden bars because the demonstrators were trying to push their way in to beat them. The mob stoned our dog to death.

The group that carried out the *acto de repudio* that day included not just the students but people from our block—including people I saw here in Miami a year later. When I saw one of them, I asked her, "You're here? Didn't you carry out an *acto de repudio?*" She said, "Well, at that moment we had to be that way." That was true, as even relatives who were Revolutionaries behaved that way. A cousin of mine wanted to kill my husband because he'd sent us to the United States; my own relatives carried out *actos de repudio* against them. These were people whose minds had been worked over, whose minds had become rotted. It was horrible.

My husband looked for work everywhere. But to get a job, he'd have to show his identity card. When they'd see the stamp, they wouldn't give him one. He sold everything in the house in order to eat, but had to do it surreptitiously because the CDR was watching to see if he'd take even a little package out. Also, we had some guava trees in our yard and so he'd make some guava jelly and secretly venture out with two or three little bottles and sell them at the tenements in Old Havana—trembling the whole time, thinking that a policeman would inspect his package.

For our son to receive his release from military service, my husband went to the library and studied all the symptoms of schizophrenia. A cousin of his who worked at Mazorra [Havana's psychiatric hospital] had told him that youths diagnosed with schizophrenia were given release from military service. He started by taking the boy to the local medical clinic and describing to the doctor all the symptoms that he had studied. He said, "Look, Doctor, my son doesn't want to bathe, he doesn't speak, and he's always depressed and with his head down. He misses his mom a lot since she left the country." So he started painting the picture, based on what he'd studied about schizophrenia, there at the clinic. The doctor at the clinic sent the boy for psychiatric treatment. They gave him some pills, which he and my husband would throw away.

Of course, my son didn't have schizophrenia but my husband was presenting that picture. He would talk to the doctors, while the boy would just sit there silently with his head down, saying nothing. The boy was reluctant to play that role; it was a struggle to make it seem as though he had that disease and also a struggle because he didn't want to cooperate. But, well, it was the only way to get him out.

Then they checked my son into Mazorra and placed him under treatment. My husband would tell him not to swallow any of the pills they gave him and he would throw them out. At the hospital, my husband wouldn't separate himself from the boy for anything in the world and spent three days there without even bathing. He finally reached the point where he said, "I'm going home to bathe and change clothes because, if not, I'm going to raise suspicions here." He called his half-sister and told her, "Listen, come here and stay with the boy and make sure they do nothing to him. I'm going home to bathe and change." He explained to her what he was up to.

While my husband was away, they came in to give my son electro-shock treatment. When the boy saw that, he escaped through a hospital window. He got on a bus, in his pajamas, and went home. His father was still there when he arrived. My son told him, crying, "Dad, please, don't make me do this anymore." My husband said, "Well, son, it was our way of leaving; it was only so that they would give you release from military service. Let it be as God wills." It hurt him a great deal to have his son play that role, but there was no other way for him, a completely healthy boy, to be released from military service.

Then the hospital gave him a document stating that, because he had escaped, he was even worse than they had thought! That paper was enough for a military committee—made up of five doctors who were rabid dogs—to see if he was really schizophrenic. They had to demonstrate that they were guided not only by the diagnosis from Mazorra, but that it was confirmed by military doctors.

God put His hand in things.

My son didn't want his father to go in with him to meet with the committee—he wanted to go in alone. At the meeting, he confessed nothing; he just lowered his head and didn't answer any of their questions. He walked out of there with his release from military service.

They were allowed to leave immediately after my son received his release. The ordeal took two years and two months. Right away, I arranged for tickets for them to fly out of Cuba to Venezuela. My mother-in-law, who was an American citizen, claimed them. I remember the tickets cost $750.

We arrived at the Abreu Fontán at night. There was a huge ocean of people there, hundreds of them, sleeping on the ground in makeshift tents. We heard that some people had been there for days.

We spent the night on the ground in an open field by the ocean. I remember looking out and thinking, "Wow." It was almost like I could see the U.S. on the other side of the water. The feeling was pretty cool. I thought, "Pretty soon, I'm going to be on the other side and I'm going to be out of this country." It was a feeling of renewal, of hope that something better was coming despite the fact that everything was so horrible at that moment.

The next day at around noon, our names were called and we were put on a bus. Besides the driver, there were two guys from the police on board. After we were traveling for around ten minutes, the driver announced, very nicely, to the passengers, "Let me tell you all what's coming. We're going to go to this place, but once you get there you're going to be checked. They're going to confiscate everything from you. So if you have anything that you want to give away—money or whatever—I'll be glad to take it right now so they don't take it away from you by force." As one might imagine, the people on the bus emptied their pockets right away. Those guys probably made out like bandits.

The Mosquito was probably the most sinister place I ever encountered in my life in Cuba. It was there to create fear; it was almost like they were saying, "This is your last taste of Cuba, and we're going to make you pay." For a child of my age to get there and see that camp . . . it was almost like those scenes you see in Nazi films, with barbed wire everywhere. I had never seen policemen with machine guns and dogs before. The treatment we received was very rough, with the guards shouting, "Get in line!" Those were the guys who were there to give you a farewell.

When we got there, we had to wait in a huge line. During the searches, it was very intimidating when they would take your parents. They'd say to the kids, "You guys stay there," and there would be a guy standing there with a machine gun and a dog. Then they'd tell the adults, "Go in here," and they'd conduct a full strip search on them. My mother was pretty bothered by it. My father had a gold chain with him that had been in the family for generations; he didn't want to give it up and had hidden it somewhere—I don't know exactly where. Anyhow, they found the chain when they checked him and he lost it.

There were military tents everywhere, with cots and bunk beds in them. Then there was a fence, and you could see they were keeping only men on the other side of it; they were obviously being kept separate from the families.

We were there for three hours. That same night, at approximately nine or ten o'clock, we were called. They took us on another bus to the Mariel port.

Lourdes Campbell

When we got to the Abreu Fontán . . . wow, it was like that moment in *Total Recall* when Arnold Schwarzenegger gets to Mars. The area was enclosed by barbed wiring; armed guards were on patrol with German shepherds and people were sleeping on the ground. There was a mob outside the entrance throwing eggs and hollering vulgarities. I had never experienced such anger and hostility. When we made our way inside, it was full of people ranging from small children to the elderly. There was no cover, no tents, and no access to any of the buildings—other than the deplorable bathrooms. The guards treated people roughly. People who were sick were not getting any medical attention and children were crying. Day and night, we could hear the mob outside shouting, "¡Escoria!" "Scum of society!" "Parasite!" "Traitor!" My dad and I were there for at least five nights.

The next step in the process to get to Mariel was to listen for your name to be called. If you missed your name, you were done. So everyone teamed up, trying to help each other. Small groups of people found out each other's names so that if you fell asleep when your name was called, they would wake you up. When you left the Abreu Fontán, you had to leave behind any money you had. So when they called your name, you gave your money to someone else; then that person would give whatever they had left to the next person, and so on. When we were handed the roll, it contained a nice little bit of money and we were able to buy food and beverages.

When our names were finally called, we were transported to the Mosquito. It was nighttime and very dark. After exiting the bus, we were searched in some tents. I had to strip down completely. I was fifteen, without my parents, and in a room with this strange person; at least it was a woman. I felt completely violated. It was horrible.

The place had dirt floors and little bulbs that barely gave off any light. I remember there was a Santera there with a little white turban; they made her take the turban off.[22] She had a lot of shells and other things in there and when they told her that she couldn't take them she threw a big fit. The treatment was terrible. People were cluttered everywhere; everyone was mentally and physically exhausted, dirty, and feeling insecure and vulnerable. The guards were uncooperative and aggressive. They'd shout, "Get over here! Go over there! Shut up! Don't speak!" I don't think they physically pushed me, but they might as well have. I definitely felt bullied.

Thank goodness that we spent only around fifteen minutes at that location before they called our names to go to where the boats were. My dad was quite surprised. We walked toward the water and boarded our boat.

Javier Delgado

Javier Delgado was born in 1972. His father had opposed Fidel Castro and had consequently served time in political prison. His father later became a civil engineer. His mother worked as a manicurist and hair stylist, and was also an employee at a toy store. Javier's parents divorced when he was around a year and a half old, and he was raised in a household with his mother, grandmother, and uncle in the Marianao section of Havana. He was seven years of age when he left Cuba.

As kids, we had heard things about the Boatlift but didn't really know what was going on. One day I was in a relative's car with my mom and all the kids [his cousins] coming home from somewhere. We ran across a huge mob and everyone in the car was saying, "Oh, my gosh! What's going on?" The people in the mob were hoisting a man up above them and carrying him down the street; they were yelling and beating him, calling him "*gusano.*" A woman was screaming and she came up to our car and started banging on the window; she was asking for help because they were going to kill whoever that person was. I was thinking to myself, "What's going on? Why aren't we helping him?" The adults obviously knew that if we did we would have been next.

My grandmother's side of the family left Cuba during the Boatlift; they had been picked up by family members in the United States. Before they left, my Uncle Manolo promised my mom that they would bring us here to the United States, because she had immediately wanted to go.

The next thing I remember was that my mom and I were at some type of government compound where there were a lot of people. My mom, who was around twenty-eight years old at the time, couldn't leave with me until my father had given away his rights as a father. He was working as a civil engineer for the government at the time. My father and I sat down—I remember it was at night—and he explained to me why he thought it was better for me to leave Cuba. He obviously felt it was in my best interest and told me so. He had to give up all his rights. I didn't know my dad that well; I had spent some time with him and I had spent some time with my grandmother on his side of the family, but we didn't have Sundays together or anything like that.

The next thing I remember was that my mom and I were on a beach and that there were huge tents there with cots inside them. I recall my mom talking about how embarrassing the whole strip search was. I played with the other kids there on the beach; for me, it was like going to the beach except that I was sleeping on a cot and didn't really know what was happening. As a kid, they'd give you a box lunch—maybe once or twice a day, I don't remember.

There were a lot of men at that place and I remember my mom being very nervous in general about my safety. I remember she also worried over whether or not a boat would come for us. She tried to reassure me and told me that we would be seeing my cousins really soon. We were there for at least three or four days.

Ivonne Cuesta

Ivonne Cuesta was born in Havana. Before the Revolution her pa-
ternal grandparents were professors at the teachers' school in Pinar
del Río and her maternal grandparents were merchants. Her parents
moved to Havana after marrying and her father fought in Cuba's war
in Angola. Her parents subsequently tried to emigrate to the United
States via Spain, but were unsuccessful because of her father's war vet-
eran status. Ivonne was seven years of age at the time of the Mariel
Boatlift.

Relatives on my father's side of the family had left Cuba in the early
1960s and settled in Puerto Rico. My grandmother in Cuba, my father's mother, convinced them to come and take us away from the island during the Mariel Boatlift. My grandfather already had passed
away, and she had wanted to leave the island for a long time. Anyhow,
she was the catalyst for us leaving; she was the engine. She died when I
was fifteen years old, and I remember her as a person who loved freedom, loved democracy, and loved everything the United States stood
for. She was like the matriarch of our family.

My parents divorced when I was very young, but my mother stayed
close to my father's family. The plan was always for all of us to come to
the United States together. I was seven at the time of the Boatlift and
conscious, to an extent, about what was going on. I didn't have a full
grasp of the situation, but I would hear the conversations and knew
that we were leaving. My mother would tell me, "You can't tell any-
body. You can't say anything to your teachers in school. You can't talk
about this with your friends."

I lived with my mother in an old, Spanish-style house with high
ceilings. The *actos de repudio* had been occurring and she didn't want
to get caught in one with a seven-year-old, in a house by herself, and in
the middle of the night. So every evening she packed up some clothes
and a few personal things and we would go sleep at my maternal
grandmother's house just in case they came for us. It became a routine for us. I recall—and perhaps because the memories are still alive

through the conversations my family has to this day—that my mother was very tense throughout this time.

One of the nights we were at my grandmother's house, there was a knock at the door. A person from the government was there dressed in uniform. He said, "You're leaving." He had a list of people who were supposed to come to the United States. At that point, there was a discussion between my mom and my dad. My mom realized that she wanted her family to come with her. She said, "I want to bring my mother with me. I want my brothers to come as well." They were somehow able to work that out, so the people who ended up leaving were: my mom, her two brothers, my maternal grandmother, my paternal grandmother, her sister, my father, and me. They put us in a car and took us to a beach called the Abreu Fontán.

I remember the Abreu Fontán was very crowded. We set up camp there; my mom and my uncles had brought blankets and sheets and literally built a tent on the sand. There were a lot of families there and a huge line to use the bathroom. Everybody was on edge; nobody really knew what was going to happen next. My mom tells me that she was very tense.

We must have been there for a day or two when they sent someone from the government to where we were and pulled my dad out. That's when he was told, "You're not going anywhere" [because he was a veteran of the war in Angola]. The official then asked, "Are you going to let your daughter leave?" The official didn't want my father to let me leave. My father tells me it was a very hostile conversation. Anyhow, at that point my dad had a decision to make. He signed off and gave his permission to let me leave.

We were at the Abreu Fontán for seven days. Because of what happened to my dad, things got worse for us. We wondered, "Who else are they going to pull? Who else are they going to separate? What else is going to happen?" We went the Mosquito, but we must have been there only hours. Then we went to the port of Mariel.

Andrés Valerio

Born in 1934 in Havana, Andrés Valerio was the son of a long-time
employee of the University of Havana. Although Andrés had studied
to become an art teacher and graduated as such in 1958, he never
taught, becoming instead a full-time artist. He was prevented from
leaving Cuba in the early 1960s by the cancellation of flights to the
United States following the Cuban Missile Crisis. During the Camari-
oca Boatlift, he received permission to leave the country but his wife at
the time did not want to go. His mother and younger sister, who had
left for the United States in 1970, claimed his family at the outbreak of
the Mariel Boatlift.

I got to the Abreu Fontán with my wife and our daughter. There was
a huge hall there filled with long, rectangular tables large enough for
twelve people. They'd sit you before a group of individuals, who were
back and on the left, and they asked a whole series of questions. We
were at the Abreu Fontán for around two hours. We filled out some
papers, signed them, and got picked up with a group of others by a bus
that took us to the military base at Mariel—the Mosquito.

When you got to the Mosquito, you had to leave everything behind:
your rings, your money, everything. We were there for eight days.
When we first arrived, people were sleeping outdoors on pieces of
cardboard, exposed to the sun, the light, and the air. The tents were put
up because two other people and I spoke to a colonel there, the head of
the base, and said to him, "Look, we have young children here and we
can't live like this. As of now, we don't even know when we're leaving. If
it rains or if anything else happens, we have nowhere to go." The colonel said to me, "If you want to, form a brigade." Then he showed me
where there were several large canvas packages outside. He said, "The
tents are over there. Set them up." We asked, "Where do we sleep?"
He said, "There are also some wooden bunk beds that only need to be
assembled." So we formed a brigade and put up the first seven tents.
Then we started assembling the bunk beds and set them up them inside the tents.

Two or three days passed and I thought, "No one is going to leave this place." There were, by then, between 2,000 and 2,500 people at the Mosquito. And I knew more were arriving every night because I would hear the dogs that had been brought in to guard the people they were bringing in from the prisons. The prisoners were also being watched by guards armed with bayonets. The prisoners were kept separate from the other people, but when we got on the bus to go to the port they were put on board with us.

Andrés Reynaldo

When we got to the Abreu Fontán, there was a mob waiting outside to beat people up and to throw eggs at them. It was organized into two lines around four feet apart, and you had to go in between the two lines to get in. The policeman entered in front of us; of course, the advantage of that was that the mob had to wait until the policeman went by before they hit you—but, if you went quickly. . . . So this other guy and I ran through there very fast. Plus, there were people coming in behind us that the mob had to get ready to hit.

The Abreu Fontán was the center where they did the final processing. There were some long tables there where uniformed State Security people were seated. You had to turn your papers in and they would check them. That's where they told you, "You can't leave," or sometimes, if they saw large families, they would say, "No, you can't go, you're staying; the woman and the child are going, but you're staying." It was terrible.

They were overwhelmed with work at the Abreu Fontán, so they processed you as quickly as they could. Then you went outside. There were two or three places where they sold pizza and things to eat, but it was very, very expensive. I had taken two hundred pesos with me, and I must have eaten a pizza and had some coffee; by the time I left, I only had seventy pesos left. I spent the night of May 17 there, and on May 18, in the late afternoon, I was taken to the Mosquito. When they called people to go to the Mosquito, they did so over a loudspeaker. They'd say, "A bus is leaving for the Mosquito. The following citizens present themselves. . . ." Since I knew that at the Mosquito they would take everything away from you, I gave my seventy pesos to one of my father's workmates I had seen at the Abreu Fontán with his family.

The Mosquito was a military camp, and it had the characteristics of a concentration camp. They took everything from you when you went in, including your money and your jewelry. Once inside, your pockets were empty—you only had the clothing you were wearing. They had set up some large tents there, the type they used for battalions, and they were packed with people. Problems surfaced, like rapes, because common delinquents were mixed with the people. I slept outside that night on a board, near a loudspeaker. I remember that at around ten o'clock they brought in little food boxes: one hundred little boxes for thousands of people. I was there for one night, May 18.

On May 19, in the morning, they called me to go to Mariel. I boarded another bus and a group of people was there to throw rocks at us again.

4

A Perilous Voyage at Sea and Arrival in Key West

WHILE THE DRAMA AND VIOLENCE of the Boatlift unfolded on the island, thousands of Cuban Americans in the United States were making a southward dash. The iconic fishing and vacation city of Key West—also home to a naval air station and the closest point in the United States to Cuba—quickly became ground zero on the American side of the Mariel exodus. During the height of the crisis, simply getting to the small island city was challenging, as the only overland road, U.S. Route 1—in many places consisting of a single northbound lane and a single southbound lane and containing countless bridges—became congested with vehicles and boat trailers.[1] An accident or breakdown along the way could easily turn the normally three-and-a-half-hour drive from Miami into an all-day affair. For businesses along U.S. 1, such as restaurants, grocery stores, and gasoline stations, the crisis was no doubt a boon.

With thousands of people pouring in, Key West, having just entered its off-season, experienced a massive (if brief) population explosion. Those on their way to Cuba made final preparations for their journeys and searched for places from which to launch their boats.[2] Others nervously awaited the return of vessels sent to retrieve their family members. When hotels, motels, and boarding houses in the city and nearby areas filled to capacity, visitors—having come in not only from Miami but from all over the United States and beyond—slept in their vehicles.[3] Volunteers, ranging from health care workers to those simply looking for a way to assist, likewise descended on the city, along with a constant stream of federal, state, and local officials sent in to help manage the crisis.

As already mentioned, the boats heading for Cuba were often owned and piloted by actual family members of those being brought from the island; others were piloted by captains-for-hire who may or may not have taken along one or more of the relatives who had hired them. The flotilla, in any event, consisted of boats of every size and make. *Newsweek* reported from Mariel: "Hundreds of boats were there—huge freighters, steel-hull shrimpers, sleek pleasure boats and 18-foot uncovered wooden tubs that had no business on the water at all."[4] Some of the vessels made the treacherous 125-mile crossing alone; more did so in groups to enhance safety.

During the first days of the exodus, boats arriving at Mariel found a good degree of organization. They were met by Cuban patrol boats at the entrance to the harbor and accompanied to the dock, where authorities checked identifications, searched the vessels, had those aboard to fill out forms, and issued temporary visas.[5] Each boat was given a number and then waited; when its number was announced, those picking up the refugees turned over the list of the people they had come to retrieve. The boat would later be called back to the dock, where it was loaded with passengers.[6] They might include all or some of the people on the list and, almost always, others determined by Cuban officials.

As the number of boats arriving at Mariel increased, the process slowed and then quickly deteriorated. With Cuban authorities overwhelmed, boat captains were now forced to wait days, and later weeks, to be called dockside. Earlier official procedures, such as filling out forms and searching vessels, were abandoned.[7] The Cubans nevertheless kept track of the boats by photographing them from their own vessels and monitoring the scene from above in armed military helicopters. "Several times," wrote photojournalist Ron Laytner, an eyewitness to the scene at Mariel, "a Cuban helicopter flew over the rescue fleet, rocket pods and machine-guns reflecting in the bright sunlight."[8] Armed soldiers kept watch from the shoreline and search lights scanned the bay after dark.[9] Those aboard the boats, meanwhile, could only disembark if authorized to do so by the Cuban authorities. Expecting to be in Cuba for only a matter of hours (or perhaps a couple of days), few had brought enough provisions for a prolonged wait.[10] Given the limits of most on-board toilets, the harbor was soon teeming with waste.[11]

Some suspected that the delays at Mariel were deliberately caused by the Cuban government so that it could extract the maximum amount of dollars from the waiting vessels. Indeed, the regime provided special boats that made the rounds, selling food, water, and other provisions to the visitors at high and ever-increasing prices.[12] At one point it even organized a party boat where musical entertainment was provided.[13] Government-authorized boat rides to the dock or bus transportation into Havana were likewise provided at inflated prices.[14] Arbitrarily setting the exchange rate of 70.2 Cuban cents per dollar, the regime was assumed to have made good profits.[15] As noted earlier, captains who wanted to sail back to the United States without Cuban permission were prohibited from doing so.[16] The vessels anchored at Mariel were as much prisoners of the Cuban government as the souls confined at the Abreu Fontán and El Mosquito.

The Tritón Hotel in Havana, built the previous year for delegates attending the Non-Aligned Conference and located near the Peruvian Embassy, was made available by the Cuban regime to those waiting aboard the boats at Mariel.[17] Immigration officials set up an office there.[18] Although victimized by the same sort of price gouging as at the port, those American and Cuban American visitors who could afford it received some measure of relief as the hotel, besides rooms, provided access to telephones, toilet facilities, and showers. The rooms themselves were in high demand, and people seeking one often had to wait days in the lobby for one to become available.[19] Despite the relative comfort of the hotel, guests at the Tritón were not free to move about: they were barred from leaving the premises, prohibited from receiving guests, and carefully counted as they came and went. Surrounded by a chain-link fence and manned by police, the hotel was christened the "Concentration Camp" by those who took advantage of its accommodations.[20] Similar quarantine facilities were reportedly used at a handful of other locations in Cuba.[21]

As mentioned, when a boat was finally called at Mariel, the captain, in addition to boarding those for whom he had come, was also required to take a number of people determined by Cuban authorities. It has been reported that the ratio was one person on the list to four chosen by the regime.[22] Mirta Ojito stated that "Castro himself manipulated the formula every day."[23] Whatever the ratios at any given moment, there was no way boat crews could predict what the authorities might require of them. Often, only some of the approved individuals on a captain's list were boarded on his vessel, along with a number of people he did not come for, perhaps with assurances that the others on the list would be sent on a different boat; or the captain might be told to make a return voyage to take the remainder on his list, along with a second group of strangers. Sometimes boats were completely loaded with strangers and the captains were told to come back a second time if they wanted to retrieve the people on their lists; sometimes they were forced to take a full boatload of strangers with merely the promise that the relatives for whom they had come would be sent on a different boat. It was by this means that the Castro regime packed the boats with whomever it chose. Some of the strangers, as aforementioned, were the among the so-called undesirables and anti-socials. It is critical to reemphasize, however, that only a portion of the strangers put into the boats at Mariel were dangerous criminals or anything of the sort, as people sent in this fashion included former and current political prisoners (many with their families), Peruvian Embassy asylum seekers, and members of Cuban society whom the government wished to get rid of for political reasons. Other strangers were everyday Cubans with no special status who had simply requested and received clearance to depart.[24] And as already alluded to, some strangers put aboard boats were sponsored family members who had been on the lists of other captains.

For Cuban Americans who had drained their savings, mortgaged their homes, and taken out loans to retrieve their relatives, it was a bitter disappointment if, for whatever reason, they were prohibited from taking their loved ones. One interviewee quoted from the story of a sister-in-law who had gone to Mariel:

> There was a man in a boat next to mine who sold his gas station in order to buy a boat to go personally to pick up his family. They denied him permission and instead filled his boat with delinquents and told him to go. The man couldn't withstand that pain and hanged himself from the mast of the boat.[25]

The vessels were not only required to take whomever the Cuban authorities designated; they were deliberately overloaded to hazardous levels by the same authorities. So many refugees were packed on the boats that water lines were sometimes plunged well beneath the surface. "One entire bus load, perhaps 100 persons," wrote Ron Laytner, "was ordered to climb onto the roof of the shrimp boat's wheel-house. Tots and babies were held by mothers, children squeezed in among adults, legs hanging over the sides."[26] Mirta Ojito reported that "Coast Guard officials estimated that 90 percent of the vessels returning from Cuba were either overloaded or filled to their maximum capacity."[27] Furthermore, vessels were sometimes ordered to depart in poor weather conditions.[28] Were it not for the omnipresence of the U.S. Coast Guard and Navy and their round-the-clock rescue missions in the Florida Straits, the death toll would have been infinitely higher than it was, which was fewer than thirty.[29]

When boats were finally given clearance to leave Cuba, they often departed (as they had done on the southbound journey) in groups. Whatever emotions may have swirled in the hearts of the refugees as they watched their homeland shrink in the distance, they now had to cross the treacherous Florida Straits in vessels usually bearing loads far exceeding those for which they had been designed. While some boats had relatively uneventful crossings, others experienced stormy weather and rough seas. With safety equipment such as life vests and lifeboats falling well short of what was required for the number of people the Cuban authorities had packed into the boats, the threat to life loomed large. Rain, wind, and enormous waves tossed about small and large boats with equal violence, sometimes in the dark of night.

The protective hand of the Virgin of Charity, Cuba's patron—who is historically depicted as saving a trio on a boat during a storm—was no doubt invoked thousands of times. May Day calls were incessant, and the U.S. Coast Guard was usually on the scene quickly, often plucking refugees and boat crews off sinking vessels and, in some cases, from the water itself, in dramatic rescue operations. It was, without question, one of the U.S. Coast Guard's greatest moments.

Finally seeing land as they neared Key West, or its lights if they arrived at night, was an indescribable thrill and relief for the refugees. They had made it. They were finally free. A new life—a better life—would begin, they believed, the moment they set foot on shore.

When the first boats arrived in Key West, local U.S. officials did not see the arrival of Cuban refugees as anything strange or out of the ordinary; the new arrivals were processed and released in the same manner as Cubans had always been. Within a couple of days, however, hundreds more refugees had arrived and, based on the number of boats heading to Cuba, all indications were that thousands more would be coming shortly. U.S. Customs and the Immigration and Naturalization Service (INS), each with only a small presence in Key West, would soon receive reinforcements from their respective agencies.[30]

On April 28, with the refugee flow from Cuba showing no sign of abating, Florida governor Bob Graham declared a state of emergency in Dade and Monroe counties.[31] Very soon, in addition to the increase in INS and U.S. Customs personnel, a multitude of agencies would be hard at work managing the crisis. They included the U.S. Coast Guard's Marine Safety Office, Florida's Marine Patrol, the Florida Highway Patrol, Florida National Guard, U.S. Marines, U.S. Border Patrol, U.S. Public Health Service, and Federal Bureau of Investigation (FBI), there to root out potential Castro spies among the refugees.[32]

The Carter Administration then charged the Federal Emergency Management Agency (FEMA) with the task of coordinating the response to the crisis.[33] The handling of an ongoing refugee situation was new for FEMA and, given the numerous problems that eventually emerged, the president's decision to use the agency would be criticized in the months and years to come. Moreover, the authority given to

FEMA, combined with the tough approach of the coordinator it sent to South Florida, initially caused no small amount of tension with those who had been overseeing the operation up to that point.[34] In any event, within a relatively short time FEMA was coordinating the efforts of multiple federal departments and agencies as well as volunteer organizations. It would continue as the lead agency until mid-July, when most of its responsibility was transferred to the Cuban-Haitian Task Force of the State Department's Office of Refugee Affairs.[35] By that time the number of refugees arriving in Key West had dropped dramatically.

In an effort to bring a semblance of order to the growing chaos in Key West, boats arriving with refugees were at first directed to stop at the Outer Mole of the Key West Naval Station. When this proved unworkable, they were instructed to dock at Pier Bravo at the Truman Annex.[36] There they were processed by authorities from the INS and U.S. Customs (an exercise that took on more of a law enforcement focus and included Coast Guard officials after President Carter's mid-May directives aimed at ending the Boatlift).[37] Captains were asked to complete arrival forms, and the refugees aboard were counted and then escorted off the boats with the assistance of National Guardsmen and later U.S. Marines; they were interviewed, checked medically, offered nourishment, and then turned over to FEMA at a structure at the Naval Station.[38]

Meanwhile, anxious Cuban American relatives waited outside a fence near the docks. Some Cuban Americans were there simply to cheer and welcome the newcomers, in direct contrast to the hostile and often violent farewell the emigres had received in Cuba. Some of the well-wishers shouted anti-Castro slogans and sang the Cuban national anthem.[39] During processing, the refugees were asked if they had ever been arrested in Cuba. If they answered in the affirmative, they were usually separated and detained. This quickly became controversial because, as previously mentioned, many individuals had been imprisoned in Cuba for minor infractions or for actions that would not have been considered crimes in a democratic society.[40] The speed at which the refugees were processed, as well as complications arising from the language barrier, only exacerbated this problem.

When the number of refugees swelled, temporary housing and feeding were moved to an old seaplane hangar at Trumbo Point on the northern shore of Key West, which could accommodate a large number of cots, portable showers and toilets, a health care station, and areas from which to distribute food and clothing. Donations, many of them provided by Cuban Americans, poured in along with American and Cuban American volunteers. Arturo Cobo, a Cuban exile and a veteran of the Bay of Pigs invasion, played a leading role in coordinating the volunteer efforts.[41] In early May, Miami archbishop Edward McCarthy, with the assistance of Monsignor Bryan Walsh (who had vast experience working with Cuban exiles and had been the key figure in Operation Pedro Pan, 1960–1962), delivered a Mass to over four thousand refugees at Trumbo.[42]

Mariel refugees arrived in Key West exhausted, bruised, hungry, and confused. Their first encounters in the United States were nevertheless positively memorable. Most recall the extraordinary kindness extended to them by the soldiers who helped them off the boats. It was not at all what some had expected when they saw soldiers waiting for them dockside, given their recent experience with military personnel in Cuba. They remember being surrounded in Key West by generous strangers—American and Cuban American Good Samaritans—who made it their task to feed the refugees, house them, tend to their injuries and illnesses, and reunite them with family. Beyond compassionate treatment, the material relief the refugees were given astonished them. Those whose only experience was one of scarcity under Communism had never seen so much food and clothing in a single place— much less food and clothing meant for *them*. The younger refugees experienced new and wonderful taste sensations: a Coca-Cola from a soldier at the dock or an apple or pear received at Trumbo.

Refugees with relatives present in Key West to sponsor them were eventually released to the relatives and told to report for further processing in Miami. Those whose sponsors awaited them in Miami were bussed there; those lacking immediate sponsors were taken to resettlement centers in Miami or to other facilities that were opened in different parts of the country. This latter group would add an entirely new— and somewhat painful—dimension to the Mariel Boatlift experience.

The present chapter contains testimonies from Mariel refugees covering the time from their arrival at the port of Mariel to their release from Key West. In the first two interviews, Miami relatives who had gone to Cuba to pick up family share their harrowing experiences.

Anonymous

This interviewee preferred anonymity. He was originally from a city in Camagüey Province and had left Cuba in the 1960s at sixteen years of age. When he visited his sister and her family in Cuba in the late 1970s, he promised, as many other relatives did, to get them out if the opportunity arose.

I was in the Dominican Republic with my wife and young child when I heard the news that people in Cuba had gone into the Peruvian Embassy. When I heard that they were going to allow people to leave the island, I said, "Well, I've got to take advantage of this," and I returned to Miami right away. I had a twenty-eight-foot boat with a new engine and went to Key West with it. While I was putting it into the water there, the propeller hit the concrete ramp and broke. They told me it would take a while to fix, but I couldn't delay. So I went all around the Keys for two or three days, without eating or sleeping, trying to figure out a way to get to Mariel. I found a couple of Americans in Marathon and they had a thirty-plus-foot boat. I hired them.

It was an old wooden boat, but it had a couple of new, black, inboard Mercury engines. You could have thrown away the boat, but the motors were great. We gathered plenty of provisions—including cigarettes, food, and money—and departed for Mariel from Marathon at around 1:00 p.m. on April 27. Soon after we left, some large, black clouds started looming in the distance. I said to one of the Americans, "Look at that over there." He said, "We're going to go around it." Well, we reached it at around two o'clock and ran right into the storm. It was as though we'd hit a wall. I hadn't eaten or slept in three days. I asked the other American, "Is this how it always is out here?" He said, "Yeah, it's always like this" [interviewee laughs].

The waves looked like they were forty or fifty feet high. When we were on top of a wave and looked down, it seemed as though a valley was below us. Instead of trying to navigate in that situation, you have to get on top of a wave and ride it, going neither forward nor backward; then you look to all sides to see if the wave changes position. Meanwhile, rain and lightning were coming down and the sea was churning so much it looked white—like milk. Sometimes, the propellers would be sticking out of the water and you could hear them spinning; other times, the boat would go under the wave a little and then surface again. I kept looking at the captain to see his reaction in case we had to go into the water on the life raft, which we had already inflated. I'll tell you, if I had been piloting the boat I wouldn't have lived to tell the story. Years later, we looked up the Coast Guard records and learned that a mini-hurricane had suddenly formed that day and that there were winds of seventy miles per hour. We were in the storm for around two hours, and though it calmed down, the sea was still choppy afterward; the types of waves were different from those we had encountered before, but still choppy.

We ended up in the bay of Matanzas that night. It so happened that I knew that stretch of Cuba very well because we used to go to Varadero a great deal when I was a boy; we also used to drive through that area on our trips from our hometown to Havana. So, Cárdenas, Varadero, Matanzas, and on to Mariel, I knew well. Belén School in Havana, which I had attended as a child, also had a camp near Mariel.

As we were approaching the entrance to the bay there at Matanzas, a Cuban Coast Guard boat came up to us. Two soldiers boarded our boat and I sat with them in the cabin. I took out a bottle of cognac and gave them a couple of drinks. They told us to follow them and to dock our boat. So we followed them to a concrete marina that was built during the era before Fidel. They didn't let us leave right away, and we had to spend a couple of nights there before going on to Mariel. They didn't let us make any phone calls, either. Meanwhile, my sister in Miami and the rest of my family had seen that the hurricane had gone by and everyone thought we were dead. The two Americans' families were nervous, too. Everyone was calling the Coast Guard.

We finally got to Mariel on April 29. There were over a thousand boats there. My relatives in Cuba knew that I had left for the island, but they didn't know if I had made it. I was lost for three days and they thought that something had happened to me, as there had been deaths and capsized boats in the Florida Straits during the storm. So the day after I got there, I went to the Tritón Hotel on a bus they provided and sent my sister in our town a letter letting her know I was there.

The Mariel bay was filled with all sorts of boats; some were large, some were medium-sized, some were small. There were some nice yachts there, too. But overall, it was a disaster. Imagine it, the place was full and there were people who'd been there for a very long time. They had to throw excrement into the bay and the water was filled with it. There was a very large boat there that sold pork, rice-and-beans, fried plantains, water, and other things, and we'd go to it to eat. We also had a small dinghy with a little engine, and we'd go around the bay in it. One day the motor fell into the water and we had to row back to our boat with our bare hands through the disgusting water.

On May 13 they finally called me to the dock to load my family on the boat. My sister and her husband couldn't come because they didn't let my brother-in-law leave; his parents and his grandfather stayed behind with them. So in total, I brought five relatives with me. But overall we boarded twenty-five people: my five relatives and twenty other people the authorities had picked. Among those other people was a family of five that included the parents, the grandmother, and two children; the rest were prisoners, all of them young men. The authorities told us that we had to take them, otherwise we couldn't take anyone. Eight or ten of the young men stood next to me the whole time like soldiers; if the captain raised his hand, they'd do whatever he'd ask. There were four or five who were delinquents, completely crazy. When they got on the boat, I told them, "You sit there. Whoever moves I'll cut his head off and throw him into the water." I had my family there, you know. But they behaved well. Anyhow, my relatives and the other family were in the cabin and the others were kept outside.

When we were ready to depart, along with around twenty-plus other boats near the mouth of the bay, they didn't let us go. They were waiting for poor weather to set in and say, "OK, go now," so that we'd all drown. We finally departed and, about ten miles out, we ran into bad weather and turned back. After a day or so, a southeast wind started to blow and I told the captain, "Listen, let's get out of here." We left through the mouth of the bay and five or six others followed us. The Cuban Coast Guard was out there on a vessel with a 50-millimeter gun. One of the guys from the Cuban Coast Guard told us that we couldn't go. I told him, "Listen, I'm leaving now. No one is going to stop me." He signaled to me that the order was coming from the top. So, I said, "the hell with it," and kept going.

After we were at sea for around half an hour, following another boat, our boat all of a sudden started losing speed. One of the Americans checked the motors. He went back, opened the engine cover, and saw that the engines were inundated. The other American immediately called on the radio, "Mayday! Mayday! We've got twenty-eight people on board." I told the young men near me to start throwing everything into the water; we threw everything out, including the coolers, and the garbage was soon floating all around the boat. I took a yellow shirt from someone and went to the front of the boat and waved it at the boat we were following. It took a while for them to see us, but they finally did and turned back. It came and pulled up next to us. The American again started calling "Mayday!" into the radio.

There was an American ship nearby, the *Diligence,* a U.S. Coast Guard cutter. From the distance, it had seen all the garbage floating in the water; a sailor later told me they had thought it was people that were in the water and had sped up. A helicopter flew to where we were with a message that the Coast Guard was on the way to rescue us. Around twenty minutes or a half hour later, the *Diligence* got there and took out a small rescue boat for us to board. We got on it and then they hoisted us up on the *Diligence.*

When we got to Key West, my younger sister and her husband were there waiting. I gave the boat owners the flat fee I had promised them, plus $30,000 for the boat they lost, which was a good price. I didn't have to do it, but they were good to me.

What inspired me to do this—and other things for my family—was that I promised my father before he died that I would take care of the family. I told him to be at peace on that count. He died a year after I left Cuba and I had told him that over the telephone. I was in shock for a long time after his death. He was my best friend. Before he died,

I also sent him a copy of Douglas MacArthur's prayer for his son and they read it later at the funeral. I had him on my mind the whole time, and I wanted to do what he couldn't to keep the family together. He must have been very proud of me.

Andrés Manso

Andrés Manso was born in Nuevitas, Camagüey Province, in 1935. He joined the anti-Castro resistance not long after the dictator's seizure of power and left Cuba for United States exile in September 1960. He took part in the Bay of Pigs invasion as part of Brigade 2506 and was imprisoned by the Castro regime until December 1962. Upon his release he took part in anti-Castro operations for a time from a base in Central America. He eventually returned to the United States, moved to California, and later settled in Miami, where he worked for Eastern Airlines for more than twenty years. In the years preceding the Mariel Boatlift, he also owned his own marina on the Miami River, where he built and repaired boats.

When Mariel started, everyone was going to Cuba to retrieve family; I had relatives there and so did my wife. In my case, I had a sister and her husband still on the island. I didn't want to pressure my sister to come, and when we communicated with her by telephone, she said that she would let us know if she would leave, that it depended on conditions she saw on the island. In the end, she didn't make a decision; when we got to Mariel, she didn't want to leave because of all the brutality the Castro people were committing.

Anyhow, I departed for Mariel the first time—still without knowing if my sister would come—around April 20, on a forty-two-foot boat. The trip over was good, but I had miscalculated the fuel and when we were around ten miles off the Cuban coast we ran out of gas. So I contacted the Cuban Coast Guard and spoke with their base at Varadero. I told them that I was one of the boats going to Mariel to retrieve family and asked if they could either supply gasoline or tow me in. They sent a small tug boat out to get me and it towed me to the bay there. We spent like $200 or $300 on gasoline. They didn't give me any problems, but they did tell us that we had to leave immediately and sail out to international waters. I did so, and eventually made it to Mariel. It was the first time I was in Cuba since 1962. I felt very sad.

When I got to Mariel, there were more than two hundred boats anchored there, both outside and inside the port. I was with the mechanic from my marina, who was Cuban, and two other people who were friends of mine that wanted to get their relatives out. I had told these friends that I would not charge them anything, as long as they helped me with the expenses of the trip. Anyhow, we anchored outside the port and waited until they ordered us to enter. We were finally called in and they told us where to anchor. Then one of the Cuban immigration officers boarded our vessel; he took down some information and asked me for my identification. Because I had been in the Bay of Pigs invasion and in prison, I thought that if I showed up in Cuba something might happen to me. Fortunately, I had a relative in the Coast Guard and he was able to change the last name on my captain's license so I had no problem with that.

We were anchored there for around two weeks. While we waited, a tropical storm went straight though Mariel. It was very sad, because we saw how all the smaller boats crashed up against the shoreline. I had to weigh anchor and maneuver toward the entrance of Mariel in order to get away from the smaller boats that were being pushed toward me by the wind and didn't have the power to stop; they would have crashed right into me, but I had the power to move from one place to the other. In fact, I put one of the people in my boat on the bow so he could signal me and tell me where the smaller boats were coming from so that I could move.

After two weeks of waiting, I had run out of time and had to go back to my job. I went to the dock and told the authorities that they had to release my boat. The captain there told me that the relatives we had requested had not yet shown up; I told him that I couldn't wait any longer and that I was leaving. We had a bit of an argument, and I asked him if my boat was being detained. He said it wasn't, but that if I left he would not let me return. So I said to him, "What do you want? For me to take someone with me? Give me six or seven people and I'll take them with me." Well, six or seven people turned into sixteen, all of them strangers. I think there were prisoners in the group, but I didn't ask a lot of questions. Most of them were young men.

So I departed, made it to Key West, and left those people there. At that time the authorities didn't do anything on the boat. They took the people and asked me where I was going to dock. I told them that I was going to a nearby marina, and did so. The boat had had some mechanical problems that needed to be worked on. At Key West I spoke to my wife and she told me that someone from her family in Cuba wanted to come over, and that a niece of mine, her husband, and their newborn baby would also be coming. Then my brother, who lived in Puerto Rico, showed up in Miami to go back to Cuba with me—he had been my mechanic on the boats during the Central American missions with Manuel Artime in the 1960s. The niece we were going to retrieve was his daughter.

So I made some repairs to the boat and departed for Cuba for a second time in late May. This time my wife, a friend of my wife, a sister, my brother, my mechanic, and I went over. We got to Mariel and went through the process again: anchor outside the port, wait to be called in, go in, anchor inside the port, wait for the people to be sent. This time, I had to wait for thirty days. Also, on this trip my brother and my wife would leave the boat and go to the Tritón Hotel. I never left the boat since I didn't know what might happen to me; plus, since my wife and brother were already going to the Tritón to make telephone calls and all that, I had no reason to go.

After thirty days they called me to the dock and we picked up our relatives. My niece and her baby came, but they had not allowed her husband to leave. My wife's friend brought her mother and a sister with her husband and two girls. The authorities nevertheless put sixty-six people on the boat—those who were not family were strangers, and there were prisoners among them, but you weren't sure because you received no information about them. The trip over this time was difficult because the Cuban authorities waited for bad weather to arrive before they let us leave. The sea was very rough and people got seasick. On top of that, the boat was packed and didn't have enough life jackets for everyone. I had to tie a number of ropes across the boat so that people could hang on to them and not bounce around.

When I anchored at Key West, the Coast Guard was waiting. They gave me instructions, and I told them that I had a couple of sick people aboard; they immediately sent a small boat and took them ashore. I had an incident in which a couple of the people aboard jumped into the water, and the Coast Guard didn't want them to do that and so they came back on board.

When we finally docked, Immigration came aboard. I indicated to them who my relatives were, and those of the people who had gone over with us; but when they asked about the others, I told them that I didn't know who they were. So they were separated. The authorities let my relatives and those of our friends stay with me, under my responsibility. I was told to take them to Opa-locka the next day in order to fill out all the papers.

Then they confiscated my boat and stuck a citation on the windshield. They levied a fine of $1,000 for each person who didn't have a life vest—a total of more than $40,000; then there was, I think, a fine of $1,000 for the illegal entry of undocumented immigrants. I called my contact in Miami and he called the Coast Guard commander there. They made a concession: they placed a red seal on the windshield and told me to take it to the marina where it had been before and to anchor it there until my problem was solved. So I took it and anchored it at that place. Then my wife, along with all the relatives, picked us up at the marina in a station wagon. We went to eat at a restaurant, and from there we went to Miami.

I fought the fine at the Coast Guard in Miami and it cost me a heart attack. I had an argument with a Coast Guard captain who wanted to take away my boat and fine me more than $60,000. I had experienced heart problems previously, but this finally did it because the man was the sort of person who was completely intransigent. Anyhow, when I left the Coast Guard that day, I boarded a car with the friend who had gone with me and told him, "To Mercy Hospital." My friend said, "What?" I said, "To Mercy Hospital because I'm about to have a heart attack." I spent a week in intensive care. In the end, after I got a lawyer, the fine was lowered to $4,000. I paid it and they allowed me to have my boat back; they had earlier allowed me to bring the boat up from

Key West and anchor it at my marina in Miami, but I had not been allowed to move it. After I paid the $4,000, I decided to sell it.

All those relatives are still here and doing well. The girls are now grown women with children of their own and they love me dearly, the same as the other relatives. And my sister eventually left Cuba, too. Her husband had been an officer in the Cuban Navy and he had served in the U.S. Navy during World War II. As such, he went to the U.S. Interests Section in Havana and they gave him and his wife the visa they needed to leave Cuba.

Marino Mederos Sr. and Marino Mederos Jr.

[Marino Sr.]: At around four o'clock in the afternoon they took us to the boat. They made us wait in a line, and they had a separate line for the delinquents. They counted the delinquents first, and then they let us on board.

[Marino Jr.]: It was a big shrimp boat, around ninety to a hundred feet long, and it was carrying more than two hundred people; plus, it was towing three smaller boats that had broken down. We left in a flotilla of around forty or fifty boats, with a large boat in the lead and another large boat at the rear; the smaller boats traveled between the two larger ones. We departed on May 18, but they turned us back because of bad weather. We anchored in the bay and spent the night aboard the boat. Then the next day, May 19, at eleven in the morning, they gave us permission to depart.

After twelve miles or so, the sea got really bad. I remember that one moment all you could see was a wall of water; then the boat would go atop the wave and you could see everything all around. Then you'd go down again and you couldn't see a thing, even the large boat at the end of the flotilla. Even the tips of the boat's stabilizers were going under the water. There were a lot of people aboard who got sick and were vomiting. The captain, who had departed towing a few boats, picked up more broken-down boats along the way. We also took on some people who were floating in the water—a wife and husband with their son. The people operating the boat behaved well with us.

I remember there were a couple of Americans there who didn't speak any Spanish.

At night, things calmed down quite a bit. I remember when we saw the first light on the shore. Everyone started shouting, "Land! Land! There's land!" After that, it took us around four hours to reach land. Anyhow, soon after we saw that first light, we saw two lights, then three lights, then four lights; then you saw the whole place illuminated.

We landed at the naval base in Key West just after midnight and that's where I had my first Coca-Cola. There were a lot of volunteers there from Miami and there were Cubans from other places as well. Everyone spoke Spanish. They had an area at the naval base with portable showers and we took showers right away.

[Marino Sr.]: After we were processed, we went to a hangar that was filled with fruit and all sorts of other things. You went all around until you came to a place where they gave out coffee and cigarettes. When you finished there, they sent you to the sleeping area and gave you some clean cots.

[Marino Jr.]: They called for the people who had family in Miami—those who had no family in Miami were already being taken to other states. We were about to go to sleep when they called us to board a bus.

José García

We got to the port from the Mosquito in ten minutes and right away we were escorted to a boat. My uncle had originally come to pick us up with the captain he'd hired, but they had been forced to return to Key West without us. The authorities in Cuba had filled their boat with other people instead—many of them Jehovah's Witnesses—and they had no choice but to take them. The authorities promised him that they would send us on a different boat later.

The boat they put us on was pretty nice, a double-decker, not very big and not very small. We were all families on board, but it was overloaded. Because there were a lot of kids among the families, some of the people started complaining, saying, "We have families here with kids. Is there any way we can get some of these people out and put them on a different boat?" But they never took care of it. The captain, a Cuban American from Puerto Rico who had gone to pick up his family, was pretty concerned about it as well. I don't think any of his relatives were on board; they might have been sent on a different boat.

The next morning, we took off. While we could still see the Cuban coast, the motor all of a sudden stopped and the boat started taking on water. The captain said, "We've got to go back," so he turned around and went back. When he got to the dock, he spoke to the captain of a shrimp boat, another Cuban American, and asked him, "Is there any way we can sail near each other?" The other captain said, "Yeah, no problem." We were getting ready to sail again that day but we couldn't get out of the bay because there was a storm coming. We spent the next four days at the port of Mariel. We didn't get out of the boat that entire time because the Cuban authorities would not allow it.

We finally left on June 3, 1980, sailing within view of the shrimp boat. I remember that you could just stick your hand out and touch the water [above water line, because the boat was overloaded]. When we could no longer see the coast, the engine stopped and we started taking on water again—and it was coming in fast. Everyone on our boat started bailing out the water, but within twenty minutes it was up to our knees. I remember seeing fear in my mother's eyes; I'd never seen that look in her before. The Cuban Coast Guard, meanwhile, just sat there watching the whole thing. I want to think that as human beings they probably would have wanted to do something. Anyhow, the guys on the shrimp boat we were following came over to help us. The men on our boat started grabbing the women and children, including me, and putting them on the shrimp boat before they boarded it themselves. The shrimp boat had already been packed to double capacity.

Being on the shrimp boat was even scarier. There were prisoners on it. Anyhow, we towed our empty boat for around twenty minutes and then it started to go under. They let go of the rope, and it sank. It was very frightening to think that I had been on there. I can't even imagine what my parents were going through. After that we all sat on the shrimp boat's floor. The stench was horrible; it was all the smells you can think of all mixed together. It was a unique smell that, if you ever smelled it again, you would just want to die; but it is amazing how, after a while, you just became immune to it.

It seemed as though the ocean was going in all different directions. The waves were probably as high as a four-story building. All of a sudden you were on top of the building and you looked down and saw a precipice; then suddenly you were at the bottom of the precipice and looking up at the waves. Every five minutes the captain would say, "Everybody, please roll to the other side." I was in a constant state of fear for eighteen hours. I really thought we weren't going to make it. After a while, you could see that some people were completely dehydrated; they looked like they were dead, lying on top of each other. I hadn't prayed since I was a kid, but for the first time I started praying again.

When night came, it got really scary. I think people started hallucinating, because every few minutes you could hear somebody say, "I think we're getting there; look, there are lights." I don't know if I fell asleep or what, but all of a sudden I saw another boat for the first time: it was a U.S. Coast Guard boat. It was still dark, maybe four o'clock in the morning. The Coast Guard boat helped guide us to the port.

It was pretty moving when we finally saw land. I couldn't believe we had reached the U.S. Some people on the boat started clapping and hugging; other people were half dead and didn't even know what was happening. At the port, they carried some people away on gurneys. After disembarking, we went into a huge tent where they questioned us. "Were you a member of the Communist Party?" and "What was your profession?" The whole thing was surreal; it was like I was watching this at the movies.

But there was something different from Cuba that was very eye-catching: the way you were being treated. There were military guys there, but they were incredibly nice and helpful. They would come over right away and carry the ladies off the boat. I was thinking, "We just left our country—our brothers—and these people are doing all this for us. In Cuba, we were treated like crap." Here, the soldiers didn't have dogs or heavy weapons. They weren't intimidating. Plus, the Cuban Americans there at Key West had a sense of brotherhood with us and they were very welcoming. It was a completely different sensation.

The interrogation was very quick and after that we went to a huge cafeteria. You can imagine the amount of food they had there. "Can

I have some more?" I asked when I finished eating. "You could have all you want," they said. They had a pile of clothes there for us, too. I thought, "In Cuba, it's so hard to get any of this stuff, and here they're just giving it away!" These things seem trivial, but to us they were a big deal. You had a sense that you'd arrived in the Promised Land.

Ivonne Cuesta

We got to the port and saw our relatives from Puerto Rico who had come for us. I didn't know them, but my paternal grandmother did. The Cuban government had promised her that they would send my father [who had been denied the right to leave the country at the Abreu Fontán] shortly thereafter; they even said, "We promise, we swear on the Revolution, he's going. He just can't go now."

We boarded a boat called the *Mahogany Manor*. It was a nice boat with two cabins. Then they started boarding strangers. I think a few families had chartered the boat and what was supposed to have been around fifteen family members turned into around seventy people. We were in the boat for a day or two because the weather was bad. Then, even though the seas weren't getting any better, they sent us off. We set sail for the United States on June 2. The seas were very rough—that's the reason I don't like boats.

I don't remember how far we got into the trip, but the boat started sinking in the middle of the ocean. The tension was high and the boat was overcrowded. Everyone was scared to death. Water started coming in and everyone was sick to their stomachs. They gave us garbage bags and told us to sit. My uncle, who came with us from Cuba, would go up and down the stairs to report to us what was going on. He clearly recalls that the water was knee-deep. They finally called the Coast Guard and the Coast Guard came.

I have a different memory than my mother, but I remember that, all of a sudden, a helicopter was hovering over us. I remember the deafening sound of the propeller. They took us from the boat, and the next thing I remember was being hoisted up into the helicopter. I remember being close to my mother on the helicopter and looking down and seeing the water below. Then I remember landing on a landing strip on an aircraft carrier. But the sound is what stands out in my mind the most.

We were soaked to the bone. They gave us blankets to cover ourselves and ushered us into what seemed to me a huge room lined with metal folding chairs. I was seven—and I know the perspective is maybe a little different—but as far as I'm concerned there must have been five hundred metal folding chairs there. We were seated toward the middle of the room, and I recall a gentleman from the Coast Guard dressed in uniform pacing back and forth and talking in a language I didn't understand. They gave us a red can of Coca-Cola and a red apple. That was essentially our welcome. I had never before seen an apple. It was very symbolic for me.

We went straight to Key West. There were a lot of people there but, because we had family members who were U.S. citizens with us, we were able to bypass whatever lines or checkpoints other people had to go through. From there, we went and stayed at a Howard Johnson's in Key West. I remember there were bags of clothes in the hotel room for us, mostly men's clothing. Our family took us out to dinner that night and several tables were put together for us at the restaurant. There must have been room for thirty people. My family ordered steaks and they brought each of us a plate. When my mother saw the size of the steak, she thought it was for the whole family! When she saw that everyone got the same portion, she said, "Oh, my God!"

Miriam Vilariño

After we had spent several days at the Mosquito, they informed those in our tent that we were going to board. When we got to where the boats were, they told my father that only three or four of us could board and that the rest of us could go on a different boat. My father said, "Send us however you wish. Separate us if you have to—the issue is to get us out of here." My mother began to scream, saying that if we were going to drown that we would all drown together.

They put us all together on a boat that had been sent from Miami by a different family to claim its relatives. I don't think the people who'd sent it were actually on board; I believe only a captain had come. On the boat there were members of the family for whom it had been sent and there were also political prisoners and their families, like ours, as well as many common, violent prisoners. In order to protect the women and children from the common prisoners, the women and children were put on deck near the captain. The common prisoners were placed at the rear of the boat near the engines. Between the two groups the family men formed a human line and agreed that if any of the common prisoners moved, they'd push them over. They didn't move from there the entire crossing.

We boarded at around seven in the morning on May 20. The trip over was horrible. The weather was bad during the crossing, with the May rains of the Caribbean and sixteen-foot waves. There was a moment when we didn't think we'd make it. My mother didn't stop screaming until we saw the lighthouse at Key West.

When I saw land, I experienced a whirlwind of emotions. Everything we knew about the United States we had learned from my father. We knew we were coming to the land of freedom, to a place where my father would no longer be persecuted, to a place where we could attend school and not have to work in the countryside. We knew that in the United States an honest person who arrived could work and earn respect and would not be persecuted; we knew there was opportunity here for all who wanted it; we knew that if we had a company it would not be taken away, like they had taken away my grandfather's land.

We arrived in Key West, and the place was filled with beautifully dressed American officers. Everyone was very cordial. They helped us off the boat and took us to a dining hall. When we went in, my eyes popped out. Never had I seen so much food. Much of it was unknown to me—I had never seen an apple, I had never seen a pear, and I had never seen a grape. We didn't know what to take. We bit into the apples and the aroma was all-consuming. It was such that they have never since had the same impact on me. My mother and father, who had eaten apples before, grabbed them. They were euphoric. They said, "Look! Look! An apple! An apple!" It was euphoria.

When we left the dining hall, people were waiting to give us little bags filled with tooth brushes, soap, and towels. They took us to the bathrooms and we took a good shower.

Isis Gottlieb

A relative had come down from Chicago to get us. I remember seeing the boat—it was called *El Angelisa*—and that people were happy. My mom's godmother in Chicago had paid the captain $1,000 for each of us.

They let the ones who were claimed by family get into the boat first. Once my family was in—along with the other families who were supposed to be there—the captain was asked by a person from the Cuban government, "How many people fit in the boat?" He said, "Fifty." There were already fifty people on there. It was extremely overcrowded. The person with the Cuban government then said, "OK. Put on fifty more." Then they put criminals, prostitutes—the works—on the boat.

My mother had brought along a little water bottle and jackets made in Poland for us. During the crossing, she would tell me, "You cannot leave my sight. You have to sit next to me because there are a lot of criminals here. There are a lot of crazy people on this boat." But the criminals were fine during the trip. One lady on board got very sick—I guess she was nervous—and had diarrhea. There was an enormous aluminum pot on the top of the boat; if you needed to use the restroom, these men would just take this pot down, you'd use the restroom in it, and they would empty it out into the ocean. The lady had to use it every ten minutes. There was no privacy. Everybody was really embarrassed.

While we were sitting on the boat, you could actually reach out and feel the water [because the boat was weighted down due to overloading]. Then when it started getting dark, we ran out of gas. That was really bad. People had mixed feelings when they saw the Coast Guard approaching; they didn't know if they should be happy or sad because they had been brainwashed in Cuba. They didn't know exactly how to feel. But the Coast Guard people were all very nice. They jumped into the boat and the first thing they did was to talk to the captain. They gave us a fill-up and followed behind until we got to Key West.

It was dark when we arrived in Key West on May 25. Everybody was really happy, and they were praying, "Thank you, God! We finally made it here!" Everyone in Key West was nice to me since I was so little. The soldiers put me on their shoulders, they tried to teach me some English, and they taught me how to "give five." They gave me a Coca-Cola for the first time. I had never used a straw and they taught me how to use one. They also gave me a hot dog, but I didn't like it.

We were in Key West for five to seven hours. We had really good food—and Coke. Then my dad's relatives in Miami came to pick us up.

Ramón Dueñas

Ramón Dueñas was born in 1966 in Santiago de las Vegas, near Havana. His family owned a tobacco farm prior to the Revolution. His father was imprisoned for four years in Cuba for trying to escape the island during the 1960s. Prior to the Mariel Boatlift, the family had exit permits to Venezuela because of Ramón's father's political prisoner status.

My father was a political prisoner and he had to leave the country via Mariel. They sent us to the Mosquito on May 15. We were there from seven o'clock in the morning until six o'clock in the evening, and we were then put aboard a shrimp boat at the port. We didn't know the person who owned the boat. Seventy family members and political prisoners were put on board initially, but then they brought in four hundred female prisoners on buses and boarded them as well.

The sea was very rough during the crossing and there were too many people on board the boat. The waves were twelve to fifteen feet high. When you went up, it seemed as though you were going to touch the sky; then, when you went down again, it seemed as if the sea would swallow you. There were almost five hundred people aboard. It was horrible; people were sitting against each other, and everyone was seasick and vomiting. We looked like slaves. The crossing took all night.

When we saw the lights, everyone was happy and screaming, "Miami!" But, of course, it was Key West. We arrived at six o'clock in the morning. My mother injured her finger between the boat and a post, and they took her away for treatment. The National Guard, meanwhile, took everyone off the boat but left my family there waiting for my mother to return. She came back two hours later.

The treatment we received from the National Guard was phenomenal. They took us to an enormous cafeteria there. They had everything and you could eat anything you desired. From there, we were going to board a bus to Fort Chaffee [refugee camp in Arkansas] but there were only five seats and we were six in our group. So they told us we'd get on the next bus. At that moment, my uncle got there and picked us up. We spent two weeks at his home in Hialeah.

Manuel Vega

They called us at around five in the afternoon to get on some buses to take us to the boats. When we were aboard the boat with my brother, who had come from Miami, we felt free. The authorities put two people from the Peruvian Embassy on the boat with us. They didn't let us depart until midnight.

The moon was full that night. I drove the boat for part of the trip because my brother was tired; he and the friend who'd gone with him had been at Mariel for many days. To be honest, if I had to do it all over again, I don't think I would. I found myself in the middle of the Gulf with my children, my parents, my wife, my brother, and the other people. It was a small boat, and it was overloaded—it was a boat for maybe six people, but we were ten! Do it again by myself? Yes, I would do it. But with an eight-month-old child? And a nine-year-old girl? And your parents? And your wife? Think about what happened to other people, whose vessels broke and cracked along the way and they ended up floating in the water. If something like that happens and you're with an eight-month-old, how are you supposed to keep him afloat? Or your parents? Or your daughter? Who are you supposed to let go of? Your son or your daughter? Your father or your wife? Every time I think about that, I don't sleep. It gives me nightmares.

When we saw land, the boat stalled because water had gotten mixed in with the gasoline. We tried to start it again, but it wouldn't start. Luckily, within five minutes another boat came by and threw us a rope and started towing us. Then we tried the motor again and it started. We landed in Key West under our own power at six thirty in the morning on May 1.

When I stepped on land, I was the happiest man in the world. The Cubans who were there in Key West received us very well. There was a man selling *pan con lechón* [Cuban pork sandwiches] there at the marina and he gave us some. It was the first thing I ate. He gave us three important things: Cuban coffee, *pan con lechón* for everyone on the boat, and my first five dollars—five for me, five for my father.

The contrast between Cuba and Key West was incredible. In the Mosquito, there were dogs and soldiers. While I was there, I saw a dog attack a man who was looking for food for his mother. A guard had told him, "You can't pass here." The man said, "I just want to see if I can get a little food box for my mother, who is in a wheelchair." The guard said, "Well, go on then." As soon as he walked past, the dog attacked him. The guard pulled the dog back, but it had attacked the man. It was something I saw that caused me great grief. In Key West, it was the opposite. The National Guard and the Navy people took us to a dining area and gave us all we wanted to eat. They had apples, pears, ham, cheese, crackers, everything.

My brother later called his wife in Miami from a public phone and told her to come pick us up.

5

Reception and Resettlement

AMONG THE EARLY DILEMMAS the Carter Administration faced during the Mariel Boatlift was determining a legal status for the refugees. They were initially given "temporary but renewable parole," under the Immigration and Nationality Act, rather than official refugee status under the recently passed Refugee Act of 1980.[1] Those officially classified as "refugees" under the new Refugee Act were entitled to a more expansive range of services.[2] Among the many factors that prevented granting Mariel Cubans refugee status was that advocates for the tens of thousands of Haitian boatpeople who had arrived over the previous years (and were considered to be illegal immigrants) demanded, understandably, that Haitian boatpeople and the Mariel Cubans be treated equally.[3] Whereas considering the Cubans to be refugees would have been consistent with past practice, declaring Haitians as such would have reversed the government's stand on a group it had always considered, however incorrectly many may have viewed the government's stand, to be economic rather than political migrants. In the end, under pressure not to grant Mariel Cubans a more favorable status than Haitian refugees and fearing that conferring refugee status on Haitian boatpeople would touch off a mass wave of economic migrants, especially from Caribbean and Latin American nations, both groups were denied refugee status.[4] In order that Haitian and Cuban refugees be treated in the same manner, Haitians who arrived after the commencement of the Mariel Boatlift were also given parole.[5]

On June 20, two months after the start of the Mariel exodus, the administration announced legislation that would create the classification of "Cuban-Haitian Entrant (status pending)" with a six-month renewable parole. It would apply to Cubans who arrived between the start of the Boatlift and June 19 and were in INS processing, and for Haitians who likewise were in INS processing by June 19. The proposed legislation would allow the "entrants" to apply as permanents residents after a two-year period.[6] It would also entitle them to some federal benefits, but fewer than if they had been legally designated as refugees.[7] The legislation further proposed to reimburse state and local governments 75 percent of the costs associated with assisting and resettling the entrants.[8] Many in Congress—who viewed the administration's handling of the situation as incoherent, indecisive, and falling short with regard to the needs of the states impacted by the Mariel crisis, especially Florida—preferred the idea of applying the Refugee Act, as it would provide far more federal aid and impose better organization on the Mariel resettlement efforts.

The president's plan met stiff opposition in Congress. The Florida congressional delegation, which was especially opposed to the president's plan, succeeded later that year in adding the Fascell-Stone Amendment to the Refugee Education Assistance Act (REAA). The amendment called for extending full refugee benefits to the "entrants" and reimbursing local and state governments for 100 percent, rather than 75 percent, of the costs incurred.[9] Although the White House preferred its own proposed legislation, it conceded to Congress and signed the REAA into law. The administration's window ending on June 19 was extended to October 10, the date of the REAA's enactment.[10] The long-term immigration status of Haitians and Mariel Cubans remained an open question.

President Carter lost his bid for reelection to Ronald Reagan shortly after the REAA's passage, thus leaving the issue of long-term, permanent immigration status unresolved. The Reagan Administration had found an important base of support among Cuban Americans during the campaign. Sharing the new president's antipathy for Communism and the Castro regime, the Cuban American community had voted for him by a wide margin and had become an important political ally.[11] The Mariel Cubans (except for those deemed "excludable") were thus allowed to become permanent residents, according to the provisions of the 1966 Cuban Adjustment Act. The majority had done so by the end of 1987 and eventually became United States citizens. The Haitians were later allowed to adjust their status as well, in their case through the 1986 Immigration Reform and Control Act.[12]

Processing and Resettlement

At the very start of the Boatlift, City of Miami assistant city Manager César Odio, a First Wave Cuban American, arranged for the Artime Center in Miami's Little Havana to be used for receiving and processing the Mariel arrivals coming from Key West. It took only a short time, however, to realize that the small center was not suited for the mass wave of people reportedly making their way north.[13] Operations were therefore moved to the Dade County Youth Fair grounds at Tamiami Park in suburban, unincorporated Dade County. Assistant County Manager Sergio Pereira, also a First Wave Cuban American, became the lead player in the county's efforts.[14] The Tamiami Park center had large indoor facilities where the refugees could be processed, checked by the INS, and turned over to sponsors.[15] Manned largely by county employees and an endless stream of Cuban American volunteers, the twenty-four-hour center operated between its opening on April 21 and the time of its closing in the second week of May. During that time donations of food, clothing, and other items poured in from local residents, community groups, and private businesses.[16] In addition, several temporary holding facilities scattered across South Florida were created to house refugees.[17]

When FEMA took over in May, processing was relocated to a hangar close to Opa-locka Airport in northern Dade County.[18] The City of Miami, meanwhile, offered temporary use of the Orange Bowl to house the refugees still being brought up from Key West.[19] The arrivals stayed at the stadium until being driven to Opa-locka, where, upon completing their processing, they were released to sponsors, if available; those without sponsors were returned to the Orange Bowl until sponsors could be found.[20] Besides the Orange Bowl, some arrivals were taken to a holding center on Krome Avenue near the Everglades, on a site formerly used as a missile base.[21] Refugees whose families had taken them home directly from Key West were also required to appear for processing at Opa-locka.

Because the Orange Bowl center eventually had to be closed due to the approaching football season—and because of the increasing number of homeless Mariel refugees on Miami's streets—a "tent city" was opened under an Interstate 95 underpass in downtown Miami, near the Miami River, to house between seven hundred and eight hundred refugees. Clark, Lasaga, and Reque said Tent City was "considered to be the first Cuban slum in the U.S."[22] A *Time* magazine article described the camp:

> Some 750 Cubans live in Campamento del Rio (River Camp), a group of Army squad tents nestled under the elevated highway Interstate 95. People wash at spigots; laundry flutters from wire fences; young, bare-chested men wander morosely among the tents. An ominous new note: the residents of the tent city include not only refugees who have been unable to find a home but some who lived with sponsors for a while and then were turned out onto the streets because their benefactors decided they no longer wanted to keep them.[23]

Within a few weeks of the start of the Boatlift, resettlement camps were also opened in other parts of the country to house those refugees with no one immediately available to sponsor them. Some were sent to the camps directly from Key West, others after short stints at facilities in Miami. The first of these camps was established on May 3, at Eglin Air Force Base on North Florida's Gulf Coast, and in less than a week it reached maximum capacity at 9,700 people; a camp was then opened on May 8 at Fort Chaffee in Arkansas, which reached its maximum of 19,000 in just over a week; a third facility, at Fort Indiantown Gap in Pennsylvania, was full by May 29, with 18,311 people; Fort

McCoy in Wisconsin was then opened and reached capacity on June 16, with 13,258 refugees. Around a month later, resettlement matters were passed to the Cuban-Haitian Task Force.[24]

The camps outside South Florida all experienced difficulties, and each had its own unique challenges. Although it would be impractical and impossible to give a detailed rendering of what transpired at each facility in the present context, some general comments are nevertheless possible. Conditions at the refugee camps deteriorated at different times and to varying degrees. Painfully slow and inefficient processing was the major problem. Cuban Americans who traveled to the camps to sponsor relatives and were ready to take them home often encountered exasperating delays.[25] Meanwhile, inside the facilities, a lack of security, the absence of information, and overall idleness ate away at morale.[26] In some cases, camp authorities mixed criminals and the mentally disturbed in with the general camp population.[27] Given the lack of security within some of the compounds, criminal gangs were sometimes able to emerge to take unofficial control inside and reportedly abused and menaced fellow refugees and vulnerable refugee families.[28]

Although the refugees were fed and provided for materially, the prison camp atmosphere, the disorder, frustration, lack of security, and bureaucratic chaos brought tensions to boiling point. Riots broke out at Fort Chaffee in June and at Fort Indiantown Gap in August; disturbances were reported at Fort McCoy in September.[29] It is important to note that only a small number of the refugees were involved in the disturbances at the camps; many of the camp residents, in fact, assisted the authorities in stopping them.[30] Some of the immigrants were convinced that these incidents were started by Castro agents infiltrated into the refugee population.[31]

Around two thousand unaccompanied minors, most of them males in their late teens, were among those sent to the camps. Over 40 percent of this group reported that rather than their parents having made the decision to send them to the United States, they were deemed "troublemakers" by their local CDRs and forced to depart the country.[32] Around 37 percent of them had experienced institutionalization of some form in Cuba.[33] At the camps, alone and initially mixed in with the general camp population, some of the minors reportedly became victims of abuse and violence—including instances of rape and assault—by adults and fellow minors.[34] Also, excessive disciplinary measures—such as handcuffing their hands and feet to beds or fences—were used by authorities against the teens.[35] This situation was reportedly not the same in all the camps and seems to have been worse at Fort McCoy.[36] Although the problems faced by unaccompanied minors became well known, bureaucratic wrangling and disputes between the federal government and state authorities over who was responsible for the youths delayed a solution. Eventually, legal challenges, the passage of the Fascell-Stone Amendment, and other interventions helped ameliorate this situation.[37]

Clark, Lasaga, and Reque attributed the overall problems at the camps to a variety of factors. Among them was that many camp administrators were unconcerned with the plight of the refugees. The authors stated that for some officials, being assigned to work at the camps represented little more than "the opportunity of making good money." Moreover, those in charge of the camps outside South Florida were ignorant of the repression the refugees had suffered in Cuba. The authors pointed out that the problems experienced at the camps did not occur at the Miami facilities, where Cuban Americans helped care for the refugees. The authors also believed that the federal authorities' failure to accept offers of help from Cuban American organizations had "very negative consequences at the refugee camps." Despite these problems, the authors believed that "there were also dedicated individuals who disregarded the language barrier and worked with dedication and personal sacrifice for the welfare of the refugee population."[38]

Mariel refugees sent to the camps were sometimes met harshly by local residents. At Eglin, Fort Walton Beach residents protested, and at one point an airplane flying above pulled a banner reading, "The KKK is here."[39] In Arkansas, rumors spread about diseased refugees at Fort Chaffee; when the rumors were added to media accounts grossly exaggerating the criminality of the camp's residents, fear spread among citizens and political leaders from the surrounding community. Locals reportedly armed themselves in preparation for a conflict, and branches of the Ku Klux Klan reportedly demonstrated outside the camp and at the airport where the Cubans landed.[40] Moreover, disturbances inside Fort Chaffee, the capture by law enforcement of individuals who had fled the camp, protests by the refugees and their sponsors over the delays, and the June riot exacerbated tensions and resulted in friction between the state government, headed by Governor Bill Clinton, and federal officials.[41]

Besides bureaucratic delays at the camps, a series of other factors impeded resettlement efforts. Early on, sponsors had to assume almost full responsibility for the person or persons whom they sponsored, as little federal aid was made available. Whereas this could have been a burden for relatives, it must have seemed even more so to those with no family connection to those they hoped to sponsor. Stories about the Mariel refugees' alleged criminality, along with the news reports about the camp riots, further contributed to the challenges in finding sponsors for those with no relatives in the country to take them in.[42] In addition, caution had to be used as some people who stepped forward as sponsors had ill intentions, such as using the refugees "for cheap labor and even illegal activities."[43] It was also somewhat more difficult to find sponsors for Afro-Cubans—who represented 20 to 40 percent of Mariel refugees—due to prevailing racial attitudes and because it was far less likely that an Afro-Cuban would have relatives in the United States.

Nevertheless, by the fall of 1980, most of the refugees at the camps had been resettled. Private volunteer agencies helped connect them with relatives for whom they had to search and found sponsors for others without family or friends in the country. Among the agencies involved in resettlement were the U.S. Catholic Conference, the International Rescue Committee, and Church World Services.[44] As one might assume, some of the sponsor relationships did not go well and fell apart. In any event, as resettlement moved along, the population at the camps dwindled, and the people remaining were consolidated at Fort Chaffee in October, creating a camp population of just over 8,300; by June 1981 only 1,600 remained, most of them single Afro-Cuban males, which led to charges of racial discrimination and added to an already tense situation. By August 1981 the number had been reduced to less than six hundred. In January and early February 1982, the remaining refugees were sent to halfway homes, mental institutions, or federal prison.[45]

Mariel refugees sent to federal prison, the majority of them Afro-Cuban, presented the greatest long-term issue associated with the Boatlift. Throughout the 1980s this group emerged as the sector of the Mariel population perhaps most frequently in the public eye. In his book *The Abandoned Ones: The Imprisonment and Uprising of the Mariel Boat People,* Mark S. Hamm, professor of criminology at Indiana State University, believed that a large percentage of the Mariel refugees detained in federal prison were held unjustifiably and that for several reasons, their incarceration was politically motivated. In his study Hamm identified four cohorts of Mariel Cubans sent to the federal prisons in Atlanta, Georgia, and Oakdale, Louisiana, the two facilities holding the largest number of Mariel inmates. His "Original Cohort" included the small number of Mariel Cubans who were believed to have had "significant criminal histories" in Cuba, although he questions how dangerous they actually were. The other three cohorts were made up of those who had violated the parole they were given upon arrival in the United States. Among these were the "Disadvantaged," who "were incarcerated because they had no visible means of support or fixed address, or because they did not have an appropriate sponsor;" the "Petty Criminals," who had their parole revoked for minor crimes such as "driving without a license, shoplifting, or possession of small amounts of marijuana and cocaine"; and the "Doubly Punished," who had committed a crime, served their sentence, and were then rearrested and detained by the INS for having violated their federal parole.[46]

Whatever their path to federal prison, the government believed it could detain these individuals indefinitely. Caught in a legal limbo and referred to as "excludables," they were being "warehoused" in maximum-security prisons and could remain incarcerated until Cuba accepted their return or until they passed away behind bars.[47] They were not considered to have entered the country and thus were denied basic constitutional rights and due process.[48] The conditions in which they were held, moreover, were reportedly deplorable. Hopelessness, uncertainty, and despair led to multiple suicide attempts and acts of self-mutilation by the desperate imprisoned refugees.[49] A U.S. district judge ruled in 1983 that the government could not detain illegal aliens on an indefinite basis while denying them all constitutional rights; the INS was, thereby, ordered to conduct hearings for the Cuban prisoners with a party other than the INS deciding the cases. The government would be required to show that a prisoner was a danger to society in order for him to remain incarcerated.[50] In 1984 the same judge blocked the deportation of any excludables until their political asylum claims were heard.[51] The judge's rulings were appealed.

In December 1984 the Reagan Administration signed a migration accord with Cuba, under which the latter agreed to take back 2,746 of the excludables (who included mentally ill Mariel refugees in addition to criminals). The United States, for its part, would accept 3,000 former political prisoners along with their families and agreed to begin issuing up to 20,000 visas each year for family members of U.S. citizens and residents, as well as certain categories of workers. After only 201 excludables had been returned, an angry Castro suspended the agreement in May 1985, when the United States launched Radio Martí, a U.S. government–funded radio station aimed at reaching the Cuban public directly with news and information.[52]

In June 1987 an INS review plan was implemented to begin releasing Mariel inmates who were deemed not to be a threat to the community. (Although this program was highly restrictive at first, in time around 68 percent of the detainees in Atlanta would be approved to be released once they were accepted at a halfway house facility or found a sponsor.)[53] Meanwhile, negotiations between the United States and Cuba were resurrected and a deal was signed in November 1987, allowing for the deportation of the remaining excludables.[54] News of the agreement sparked panic among Mariel inmates in Oakdale and Atlanta, since they were not informed about who, specifically, would be deported. They did not know which prisons were to be affected either, as there were Cuban excludables being held in facilities besides Atlanta and Oakdale. And they also did not know if the deal included the prisoners who had thus far been approved to be released under the recently implemented review program.[55] The frightened prisoners at

Atlanta and Oakdale consequently rioted, seized control of the facilities, and took hostages.

Unlike in other prison riots, a high degree of organization and structure was established within the prison walls in the institutions the refugees captured. The hostages were mostly unharmed and well cared for.[56] The Mariel inmates simply had a message to deliver: they did not want to be sent back to Cuba. Both of the prison takeovers ended (several days apart) when the inmates accepted a deal from the U.S. government in which they were promised a moratorium on deportations and a guarantee that their individual cases would receive a fair review.[57] The prisoners accepted the deal thanks in large measure to the intervention of Miami's auxiliary bishop, Agustin Román, himself a Cuban exile.[58] A large percentage of the prisoners were eventually released over the next several months.[59] Still, it was not until 2005, twenty-five years after the Boatlift and with 750 Mariel refugees still being held, that the Supreme Court ruled that detaining Mariel refugees indefinitely was illegal.[60]

The following group of interviewees comprises local leaders in the Miami area—including the assistant county manager and assistant city manager previously mentioned as well as the then mayor of Miami—and members of the Cuban American community who worked directly with the effort to aid and resettle Mariel arrivals. Also included is an Afro-Cuban refugee who served numerous years in federal prison.

Sergio Pereira

Sergio Pereira was born in Havana and went into United States exile in 1961, at sixteen years of age. He lived in New York City for a couple of months before settling in Newark, New Jersey. He attended Montclair State University and did some graduate work at NYU. After starting his public administration career in Newark, he relocated to Miami in the early 1970s when offered a job by Dade County. He advanced quickly in his career and became an assistant county manager just months before the outbreak of the Mariel crisis.

I'll never forget when Mariel happened, because I was negotiating a bond issue at the airport with investment bankers. The airport director's secretary came in and said, "Mr. Pereira, the county manager (Merrett Stierheim) is on the line. He wants to talk to you." So I told the gentlemen, "Excuse me, I'll be right back," and went out. Merrett said, "Listen! There are like 150 Cubans in Key West coming to Miami!" I said, "And? We've already got over half a million Cubans in Miami." He said, "Well, there are more coming!" I asked, "What do you mean there are more coming?" He said, "Yeah, there are more coming. Take over! You're going to handle this!"

So I walked back into the conference room, where I was negotiating the base points for a revenue bond issue, and said, "Gentlemen, I'm sorry, I have to leave. I've got some refugees coming." You should have seen the look on the faces of these guys from Wall Street. They were looking at me like, "What the hell is this man talking about?"

I picked up the phone and called the head of the INS office here in Miami. I asked him, "What in the world is going on?" He said, "Well, there seems to be an exodus from Cuba."

At this point none of us had a profile of the people coming over and we had no idea what was going on; people weren't going to Cuba like you have today. So I picked up the phone and called [City of Miami City Manager] Joe Grassie's office and said, "We have a problem. Let's set up a meeting right away. Let's meet at noon over at the Artime Center"—which was a neighborhood center in Little Havana the County purchased and turned over to the City of Miami. Grassie was out of town and they said they would send [City of Miami Assistant City Manager] César Odio. I said, "Well, send your police guys. I'll bring my guys."

I could see what it would be like: a bunch of people congregating somewhere in Miami because word would get out that they were going to let people leave Cuba and that there was going to be family reunification. At the meeting, I said, "You can't have it [the processing center] in Little Havana. It would be mayhem. Let's do it at the Youth Fair on Coral Way." So I picked up the phone and called the director of the Youth Fair and said, "Guess what? We're going to be receiving

Cuban refugees." That was at about one o'clock in the afternoon. By four o'clock, we had it all set up. I had people there—volunteers, staff from the County—but we still had no idea of the magnitude of this thing.

So we eventually got word that the first group was coming over—a hundred-twenty-something people. That's when we began to get a little more information about how they were opening up Mariel and that people were running over there to pick people up. I said, "Holy mackerel. Here we go!"

We processed over 35,000 people in a month at that center. We had clothing and medical help there for the refugees, and I took all my guys from the General Investigation Unit and had them begin doing profiles. Jorge Valdes, who was a commissioner, was able to get food. We had trucks filled with food for the refugees and doctors volunteered to come in to pre-screen them. The federal government was kind of hands-off—it was purely Dade County at this point.

Tony Ojeda, who was an assistant county manager like me, took the night shift and I took over from eight o'clock in the morning to midnight. Neither Tony Ojeda, nor César Odio, nor I got more than four or five hours of sleep a day. County employees were taken from different departments to help staff the center and the assistant director of parks recruited some of his people. We also had people volunteering from the community who just came in and asked, "What can I do?" Cops would come in, some of whom were on duty and some who came in afterward, and say, "Hey, we're going to volunteer our time," because we were profiling and interviewing everybody. At the time, we understood that if you came in from Cuba and were asked if you were in jail and you said, "Yes," and we would ask, "What for?" and you would say, "Well, I stole two hens to feed my family," that there was a big difference between that and a rapist or a guy who murdered somebody.

When we realized what this was all about, I flew down to Key West to see what was happening. When I saw it, I said, "Holy mackerel!" I came back and told Merrett Stierheim, [Dade County mayor] Steve Clark, and [Miami mayor] Maurice Ferré, "This is not our responsibility. This is not Dade County's responsibility, not the city manager's responsibility: it is the federal government's." It took thirty-five days before FEMA took over—and that was because we said, "This is an immigration problem."

The Youth Fair was about to start, so we needed to vacate Tamiami. At Opa-locka Airport there was an old blimp hangar from World War II, so we flipped the operation over there. At that point, FEMA and the federal government took over. When the White House sent FEMA here, they spent two weeks going around with yellow pads taking notes. I would tell them, "This is not about taking notes. This is about action. Can't you see what's going on here?" They moved like molasses.

I look back at it and it's incredible. We had a job to do, we got it done, and then we moved on as a unit of local government.

[*After discussing the negative image of Mariel refugees generated by the media and its impact on established Cuban Americans, Pereira said the following*]:

On the other side, you had a very positive impact on this community. Housing vacancy had been 0.01 percent—there was no housing! After the Boatlift, small businesses began to flourish again; used car lots began to flourish. The majority of the Mariel Cubans became very productive and law-abiding citizens of this community and the majority was successful from day one. It was that small element—the criminal element—that gave the negative image. The press was not going to talk about the success stories. I used to beat up on them, saying, "I can give you the names of people here who have been very successful." But they don't follow up on Mariel; they don't talk about the success stories, they talk about the prison riots, the guys in Atlanta and Louisiana.

The Mariel Boatlift had an impact on us as an immigrant group that went far beyond what was ever reported in the media. Cubans are different from other minority groups in the United States in that other groups have achieved political power before economic and social status. We had economic and social status at the time, but we didn't have political status. We had Jorge Valdes, who was the first Cuban American commissioner in the county. Today we have five. But in those days, there were no Cuban American state representatives, congressmen, or U.S. senators. Then after the Mariel Boatlift, things took off. I think it was a direct result of people recognizing that [the lack of political status]. It was a motivation for people to begin to get involved. I view Mariel as a turning point in the history *del exilio cubano* [of the Cuban exile community]. The year 1980 was a benchmark in the growth of this community. A lot of things happened that changed us as an immigrant group and that changed this community completely.

[*After FEMA took over, Pereira worked temporarily as a special advisor to President Carter. He later served as city manager for the City of Miami and subsequently as county manager for Dade County. He passed away in 2017.*]

César Odio

César Odio was born in 1936 in Havana. Before the Revolution his family had owned a highly respected trucking company on the island. His parents were political activists and, although they had supported Batista's overthrow, quickly became disillusioned when Castro steered the Revolution toward Communism. Consequently, Odio and his parents entered the opposition to the Castro government. Odio escaped Cuba in October 1960, while being pursued by Castro authorities. His mother, Sarah, was arrested in 1961 and served six years as a political prisoner. His father, Amador, was also arrested and served eleven years. For several years in Miami, Odio worked for Maule Industries, Inc., a company owned by Miami mayor Maurice Ferré. In January 1980, just a few months before the Mariel Boatlift, he was appointed assistant city manager for the City of Miami, his first public position.

When the Peruvian Embassy crisis began, we began to feel the effects in Miami immediately. There were demonstrations and a hunger strike on 27th Avenue, next to *La Fabulosa* radio station. The city manager at the time, Joe Grassie, was in Brazil on a mission when all this happened. So the assistant city manager he left in charge, Vince Grimm, called me in and said, "Can you take care of this?" My concern was that he would send the police in there and then we'd have a problem. This was my first experience—I had never dealt with public matters before.

The protesters said they refused to leave until all the Cubans were freed from the Peruvian Embassy. So I went into the crowd down there and asked what was going on. People knew me since I had been active with political prisoners because of my father and mother. I told them, Cuban style, "Hey, you're going to have to break this up. They're going to send the police over here. Who are the leaders?" They said, "So and so." I told them, "I'll tell you what, let me see where we can meet so we can talk this out and see if we can solve it." So I met with them in the radio director's office and ordered two *media noches* [Cuban "midnight" sandwiches]—remember, these people were on a hunger strike. The moment one of the protesters took a sandwich, I knew it was over. That was the beginning of my experience in this thing.

I was sitting in my office, going back to normal, with the hunger strike over. All of a sudden, the flights began going to Peru; they had taken some of the people who had been in the Peruvian Embassy and flew them to Lima and to Costa Rica and they kissed the ground when they got there. I said to myself, "Castro cannot tolerate that these people are so happy that they're leaving Cuba." So how could Castro deal with this without losing face? Mariel. He met with Napoleon Vilaboa and filled his boat with people; that's when I got a call from Immigration saying that they needed help. I asked, "What do you need?" They said, "We need a building, centrally located in Little Havana, because we don't have a place where we can process the people on this boat." It was *a* boat. So we opened up the Artime Center on First Street, just before Twelfth Avenue. We gave them a whole floor of the new building. Below that was Catholic Services.

Immigration brought the refugees up from Key West. The problem was that it soon got out of hand and we had to call the police and close the street down; everyone wanted to know if their relatives had been sent or if they were coming. It was quickly decided to move things to the Youth Fair at the Tamiami Fair grounds. That's when it really hit. They were *really* coming in at that point.

My role ceased at that moment [because the Tamiami Fair grounds were in unincorporated Dade County, not the City of Miami], but we said, "We have to help," so me and a few others from the City went out to the Youth Fair. The Miami city manager wasn't in town, like I said, so Vince said, "Look, you represent the City. You go and stay there and do whatever you can, but it's not our problem." I said, "OK."

While I was there, the boats were coming in by the hundreds. The first problem that I saw, immediately, was that they were releasing the Mariel boatpeople and that they had no place to go because they had no sponsors. The first crisis of the Mariel Boatlift was the lack of sponsors for the people coming in. They were hanging out all over the place and had no place to sleep. So I talked to a friend of mine who ran the Talisman sugar mill and we took some of them there in buses—voluntarily, they wanted to go because they didn't have a place to sleep. At the time, the sugar mill was not in harvest time. We heard a report later that they had walked back to Miami because they thought we were going to put them to work cutting sugar cane. We also opened the Elizabeth Virrick gym in Coconut Grove, which was in the City of Miami. We placed like two hundred or so people there.

The County Commission met at Tamiami. Merrett Stierheim was the county manager. They decided that they didn't want any part of this, that this was a federal problem. That's when the federal government decided to process the refugees at Opa-locka. But the question was, "What do we do with these people in the meantime?" They kept releasing them and we had people sleeping all over the place. So at that meeting, I said, "Look, I have only one place where we can do it [house the refugees]: We have 70,000 people that go to games, we have the hallways to give shelter, and we have bathroom and food facilities." So they started putting the refugees in the Orange Bowl. They had to stay there until Immigration would come pick them up to take them to Opa-locka for processing. From Opa-locka, they would be released; but if they didn't have placements, they were kept at the Orange Bowl longer.

At the stadium we set up beds on the two floors with long hallways where the concession stands were located. The doctors set up a clinic in the locker room and we had recreation on the field for the kids. We put the single men in the west end, where I had the office. We also separated what we thought were the bad people because we had families there. Later, because we had an overflow, we set up tents out in the parking lot. We were eventually able to discover who was coming from where by their passport: if they came in with a light gray, new passport that had been issued in prison, we would immediately tell the authorities.

The overflow of refugees was so great that they opened the center at Eglin Air Force Base. Then they opened Fort Chaffee, a camp in Wisconsin, and a camp in Pennsylvania. They could get out if they were sponsored by someone. And that's when a problem began. Cubans are very smart. If they released someone from Fort Chaffee—let me use Fort Chaffee as an example because I spent a week there—he would get to Miami and sponsor someone he'd met there and get him out. But when they got to Miami, they had no housing, no work, no anything. So they would hang out at the airport or on Eighth Street [Little Havana]. And that led to the second stage: when we opened Tent City under the overpass to pick up all these people who were homeless.

At the beginning, I had total support from the community; people would bring in food and clothing for the refugees. I felt no resentment from the Anglo community—that is, until we set up Tent City. With Tent City, things blew up because of an editorial in the *Miami Herald* saying that it was a scandal. But the criticism was mainly against the federal government, never local government. The community appreciated what we were doing. I think we did very well.

Maurice A. Ferré

Maurice A. Ferré was born in Ponce, Puerto Rico, to a prestigious family of industrialists of French and Spanish descent. He attended the Lawrenceville School in New Jersey and graduated from the University of Miami in 1957. He settled in Miami, where his family had business interests, and eventually headed Maule Industries, Inc., a large cement and concrete company in Florida owned by his family. Ferré won a seat in the Florida House of Representatives in the mid-1960s and was elected mayor of Miami in 1973. He served as mayor until 1985. He was named by President Gerald Ford to the President's Advisory Committee on Refugees and later served as Jimmy Carter's Latino co-campaign manager in 1976. During the Carter Administration, Ferré served on the Presidential Advisory Committee on

Ambassadorial Appointments, chaired by fellow Floridian, Governor
Reubin Askew. In 1978 he was appointed by President Carter as a U.S.
delegate to UNESCO in Paris.

When Mariel happened in 1980, I had a solid relation with the administration. Vice President Walter Mondale was a friend of mine. I knew
National Security Advisor Zbigniew Brzezinski and his assistant for
Latin America, Bob Pastor, who was also a good friend. When this
whole thing happened with the Peruvian Embassy, I called Bob and
asked him, "What the hell is going on? This is going to affect Miami."
Nobody knew what Castro was going to do. After a couple of days,
Castro said he was going to open up Mariel. Mariel opened, and on the
first day boats started going over to pick up families. I called up and
said, "This is going to affect Miami." I was told, "It's too early to tell, I
can't tell you anything right now." The second day was worse. On the
third day, I got on a plane and went to Washington.

I showed up at the White House and had to go through clearance,
but my name was already pre-cleared there. I went to the West Wing
and the staff at the president's office said, "There's no way the president
is going to see you because he's involved in this Iran crisis" [the failed
rescue mission]. I was told that he had turned this smaller issue of the
Mariel crisis over to Walter Mondale. So I said, "Well, I'll talk to the
vice president." They told me, "The vice president is in a meeting." I
said, "I'll wait." They checked with Mondale's secretary and she said,
"Oh, yes, Mayor Ferré is a good friend of the vice president. Just tell
him to wait for him." I sat right outside of the Roosevelt Room for two
hours waiting for Mondale. Finally, he walked out—Bob Pastor was
walking out with him, along with some others. The vice president said
to me, "Listen, this is a major issue. I'm glad you're here. We need your
input. But I can't talk to you now because I'm way behind in my sched-
ule. This thing took much longer than I thought and I need to go. You
talk to Bob Pastor. See you tomorrow."

So I sat down with Bob and he sent me to see [Secretary of State]
Cyrus Vance's deputy. I stayed in Washington and chased everybody
around for two days. I met with Ambassador Victor Palmieri, who was
put in charge of the Mariel situation. He was for shutting it down. My

position was, "These are human beings. This is a humanitarian issue. How are you going to shut it down? What does that mean? These are people that are in pain and you've got to help them. The American tradition is that we welcome and help refugees. It's what we did for the Hungarian Freedom Fighters, it's what we did for the Czechs, and it's what we've done with our support for the people in Poland. How can you not accept these people?" That was the discussion. Bob Pastor had taken a much more humanitarian approach as far as the refugees were concerned and was against things like using force to send them back. Pastor later emerged as the key player in all of this, and it made him the go-to person in the administration on Cuba. Anyhow, I never got to see Mondale or the president. So I came back to Miami.

By that time the Boatlift was going full-fledged—that's when, a week later, Carter came out with the, "We welcome you with open arms." They didn't realize then that Castro was sending a lot of people from not only the jails but from the mental hospitals in Cuba. Those people really started creating havoc and a lot of them were taken to prison.

From Key West, the refugees were being transferred here to Miami. We decided to offer the Orange Bowl as a refuge because in the stadium configuration there was a sheltered area. Plus, we used the parking area; while it wasn't protected from the rain, it was at least asphalted so you could have a semblance of cleanliness to put up tents. The City of Miami obviously didn't have the fiscal ability to do much, so the County became the main player locally. The two Cuban Americans—Assistant County Manager Sergio Pereira and Assistant City Manager César Odio—worked together.

People from all walks of life came on the Boatlift, but of course they were all in crisis. They were all in shock; they had left their homes, their families, their country. This was a different country and a different language for them. César and Sergio were able to mobilize thousands of young Cuban Americans—teenagers, college students, and recent college graduates. They volunteered and worked hard. It really was amazing—they helped with kids, and women, and families. They became a tremendous support group. There were people [who came on the Boatlift] who had families here and those families took them in and others volunteered to help. Of course, when the resettlement process began, people were resettled all over the country. There was no way to control the criminal element. These people who were not mentally stable were out on the street right away. They didn't stay in the tent area—they went out and started to commit crimes and to become vagrants.

The negative image of the refugees existed for ten or fifteen years, but I would say that since then it has improved substantially. Former Mariel refugees now include journalists, lawyers, nurses, engineers, technicians, car salesmen, everything. It ended up being a cross section of the Cuban community. They were probably a couple of cuts above—a more educated group—than the people they left in Cuba. The 125,000 Mariel refugees were more like the Cubans who were here in the United States than the ones they left in Cuba. A percentage was from the middle class and a lot were members of families that had been divided and were being reunited. Of course, there were also a lot of people who were not from the middle class, who were laborers and working people.

Eduardo J. Padrón

Eduardo J. Padrón came to the United States from Cuba in 1961 at the age of fifteen via Operation Pedro Pan. He attended Miami-Dade College (then called Miami-Dade Junior College) and later earned a Ph.D. in economics from the University of Florida. He returned to Miami-Dade as a professor after having decided against a corporate career. He eventually entered the administration and, after moving up the ranks, was appointed president of Miami-Dade College in 1995. He has earned a rich variety of national and international distinctions and has been appointed to prominent posts by six presidents of the United States. At the time of the Mariel Boatlift, he was an academic dean at Miami-Dade and a well-known community activist.

Because of my prior work with the Carter Administration, as well as my knowledge of the Miami community, I was called upon to advise the White House. I was very involved with the administration and when they were desperately trying to decide what to do in terms of whether to let the refugees in or not.

As soon as the decision was made and people started coming in from Cuba, we mobilized the entire college. The various campuses offered opportunities for these students. We established programs, above all, for learning English, skills training, and also developed programs to re-validate degrees from Cuba. And we did not limit ourselves just to the educational component, but helped the refugees make a favorable transition. We developed a system of volunteers and worked in collaboration with the city administration. The ability to meet the challenge at hand was made easier because of the college's experience in past years with Cubans who arrived in our city. The main challenge was the large number of people who reached our shores in a short span of time. Finding housing, jobs, as well as all the relocation efforts, was a major task. It was a difficult time.

In addition to being at Miami-Dade, I had been very active in the community. At the time of the Boatlift, I was chairman of SALAD [Spanish American League Against Discrimination]. The organization played an important role in this regard, because that was a period of time when the relationship between the Cuban community and other ethnic groups became tense.

Part of the problem [at the college] was the lack of money to support these students. We needed to change some of the rules. The residency requirement, for example, established that if a student hadn't been here for at least a year we had to charge that student out-of-state tuition. So we had to spend time in Washington and Tallahassee to secure flexibility in the rules. An important factor in all of this is the fact that, at the time, South Florida had a very strong congressional delegation. Our delegation included the chair of the House Foreign Relations Committee, the chair of the House Rules Committee, and the chair of the House Transportation Committee. In addition, Florida had a very powerful U.S. senator, Lawton Chiles. The college's connection to our legislative delegation made it easier to get access and support to assist the refugees.

It didn't take long for the Mariel Cubans to adapt and to incorporate themselves into the life of the community. Many of the college's alumni from that era have become successful professionals in all fields including medicine, law, business, finance, architecture, engineering, etc.

Siro del Castillo

Born in Havana's Guanabacoa section, Siro del Castillo was seventeen when, only days after the Bay of Pigs invasion, he was arrested and put into prison by the Castro regime for anti-government activities. Because he was a minor at the time of his arrest, and thanks in part to family connections, he was released shortly before his twenty-first birthday. Prevented from leaving Cuba because he was of military age, he was finally allowed to emigrate toward the end of the Freedom Flights in 1972. He settled with family in Washington, D.C., and later relocated to Miami. In Miami he met his wife, who worked for Dade County's Latin Affairs office.

In 1978 the political prisoners began to arrive from Cuba. The Latin Affairs office decided to create a support group for them and I was part of it. Then, when the Mariel crisis began, the City of Miami opened the Manuel Artime Community Center to receive the refugees. They saw that place wouldn't work because of the number of people arriving in Key West, so the County intervened and moved the operation to the Youth Fair grounds at Tamiami Park. When that happened, my wife called me, told me about the new center, and said, "We're telling the people from the political prisoners' support group to see if they could help." So I went to Tamiami Park to help out. I knew a lot of the county leaders through my wife. From April 23 until May 10, outside the operation at Key West, the federal government did not involve itself directly in what was happening here in Miami.

At Tamiami the arrivals received complete processing. A person came in—and one could have spent twenty hours in there—and went in one door and out the other with his or her parole and a bag of clothes. I hated the clothes part because people would take so long choosing what they wanted and that was where the whole process would get backed up. We had food coming out of our ears there; restaurants and people from the community were all donating food. None of the arrivals stayed at Tamiami. For the people who didn't have family, the County opened several sites such as army reserve armories. They were also sent to the camps outside Miami.

There was a whole mix of people at Tamiami. The arrivals had been at a place called the Mosquito before departing Cuba; some had even arrived with dog bites from there. At Tamiami, they had a feeling of, "What's going to happen to me now?" I, and the others working for me, spent a great deal of time at the reception center explaining the whole process to them, telling them things such as, "This is an immigration process; they have to register you and they have to fingerprint you. You don't have to be frightened because of the fingerprinting." If you live in a totalitarian system and the first thing you encounter is an interviewer asking you questions, it creates a strange sensation. They'd ask, "When can I see my family?" You really couldn't tell them, "You can see them in half an hour" or in four or five hours. There were people there who didn't know where their families were. They knew they were here in Miami, but had no way of connecting with them.

A couple of days or so before May 10, they turned the problem of refugees in Miami over to FEMA so that it would supervise the operation instead of the County. FEMA worked like the military reserve, in that the agency had few permanent employees. What they had were reservists—principally retired people, technicians, and professionals— who were called in cases of disaster. It had very few people who spoke Spanish at the time, so it asked the County if it could recommend to them people who had volunteered at Tamiami Park so they could put them under contract. One of the assistant county managers, Sergio Pereira, who was a friend of my wife, talked to me about it.

I had been in charge all those days of receiving people coming in directly from Key West—and there were tons of people who had come in by then, at least 20,000—and, well, I get along with everyone, and I had more or less resolved things with the people there. Plus, unlike people who had been in Miami for more years, I had lived in Cuba longer so it was easier for me to understand the people coming over, including those coming from the prisons. I had that advantage over the others not because I was any better or any worse, but because of my experience. Anyhow, at that time, I was an art director for an international publisher. I spoke to the people there and they told me that I could do my work at night [and go work for FEMA].

FEMA closed the center at Tamiami because preparations for the Youth Fair had to get started. They transferred operations to a blimp hangar in Opa-locka and I went there to receive the people coming from Cuba. It was a twenty-four-hour operation. At the start, the people coming from Key West were being held at the Orange Bowl. They kept them there and brought them on buses to be processed at Opa-locka. From Opa-locka, they were released to their families.

After a few days at Opa-locka, it became impossible to hold the number of people arriving from Key West because they weren't being processed in sufficiently high numbers. So other holding places needed to be created. By then, of course, they had also started sending people directly from Key West to military bases at Eglin, Fort McCoy, Fort Indiantown Gap, and Fort Chaffee. Locally, they opened the Krome center in June. When the Orange Bowl closed—actually, before it even closed—they started taking people there. So I went to Krome with two other people from FEMA and five or six people as staff, and I was put in charge of one of the shifts. A few weeks later, the other two FEMA people, who were actual FEMA reservists, left and I became the first director of Krome. At that time, there were two Kromes: Krome North for the Cubans and Krome South for the Haitians. During this whole process, FEMA pulled out and the State Department took over.

[*Del Castillo continued working on behalf of the Mariel refugees at the Krome center and later at the Fort Chaffee resettlement camp in Arkansas.*]

Laida Carro

Laida A. Carro was born to a middle-class family in Havana. Her uncle, Plinio Prieto, a commander in the guerilla army in the Escambray Mountains that had fought against Batista, rose up in arms again against the Castro regime but was captured and executed in 1960. In

1962, when she was twelve, Carro's family went into exile in the United States. She later studied at the School of Applied Arts in Seville, Spain, and obtained a master's degree in art education from Florida International University. In addition to developing her career as an artist and art instructor, she emerged as a recognized human rights activist, working tirelessly on behalf of pro-democracy groups in Cuba. She attributes her activism to a desire to honor her uncle's legacy and her love of freedom and justice. During the Mariel Boatlift, she and her husband volunteered to help process the new arrivals in Miami.

They asked for volunteers to help with the Mariel arrivals. My husband and I were always active in the Cuba cause, so we went. At the processing center, there were rows and rows of tables and so many volunteers that we would have to wait in line and work in shifts. It was wonderful to see. But you could see the difference between the people who were volunteers and the people who were arriving. The people coming from Cuba had been exposed to rocks being thrown at them, to having dogs set on them. And then the manipulation of taking convicts and placing them on ships that carried families . . . [she sighs]. It's always a manipulation, it's always this manipulation of the human being that is so disrespectful. I saw a family there that you could tell just couldn't take any more.

As volunteers, we had to help the new arrivals fill out forms. That's where you asked yourself: "What happened to these people?" I saw fear in them: the fear they had in their eyes, the fear in their body language, the fear with which they looked over their shoulders, the fear of answering questions. They didn't understand what the authorities would do to them in this country as opposed to what they had experienced in Cuba. You have to remember that many of them were born under Communism so they didn't know the difference. When we would ask them, "Have you stolen anything?" they would tell you, "Well, in Cuba, people have to steal to survive." They would tell you in a way that you could tell they knew it wasn't right, but that they really had to do it to survive. The children arrived nervous too. Before they came, they had been in places where they were huddled with their families while rocks were being thrown at them.

But the fear wasn't caused only by what they had just been through—it was a fear that was institutionalized in Cuba. You really saw the results of the repression that existed in Cuba from 1959 to 1980. Fear is the Cuban regime's tool for staying in power; their only objective is to stay in power and they will do anything and everything they have to do.

There was a family I saw that was petrified. Their boat almost capsized, and they were mostly surrounded by criminals on the boat. They thought they would not survive the trip, either because their boat would sink or because of the criminals. The children in that family were beautiful. But the parents, everybody, was petrified.

We felt good about doing this because we wanted to see these people who were coming from Cuba and to embrace them. We wanted to make them feel welcome, to say to them, "We're brothers and sisters." I would tell them, "You know, whatever happened in Cuba, remember that this is a country where the rule of law prevails. When you have the rule of law, it is totally different. You have to respect authority, but at the same time you have freedoms and responsibilities." Some of them probably didn't care what I was saying at the moment, but at the same time I think that being volunteers and being Cuban—and not being of a different nationality—was a great thing for them. They felt comfortable. And remember, we were supposed to be the "mean ones" [the exiles in Miami]. They were sitting in front of the "mean ones" they heard about all the time in Cuba, yet who were now helping them out and welcoming them. Imagine that.

My experience helped me realize what they had done to the Cuban nation. It really gave me knowledge—being a volunteer was not the same as seeing things on the news. I sat with these people coming in and saw that fear in their eyes, listened to the things they told us in addition to what we filled out on the forms, and realized how horrible it was what the regime had done. My activism increased more and more until finally, in 1998, I started working with dissidents on the island. That was special. I didn't know any human rights organizations when I started—I just started sending out information. I found out where Amnesty International was, where Human Rights Watch was, and that's how I started, little by little.

Wilfredo Allen

In 1961, at the age of ten, Wilfredo Allen left Cuba with his family and settled in South Florida. At the time of the Mariel Boatlift, he was a social worker in Miami. He later studied law and became an attorney specializing in immigration matters. He appears frequently in the Spanish-speaking media to discuss both immigration law and Cuba-related issues and is an avid collector of Cuban art.

At the time the Mariel Boatlift started, I was the director of *Diálogo Familiar* [Family Dialogue], a mental health center for young kids who had issues with drugs, their families, or the courts. My funding came from private organizations, Metro Dade County, and government grants. When the exodus from Mariel began, Siro del Castillo and I went directly to the reception center they were establishing at the Youth Fair grounds. With a bunch of other folks, we helped set up the center and started talking to the people from Cuba as they were coming in. I also helped assign spaces to people and helped to set up interviews; the Metro Dade County Police Department and some of the FBI people were already there. I allowed those on my staff who wanted to volunteer at the center to go in during work hours or in the afternoon. I worked there most afternoons.

In the summer of 1980 the Miami Family Guidance Center—part of the University of Miami School of Medicine—got a contract from the Office of Refugee Resettlement to help deal with unaccompanied minors who had come in on the Boatlift. I had worked with the Center before, and they contracted me as a consultant to help set up camps for the unaccompanied minors at Fort Indiantown Gap, Pennsylvania, and Fort Chaffee, Arkansas. As a consultant, I would visit Fort Indiantown Gap every week or two. I never worked as part of the staff inside the camp, but as a consultant I helped hire and supervise the staff working with the minors. I also interviewed all of the kids and some of the psychologists working with them. Fort Indiantown Gap was separated into a camp for families, a camp for adult males who were by themselves, a camp—I believe—for single women with families, and the camp for unaccompanied children.

I would venture to say that the kids who had come as unaccompanied minors from Cuba were sixteen, seventeen, and eighteen years of age. Many of them had not been living with their parents in Cuba and a significant percentage had been taken out of minors' prisons and put on boats at Mariel. A few of the kids were gay, and being gay in Cuba was not an acceptable thing. It was an interesting cross section. Anyhow, a big part of the program was to hook these kids up with family members here in the United States and some of them were able to do so.

Some of the experiments, however, were not very successful. For instance, there were some kids who were placed with the Mennonite community there in Pennsylvania. That didn't work out 100 percent. I think it just didn't work out culturally; the Mennonites are very good people, but I believe coming from a Cuban culture that even in 1980 didn't have a lot of regulations made it so that things didn't work out very well.

Fort Indiantown Gap eventually closed and the remaining minors were moved to Fort Chaffee, Arkansas. By then, most of the unaccompanied minors at Fort Indiantown Gap were kids who had problems.

There was a camp in Wisconsin [Fort McCoy] I never visited, but from what I remember there was physical and emotional abuse committed against some of the unaccompanied kids there by staff and guards. I remember the people coming from there would tell you that the place was horrible. I didn't see any mistreatment at the minors' camp at Fort Indiantown Gap. There were house parents in the barracks to make sure there was nothing bad going on and there was a separate boys' camp and girls' camp. But it was still a jail; a wire fence surrounded them and they were restricted to barracks. In fact, right before the Cubans came in, a couple of the barracks at Fort Indiantown Gap—I think they were the kids' barracks—had been used as a set to film a movie about the Holocaust.

I remember some of the staff working there fell in love with each other. At least two or three of the guys found their true loves in life from among their fellow coworkers and married them. It was like Match.com.

Ernesto Pérez

Ernesto Pérez, the son of public school teachers, was born in Gibara, Oriente Province. He came to the United States as a teenager in 1962 via Operation Pedro Pan, and lived in a facility for unaccompanied Cuban children in Albuquerque, New Mexico. His parents left the island five years later on the Freedom Flights. He graduated from the University of New Mexico and later worked for the EPA as an environmental engineer. He was transferred to Atlanta in the 1970s, where in addition to working as an environmental engineer he hosted a weekly show on Radio Free Georgia featuring Cuban music and musicology. The show became popular among the Mariel prisoners being held at the Atlanta Federal Penitentiary. Pérez developed a rapport with the Cuban inmates by interviewing them on the air and by taking bands to give live performances at the prison. In 1987 those same inmates took over the prison when it was announced that Cuba and the United States had agreed to the repatriation of Mariel prisoners.

The moment came when a pact was signed between Cuba and the United States, whereby the United States would return the detained Mariel refugees to Cuba. The big mistake they made was to list a number in the newspapers that had been agreed to around three years earlier [the 1984 agreement that had been suspended] and had not been updated. When the prisoners saw the number, they all believed that they were among those scheduled to be sent back. Inmates in Texas—even those who were in halfway homes—started to run away. The Mariel prisoners at Oakdale Federal Prison in Louisiana took over the prison there. Bishop Agustín Román was very involved later in leading the negotiations to end the takeover there.

When that occurred, an officer from the Atlanta prison called me—it was a Sunday—and said, "Look, Ernesto, we have this situation here and we're worried about what might happen in the prison." I got along well with the prison officials. They let the prisoners use the telephone during my program so that I could interview them and they gave me permission to take the bands in. Anyhow, he asked me to speak to the prisoners and to tell them to remain calm. I asked him what the pact between Cuba and the United States included, because I've never liked to offer my assistance with things of which I know nothing. He said, "Well, we really don't know. But we're nervous. Can you do something?" I didn't agree to do it since there wasn't very much information as to what was going on.

The next day, a Monday, I was driving to my job at the EPA. At around ten in the morning, I heard on the car radio that there was smoke at the prison and that the prisoners had taken over the facility. Something made me turn around right there and drive to the doors of the prison. Congressman Lewis, who was advocating for the prisoners, was there and I greeted him. By then, the FBI had taken charge and had sent SWAT teams to cordon off the area. There was an exchange of words between the congressman and one of the military people.

I saw there was nothing I could do there, so I went directly to the radio station. The others there gave me their time slots and I went on the air. Over the radio, I asked the prisoners to remain calm and not to harm anyone they were holding. Later, I found out that the authorities had put a block on electronic transmissions, but that FM radio was still reaching the prison.

There was only one death during the takeover, when a guard shot a prisoner. But the more than seventy hostages they took were put into cells; they also separated the group of more than two hundred hardened criminals.

The authorities had a public relations person on-site through whom all news and information went. They put out word that the prisoners didn't want to negotiate. So I started to tell the prisoners over the radio what was being said about them and that if they wanted to negotiate, please to release some of the hostages. They released four of them. We received no credit for that from the press; in fact, when they asked the public relations person, "What happened? Why did they release them?" that person said, "We don't know." I'm not really sure why I got no credit. It was either because they truly didn't know or because they wanted to control everything. Anyhow, at that time President Reagan sent over a group of representatives from the Cuban exile community to negotiate and they spent around a week there. But I asked myself, "Why would the prisoners listen to them? These people have never been here." The United States must have thought that all Cubans were the same and that they all knew one another; it must have been something like, "Sure, just send some Cubans over there."

The prisoners were in a legal limbo. The only option in the agreement was to return them to Cuba, and that's what I criticized more than anything else. Some people were critical of me in return, but I would make my point by telling them, "OK, let them give them sentences: give them twenty years, ten years, five years, or whatever." But the problem was that, by doing so, you would be admitting them to the United States; their status at the time was the same as if they were outside the United States. And that was the dilemma: by giving the prisoners a sentence, you'd be giving them an immigration status and couldn't send them back to Cuba. These people preferred living in an overcrowded prison rather than being separated from their families that were already in the United States. This was not a political issue but a human tragedy.

While the negotiations were going on—all of it being done in good faith—I brought a young American reporter from the *Atlanta Constitution* to the radio station. While he was there, I asked the prisoners to release more hostages, because I saw that the authorities were squeezing them by cutting off their food and water. I told them again, "Please do not harm any of the hostages." I kept telling them not to hurt anyone and that the press was saying that they didn't want to negotiate. Then they released five more hostages. The next day, the *Atlanta Constitution* announced that a small radio station had made it so that five hostages were released. The station was soon filled with journalists from CBS, NBC—people from all over, even Japanese and Canadians.

One of the prisoners had heart problems, so he surrendered and was taken to Georgia Baptist Hospital. My sister-in-law worked there as a nurse and she snuck her way into where they were keeping him. She told him, "I'm Ernesto Pérez's sister-in-law." He responded, "Tell Ernesto we're in this situation and don't know how to get out of it."

Gary Leshaw was a lawyer who represented a group of the prisoners. He came to the station, and I told him what was happening and that we needed a legal mind to explain to the prisoners how to surrender. He asked the prisoners over the radio to release another hostage at 9:00 p.m.—but with the idea that the hostage would be exchanged for Gary. That way, Gary could stay inside and negotiate an agreement.

Then I started speaking in English on the air, saying, "Well, now we need for the government to allow [Gary Leshaw] to enter." Gary went to the prison. He called me from there, "Ernesto, they aren't letting me in." So I got on the radio saying that half an hour had passed since the release of the hostage and that now it was time for Gary to be allowed in. It was the first time the prison officials recognized me. They said, "Mr. Pérez, we have Officer so-and-so and we're about to let Gary in." I said, "Well, thank you very much," and hung up. Gary spent all night with the prisoners. He got them to accept an agreement whereby the government would review the prisoners' cases one by one; if they saw that a case wasn't serious, the prisoner could leave prison and go to a halfway house. The next day, it was accepted by the U.S. government. But then Cuban machismo stepped in. The prisoners said, "Well it's all of us or none of us." They were convinced to hold a vote on the pact. So they voted for it in the chapel—where there was a young priest whose first assignment was at the prison—on the feast day of Saint Barbara. After that, the prisoners insisted that Bishop Román from Miami formally witness the signing, and he was flown in for that purpose. Huber Matos [a former political prisoner and Cuban exile leader], with whom some of the prisoners sympathized, was also present.

I thought it was a miracle that the friendship factor would influence the surrender and that the prisoners had put faith in Gary and me. Gary only represented some of them, but the fact that we pushed, that we said, "This is the best you can get," and that they surrendered without killing anyone in the longest prison takeover ever, was a miracle.

After that, buses arrived and the prisoners were taken to different prisons. Some of them who'd been taken to Texas later called me at the radio station. They said, "They're interrogating us. They're violating the pact because they want to know who the leaders were." That was the part that made me feel most sorry for them. In truth, there were no leaders; it was a group of people who were desperate because they thought they were going to be sent back to Cuba and away from their families. These were people who had their families here and didn't want to go back.

Bartolo Díaz

Bartolo Díaz, an Afro-Cuban, was from Santa Cruz del Norte, a town in Havana Province. His father was a Communist Party member and his brother a lieutenant in State Security. Díaz was sent to Angola as part of the Cuban army during Fidel Castro's war there, but saw no combat. He returned to Cuba from his service in 1979, when the island's economy had entered a downward cycle. Although he had previously expressed a desire to leave Cuba, he was, in the end, forced to leave the country against his will, via Mariel, by the authorities of his town. The following year, he was arrested for a minor crime in the United States and quickly found himself among the thousands of Mariel prisoners who existed in a legal limbo for numerous years. The interview below was conducted at a homeless shelter near downtown Miami operated by the Missionaries of Charity of Mother Teresa, the Roman Catholic religious order founded by Saint Teresa of Calcutta, a.k.a., "Mother Teresa." He was sixty-eight years of age at the time of the interview.

In 1980, when the people entered the Peruvian Embassy, I told my mother, "I'm going to the United States." The population was all stirred up at the time and Fidel said that anyone who wanted to do so could leave Cuba. A lot of people came to the United States with their families, but many others were forced to leave. In my case, I had had some words with a Communist Party member in my town whose name was Cachimba. I told him that I was leaving the country and I told him off. He went to the police station to report that I was messing with members of the Party, and that I had told him that I would wipe my groin with his Party identification card. The police lieutenant at the station went to my house and told me, "Let's go, to the police station." When I got to the station, Cachimba was there, and he said, "Repeat what you said to me!" So, I said, "I didn't say anything. I said the I.D. you have is no good, that you're not from the Party." Then he said, "Now you have to leave here." I asked, "What do you mean I have to leave?" He said, "You have to leave here right now." They put me in a cell, and later boarded me on a small bus that was packed with people going to the United States. We went directly to the Mosquito.

When we got to Key West, they took me to a barracks there. They asked me, "Do you have family here?" I said, "Yes, I have family, an uncle and an aunt." Then they asked, "Where do they live?" I said, "In Boston." So, they did the paperwork there and sent me to Boston on an airplane directly from Key West.

In 1981 I was walking in the city of Worcester.[61] I'll never forget this—not ever. I had a marijuana cigarette in my hand and an officer stopped me and asked, "What are you smoking?" I said, "Marijuana." He said, "Throw it away." So, I threw it down and stepped on it. After I did so and started to leave, he said, "Wait a minute. You're under arrest." I asked, "What for?" He said, "For smoking marijuana in the street." I didn't know about the law or anything. So, he put me in the police car and took me to the precinct. I called my uncle from the station so that he could pay the $100 fine for me. When he came and paid the fine and I was going to leave, Immigration came and got me. I ended up in Atlanta [Federal Prison].

In Atlanta I was placed with the others who had come through Mariel. We were kept separate from the other inmates at the prison. A year passed, then another, then another—I was there from 1981 until 1987, when I finally went before an Immigration panel. They said, "You're leaving." From there, they put me on an airplane and sent me to Memphis, Tennessee. I left Atlanta a little over a month before the inmates there took over the prison.

In Memphis I was in the federal prison. I had not been sentenced, but Immigration kept me there year after year after year. When I would go before the panel, they would ask, "Why are you here? Murder? Robbery? Rape?" I would say, "No, I'm here because of a marijuana cigarette. It's there in my record." They would say, "No, you're not ready to enter society. We'll see you again next year." I was there, in Memphis, until they released me in 1999.

In Memphis I was with other people who came through Mariel.

There were around four hundred of us. No one there had a sentence. People there were imprisoned for driving without a license, for drinking, for talking garbage on the streets, and others who had completed sentences but were detained there by Immigration—as in my case, my uncle paid the $100 fine but then, as we were leaving the precinct [in Worcester], Immigration was waiting and they detained me and sent me to prison. All because of a marijuana cigarette.

Many people were imprisoned for years and years by the U.S. government. A friend of mine hanged himself; other people, young people, went crazy and killed themselves. People were held for years and years and years, until the new law in 2005 saying that the government could hold them no longer. I was already out by then.

The government of the United States put Mariel Cubans for years and years and years in federal prisons, but without ever convicting them. I never saw a judge. The only judges I saw were civilians on a board who would tell me, "No, you're not ready for society." It was either be sent back to Cuba or die in prison here—and Cuba accepted no one. Years and years and years would pass, then you'd see the panel, then another year would pass.

The treatment in prison was horrible. For instance, if you were screaming for a tube of toothpaste or something, the guard would come and hit you with pepper spray. The government of the United States did things to us they had never done to a human being. There was so much mistreatment. Many young people hanged themselves— in Talladega, in Arizona, in Oklahoma. And the guards killed, too, through excess force; they killed [name unintelligible], then they made it seem as if he had hanged himself. There was a lot of abuse from the people working for the government who took care of the Cubans in federal and state prisons. They killed—in Louisiana, and in Oklahoma too. All that mess ended in 2005. I don't know why the government put us in prison for no reason for so many years.

In 1999 I was released because of a man, a hero, called Mike, who was a lawyer from around there. He wrote a letter to the Supreme Court on my behalf but it came back denied. Then, around July, I got a letter saying I would be freed. I got out in August. All they gave me was a paper to present to Immigration.

When I got out, I went to Kansas City, Missouri. I got married there and the government got me a job as a welder. I was there until 2007. I left my marriage and came to Miami with the intention of working since there were so many Cubans here. But there is nothing here. Anyhow, I have to go in and sign every year at Immigration; otherwise, they'll send me to Cuba. I'm now waiting for my Social Security.

In 1981 I lost a great job in Boston as a welder. They completely destroyed my life when I got arrested. I lost everything in 1981 because of a little marijuana cigarette. And the others—the one driving without a license, the one who was drinking in the street—were also sent to Atlanta, or one of the other places. The government of the United States needs to take responsibility for the people who came through Mariel and who were imprisoned for no reason. There were a lot of barbarities committed, but until now the government hasn't given us even a penny.

6

In the Land of Opportunity

WHETHER THEY WERE taken home by relatives directly from Key West or had to wait to be sponsored from a resettlement camp, a processing center, or a holding facility, the Mariel immigrants eventually began their new lives in the United States (with the exception of the small number who returned to Cuba either on their own initiative or via deportation, and those in federal prison). Despite the unique challenges they faced, the overwhelming majority of them eventually adjusted well. Although precise figures are impossible to calculate, some have estimated that 90 to 97 percent of Mariel refugees made an effective transition.[1] A number of them, in fact, became quite successful. Even so, for many, their first steps in their adopted country were marked by frustrations and disadvantages their exiled brethren of the previous waves did not face.

As noted earlier, the Mariel immigrants received an immigration status that for months denied critical federal aid for them, their sponsors, and local and state government. A large number of the arrivals were herded into problem-plagued refugee camps and subjected to a chaotic and frustrating processing system at those camps. Furthermore, a lower percentage of them spoke English compared to previous exiles, and a higher percentage was working class or low-skilled. The Mariel Cubans were also disproportionately male; during the Freedom

Flights, around 42 percent of the refugees were male; during Mariel, the number was over 70 percent. Moreover, the proportion of unmarried people was more than double compared to the previous waves.[2]

Among the greatest difficulties faced by Mariel entrants was that the younger adults (a large percentage of the group) had never experienced life in pre-Castro Cuba, and despite yearning for freedom, they could have found the change from a totalitarian Communist system to a free society somewhat difficult or even traumatic; for many of them, a period of learning and adjustment was necessary.[3] On the other hand, older refugees, though they too could have struggled, were better equipped for life in a free system since they had spent all or part of their formative years in pre-Communist Cuba. As might be expected, those who came as children seem to have adapted most quickly and easily. Arrivals who went directly to relatives or close friends—which includes the majority of the interviewees in the present work—had a clear advantage, as they were quickly taken in by people who genuinely cared for them and with whom they shared an emotional connection. They also immediately entered a social network that could have led to jobs, housing, new friends, and educational opportunities.

The Mariel arrivals faced other disadvantages. In the 1960s, when the first waves of Castro-era exiles arrived, the United States felt confident, its economy was strong, and overall immigration was lower and not seen as a major issue. Americans by and large, with the possible exception of some in the Miami area, were generally unperturbed by the arrival of refugees from the Communist world, especially at that moment in the Cold War. Going into 1980, however, the country had been shaken by the Vietnam War, Watergate, an energy crisis, and a decline in optimism; the United States' inability to stop the Soviet invasion of Afghanistan, coupled with the seemingly interminable Iran hostage crisis, further eroded the nation's confidence.[4] Perhaps most damaging to the national spirit was a sharp economic decline—one felt most acutely in the form of inflation and unemployment. Also, immigration to the United States had increased markedly by the late 1970s.[5] Under such conditions, many Americans viewed the sudden influx of a large group of immigrants—from the Communist world or elsewhere—as a threat to their well-being.

Adding to the difficulties encountered by the Mariel refugees were the negative stereotypes that emerged about them. The deviant labels that the Cuban government had attached to those who left via Mariel (delinquents, social dregs, etc.) were transferred to the United States and accepted by some in the U.S. news media, who in turn ran numerous stories (some of them well after the Boatlift ended) depicting the refugees in a manner that reflected those labels. Unfortunately, certain U.S. officials, criminal justice professionals, and interest groups also seem to have accepted the labels and for years grossly exaggerated the danger posed by the Mariel immigrants.[6] In "Marielitos Ten Years Later: The Scarface Legacy," B. E. Aguirre, Rogelio Sáenz, and Brian Sinclair James explained the acceptance of Cuba's characterization of the refugees by the media and U.S. officials:

> The nuances of Marxist theory informing the Cuban government's accusations against the immigrants were never seriously examined by the U.S. press or effectively challenged by U.S. officials. Borrowing the imagery of degeneracy from the Cuban press, the U.S. mass media supported the transformation of the moral identity of the Marielitos. A naïve realism allowed the official Cuban labels against the Marielitos to be directly applied in the U.S. context.[7]

In just one example of the sort of rhetoric used to depict the refugees, a 1984 *U.S. News and World Report* Special Report running with the headline, "Castro's 'Crime Bomb' Inside U.S.," although admitting that "the majority are decent people" and highlighting some Mariel success stories, nevertheless stated, "They came—125,000 of them all at once—in the 1980 boatlift from Mariel, Cuba, with tattered clothes and soiled reputations. Fidel Castro himself called them *escoria*, 'scum,' and many Americans who greeted them with open arms now agree with him."[8] Popular culture jumped in with the 1983 film *Scarface*, which epitomized some of the worst notions people had about the Mariel immigrants' criminality. In their study Aguirre, Sáenz, and James demonstrated that as a result of the prevalent deviant label, Mariel refugees were, in many ways, treated differently by the U.S. government and were far more likely than earlier Cuban immigrants to be institutionalized, especially if they were non-white, young, male, unmarried, less educated, or disabled.[9]

The visual effect of the 1980 exodus also probably contributed to the negative views people held about Mariel immigrants. During the previous exile waves, media images of Cuban refugees mostly depicted families and individuals who were well groomed and well dressed (despite their absolute destitution) arriving at the nation's airports, especially Miami International. The Mariel entrants, on the other hand, arrived looking more like one might expect refugees to appear—a fact that did not seem to elicit much compassion. They had just emerged from a fully Communist Cuba where food, clothing, and every other consumer item had been scarce for years, and they had just endured an excruciating ordeal over many days under severely adverse conditions. News images this time showed bedraggled, disheveled, often unshaven refugees exiting boats in clothes they may have been wearing for days. Photographs and news clips also showed the astonishing stream of boats—some of them large, old, rusty, shabby-looking vessels packed beyond capacity—pulling into a U.S. port ferrying in an impossible number of aliens in a migratory wave that no one seemed able to control. Worsening perceptions was that a disproportionate number of the refugees were adult, single, and male; when these images were combined with the notion that a high percentage of the refugees were Cuba's "scum," mental patients, and dangerous criminals, negative perceptions only hardened.

But the stereotype, like most stereotypes, while containing a proverbial "kernel of truth," was largely false. The vast majority of the Mariel immigrants clearly were not the dangerous people that much of the media, certain public officials, and others in the public square led many to believe.[10] It must be remembered that thousands of Mariel arrivals were taken immediately by relatives or friends at Key West, processed, and never heard from again—at least not as "refugees." Also, most of the people sent to the holding centers and resettlement camps found sponsors (sometimes relatives for whom the resettlement agencies had to search), were released, and for the most part went on to live quiet, productive lives. In short, the vast majority of refugees eventually blended in and became largely invisible to the rest of the population (except, perhaps, in situations such as schools, where Mariel children may have entered special English language programs). The small percentage of real or perceived troublemakers—which the average person could have experienced via news reports, political campaigns, or on the streets of Miami and other cities—were simply the most visible and noticeable sector of the refugee population and not truly representative of the vast majority. Nevertheless, the heavy focus on this sector inevitably influenced how the American public came to view Mariel entrants overall and led many to associate all or most of the people who left on the Boatlift with this image. Consequently, the name Mariel, and by extension the term *Marielito*, became toxic, stigmatizing all the refugees, no matter if they were among the small number who were a genuine threat to society or among the 90 to 97 percent who were hardworking and law-abiding.

As to the overall previous criminality of Mariel arrivals, INS numbers painted a striking contrast to what was assumed by the media, the political leadership, and the public. As referenced in chapter 2, despite the accounts that circulated for years, less than 2 percent of the arriving refugees were classified as felons by the INS.[11] Although some later put the number higher or slightly lower—and let me note again the less than perfect method of determining someone's past in Cuba—it is nevertheless clear that, whatever the exact number, only a tiny percentage of the entrants had been true hard-core criminals in Cuba. There were, however, according to Clark, Lasaga, and Reque, around 19 percent who were placed into the category "non-felonious criminals and political prisoners."[12] The political prisoners (many of whom had been released in Cuba in the years prior to Mariel), presumably were not a problem since their incarceration in Cuba had been political and ideological in nature rather than criminal. Even among those classified as "non-felonious" criminals, which according to the authors accounted for more than 20,000 people, a large number had committed acts that, as already mentioned, would not have constituted crimes in the United States, such as trying to escape Cuba or participating in the black market to secure basic everyday commodities.[13]

Of course, when considering the "non-felonious" criminals' adaptation to the United States, one must take into account that some of them had just been taken out of Cuba's common (non-political) prisons. It would be reasonable to assume that for at least some, any trauma, prison behaviors, or prison-created survival instincts they had developed would transfer, even if only temporarily, to the streets of their new home. Also, having been among those who were forced, pressured, or induced to leave the country, they were probably not likely to have had anyone awaiting them in the United States. In addition, some refugees who had never previously been in prison may also have gravitated to illegal activity soon after arrival, especially those without family or friends to help them. With disoriented, socially marginalized, sometimes homeless, and mostly male refugees on the streets of Miami and other cities, it would not be illogical to assume that at least a percentage committed crimes. It has also been suggested that established criminals recruited gullible, destitute refugees for illicit purposes, particularly the drug trade. Clark, Lasaga, and Reque suggested that crime among the Mariel refugees also could have been influenced by "Unemployment, lack of financial aid, and some apparent rejection or apprehension on the part of the established Cuban community in the area."[14]

The spike in Miami's crime rate that coincided with the arrival of the Mariel refugees was often pointed to as evidence of the newcomers' criminality. The local crime rate, however, had been climbing prior to the Boatlift, much of the increase brought about by the drug trade and a bad economy.[15] Although some Mariel refugees indisputably committed serious crimes—Little Havana, for instance, experienced a substantial increase in robbery, auto theft, burglary, and assault—studies confirm that the Mariel arrivals were responsible for only a small part of the crime wave in the overall metropolitan Miami area. Clark, Lasaga, and Reque cited a survey of the Dade County Jail on December 26, 1980, showing that less than one tenth of one percent of the 90,000 Mariel refugees in Dade County at the time was among those incarcerated. The authors stated: "In this sense, it has been speculated that the Mariel refugees may actually have been used as 'escapegoats' for the increase in the crime rate in the Miami area."[16] In any case, the Mariel refugees who committed crimes in the United States, whether they had a criminal history in Cuba or not, represented only a small percentage of the overall Mariel population.

The Mariel label could have been damaging within the Cuban American community as well. For a time a degree of apprehension was evident on the part of some members of the community. The refugees' alleged criminality and overall negative depiction caused concern that the image of Cuban Americans as the "model minority" would somehow become tainted—a goal, it must be recalled, of Fidel Castro in launching the Boatlift in the manner that he did.[17] Also, a cultural chasm, it seemed, had developed between those who had spent two decades under Communism and those who had departed at the start of the Revolution (and were products of prerevolutionary Cuba rather than Communist Cuba). Differences in demeanor, speech, work habits, and values were perceived by many established exiles, especially in the younger refugees who had lived all or most of their formative years under Castro's rule. In addition, some of the Mariel refugees could have been viewed with hostility and suspicion if they had previously been active Revolutionaries or Communist Party members in Cuba, even if they were so only as a matter of everyday survival. For an established anti-Communist community whose cherished heroes were those who had bravely defied and fought the Castro dictatorship since the beginning and had, as a consequence, faced political prison, family separation, and the firing squad, the initial emotional reaction by some to those who had been part of the system, while it may perhaps seem a bit unfair to someone on the outside, was certainly understandable.

Although some established Cuban Americans were reluctant to have any association with the new refugees in the early period following the exodus, others, out of a sense of ethnic loyalty, patriotism, and compassion, placed themselves on the front lines both to assist the newcomers and to advocate on their behalf, either as private individuals or as part of Cuban exile organizations. Cuban Americans volunteered to greet the refugees and provide for their needs upon the latter's arrival in Key West, donated items and money to ease their transition, and selflessly helped them at the processing centers. Many worked with the refugees in programs launched on their behalf. Countless families took in and, at great sacrifice, assisted their Mariel refugee relatives and friends. Moreover, despite the financial downturn at the time, the local Cuban American economy gradually absorbed a large part of the Mariel refugee population and was of great long-term benefit to the new arrivals' achievement of economic stability.

Economic and Social Mobility

At the very beginning of their residency in the United States, Mariel refugees, on average, experienced a lack of housing and high rates of unemployment. One must consider, of course, the economic decline at the time of their arrival and that the vacancy rate of apartments in Dade County was less than one percent.[18] That some of the refugees had come with unrealistically high expectations about quickly securing high-paying jobs and reaping the material rewards of living in the United States only made their plight more difficult.[19] Moreover, adapting to an entirely new socioeconomic system and more demanding work patterns was bewildering and potentially frustrating, particularly for those who had been fully conditioned under Communism. Their early difficulties could have led to disillusion and depression. Some committed suicide and a few made desperate attempts to return to Cuba on hijacked airplanes or stolen boats.[20] These problems were presumably far less severe for those who arrived in family groups, possessed some understanding of life in a free society, and had relatives or close friends in the United States to help them.

By the mid-to-late 1980s, the situation had changed considerably. Most of the criminals as well as the mentally disturbed were confined (again, many of them unjustly), most Mariel entrants were permitted to attain permanent resident status and eventually citizenship, and the local economy had been revitalized. By 1986 the unemployment rate of Mariel refugees was half of what it had been in 1983 (27 percent down to 13.6 percent).[21] Miami—after taking a black eye in the news media at the start of the 1980s because of the refugee crisis, the cocaine wars, soaring crime rates, and the 1980 riots—reclaimed its status as a major tourist destination, albeit of a hipper flavor than before; that is, less Jackie Gleason and more *Miami Vice*. The Miami area, where most Mariel Cubans eventually settled, was also emerging as the undisputed commercial and financial "gateway" to Latin America, a feat brought about in large measure by the efforts of the first two waves of Cuban exiles and the vision of the local political leadership and to no small extent enhanced by the arrival of the Mariel refugees and other Spanish-speaking immigrants from Latin America. Good jobs became more plentiful and business opportunities soared in the chic, fashionable, new Miami.

The true long-range picture of the Mariel immigrant gradually surfaced. Despite some lingering prejudice, a natural assimilation process quietly occurred, especially among those who had arrived as children and teenagers. Education was crucial, as is so often the case with immigrants. Not only were ESOL (English for Speakers of Other Languages) programs at Dade County's schools a success, but Miami-Dade Community College (later renamed Miami-Dade College) continued its tradition of innovation and offered many of the new arrivals the critical first steps in attaining a college education.[22] When one adds to this the drive, ambition, and desire to do well that inspired most people who arrived on the Mariel exodus, success was not long in coming. Mariel immigrants soon joined the ranks of the area's laborers, business owners, artisans, professionals, academicians, clergy, and community activists.

Among the refugees who exited the boats at Key West in 1980, there also came an unexpected cultural boon: the arrival of talented Cuban artists, musicians, and writers.[23] With artistic expression tightly controlled and severely repressed in Cuba, many of them had been unable to produce and disseminate their work on the island. Finding their way to freedom via the port of Mariel, they established literary magazines, published internationally acclaimed novels and plays, became celebrated painters, sculptors, actors, and journalists, and blossomed into beloved musical performers in the United States. The roster is indeed long. Fabiola Santiago of the *Miami Herald* stated in 2005, "One year—1980—and a tumultuous, historic journey from a Cuban port—Mariel—mark their generation as creators. Twenty-five years later, the stamp of artists, writers, musicians, thespians and dancers who arrived via the boatlift is sprinkled over South Florida and the nation."[24]

Long before the current work was written, nearly forty years after the Boatlift, judging people by whether they came to the United States via Mariel had become far less prevalent. It has long been accepted, at least in the Cuban American community, that all but a small percentage of the refugees became anything other than good citizens. It also helped that, in time, both Americans and established Cuban Americans interacted with Mariel immigrants, often as equals, in schools, workplaces, neighborhoods, churches, community organizations, and businesses. Familiarity bred acceptance. Also, a greater respect and understanding developed between the early exiles and the Mariel immigrants, especially with regard to the adversity each group endured due to the Castro dictatorship. The former had been the first on the front lines fighting against Communism in Cuba, had paid a heavy price in blood for their opposition, and had established the successful exile community in the United States at a time when there were no other Cubans on whom to rely. The latter had had to survive the most brutal and repressive years of a fully Communized Cuba. Whatever cultural chasm may have existed between the established exiles and the Mariel arrivals gradually dissipated, as the Mariel refugees, especially those who had come as children, increasingly became indistinguishable from the rest of the community.

Equally critical in rendering the Mariel arrivals as nothing more than members of the Cuban American community who were veterans of an important immigration event from long ago was the arrival of the next major wave of Cuban refugees more than a decade later as well as subsequent migrations from Cuba. The presence of newer Cubans made the Mariel refugees—who by then had largely assimilated—look even more like the exiles of the first two waves. Even the terms *Marielito* and *Marielita* (for females), which at one time had been pejorative labels capable of conjuring up the most negative of stereotypes, had been rendered almost meaningless. "He came through Mariel" or "She came through Mariel" became more likely to be heard among Cuban Americans than, "He is a *Marielito*" or "She is a *Marielita*." And if *Marielito* and *Marielita* are used, it is not usually done so in a disparaging manner. In fact, if it leans in any direction, it is now probably to the side of affection once again. Mariel refugees themselves, many of whom were at one time reluctant to reveal that they had come on the Boatlift for fear of being rejected, stigmatized, or stereotyped, became far more likely to share their stories and their *Marielito/Marielita* beginnings to frame tales of subsequent success.

The testimonies that follow trace the stories of several interviewees from the time of their arrival in the United States through their eventual assimilation and development. The occupations of the individuals at the time of their interviews have been indicated after their names.

Miriam Vilariño, Restaurateur

In Key West, they took us to a big airplane hangar which was filled with thousands of cots. The next morning, they took us to receive clothes; the mountains of clothing there reached the ceiling. We had nothing at the time, only the clothes we had on when we left Cuba, which had been vomited on during the crossing. We were able to pick the clothes we liked.

We spent several days at the base in Key West and then they transferred us to the Orange Bowl, where there were tents and cots set up. Even though we were still sleeping on cots and moving from base to base as we had done before our departure, there was no comparison—in the treatment we received, in the sanitary conditions, in the abundance of food—with what we had left in Cuba.

We didn't have family here, and if you didn't have family or a sponsor they transferred you to other states. When they told my mother that, she became very upset because she knew there were people in Miami from our home town. She went out to the fence at the Orange Bowl, where there was a multitude outside looking and screaming for their relatives. She noticed a young woman who had left our home town as a girl. My mother told my father, "That's Irais!" My father said, "Do you think so?" My mother said, "There is no other." They started to shout her name and the girl started looking all about to see who was calling for her. When my mother saw her react, she knew it was her. My parents kept calling her name until she saw who it was coming from. My mother told her who we were and said, "Find your father

Pompa for me! Find Chichí and Idela! Tell them we're here!" They came and sponsored us and we got out immediately.

That's where the disputes began, because all of my father's friends wanted us to go to their homes. We ended up going to West Palm Beach with an ex-political prisoner who had been in political prison with my father. We spent months in his home and he wanted my family to stay there until my parents were financially stable enough for us to rent our own place. Anyhow, within days of arriving, my parents began working at a nursing home for the elderly. But my father knew where he was and what he needed to do. He was very clear on his mission in the United States.

My father later got a job at Tropical Shipping repairing the containers that were used for importing and exporting. His bosses noticed the value of his work and they immediately gave him a raise. Then they gave him another raise. When they gave him the second raise, my father went and told them that he had to leave because if they kept raising his salary he was going to end up staying there—and that he could not do. He had come to the United States to be an entrepreneur.

During that time, my father had been going every day after work to the Latin businesses in West Palm Beach to talk to the people there. He went out to discover the United States, to discover what he had around him. He went to gas stations and to grocery stores to study how businesses here worked. He went into a bodega and asked for a job as a butcher, since he had done that his whole life on my grandfather's cattle farm. They gave him the butcher job—this, after he had left a job that paid well and provided all of us with medical insurance.

The distributors who came to the bodega to deliver merchandise dealt with my father. My father would ask them how the distribution system worked, how they sold the product, and what the costs were. One day, one of them told him there was a bodega for sale in Fort Lauderdale. He said, "That's for you. You have what it takes, don't be afraid." My father called two friends in Miami—my father had nothing at the time—and they put up the money to buy the bodega. My father was the butcher and we [the interviewee, her four sisters, and her mother] were the ones who cleaned, sold products, and took the food out to the customers' cars. Our service was very personalized. When we'd close for the day, we'd go to Publix Supermarket and Winn Dixie to study how the American grocery stores were organized. My father would observe and think about how we could imitate the American chains in the little place we had.

After the bodega succeeded, my father separated himself from it; there were three partners and not all of them could fit in it any longer. That's when someone told him that there was a restaurant for sale in Hollywood. I think the hand of the Divine was involved in that. My father has always been a good man, and everyone always tries to help good people. He bought the restaurant.

The restaurant had a chef who had worked at a world-renowned hotel in Havana. He was an older man with an incredible work ethic, and he was a magician in the kitchen. My father immersed himself in the kitchen, since it was the only way he could learn the business. He had never before entered a kitchen, even to brew coffee. He soon dominated cooking to perfection. The restaurant was called Las Vegas; my father loved the name and kept it, because it was like the "vegas" of tobacco in the countryside in Cuba. We didn't know at the time what the significance of "Las Vegas" was for Americans. In the end, it was good because the Americans remembered the name and associated it with Las Vegas, Nevada; plus, it was a name they could mention.

We now have fourteen restaurants. The first one we opened in Miami was in Miami Beach. We also have one now at Miami International Airport called "Ku-Va." All of us are involved in the family business. How did we get here? Because I have never met anyone with more tenacity and more determination than my mother and father. And my family has something that I have not seen in many people: When things are difficult, we double our efforts and find a solution. That is not very common. Many people tire or give up when things get difficult, but that is not how we are. And it's not just my father and mother. Since we were girls, my mother taught us to help my father if he was working. It's the culture of the countryside, a culture of work. That's the culture of the Cuban people.

José García, Ph.D., Professor

The day after we got to Miami from Key West, my uncle flew back down from New Jersey. We went to Opa-locka to do all the paperwork and stayed in Miami for approximately a week. My uncle took us to stay at some really nice hotels in Miami Beach, trying to give us the best. I thought it was so strange that we had just gone through this huge fiasco in the middle of the ocean and here we were sitting poolside in Miami.

After that, we took off for New York City. My family lived in Washington Heights, a poor neighborhood in upper Manhattan that was mostly Dominican. The first time I ventured out alone, I went to a store; on the way back, these rough kids started picking on me—they must have noticed that I was scared because I didn't speak any English. I was so traumatized by the experience that for two weeks after that I didn't want to leave the house. I remember that the floors of the building we lived in creaked—it was one of those huge buildings, a tenement, which belonged to the Industrial Revolution era. I thought, "Why are we here? What is this about?" The U.S. was all of a sudden on television—it was not what I was living.

When school started, I entered the ninth grade. They had bilingual education at the school I attended and so I started learning English. But it was a Hispanic neighborhood, so everything outside school was in Spanish. I was transferred to English-speaking classes in my second year, which was pretty traumatic. I could understand a little bit here and there, but I really couldn't speak the language yet.

Drugs were everywhere in that area. When you walked into my building, you couldn't get past the front entrance without somebody offering you marijuana or whatever. I was never interested in that, plus I was aware of everything my parents had done for us to come to this country. In school, I saw a lot of people being mugged and, a few times, I saw people getting stabbed. It was a pretty ugly picture. But I knew I had to go to school. My father was working two jobs trying to get us out of there. Still, for a while I was asking him, "Why are we here? I want to go back. I don't think I want to live here." He would say, "Just be calm, be patient, we're going to be out of here pretty soon." I felt for him and my mother because they had made this huge sacrifice for us.

My dad was quite a hustler, but in a good way. He wanted to work at Goya Foods but didn't speak English. My uncle, who worked for Goya, asked him, "Where are you going to work?" My father said, "Well, they can put me in a Hispanic neighborhood." My uncle got him an interview. They probably felt pity for him, and so they told him, "We're going to give you a shot. We're putting you in this neighborhood in the Bronx and you're going to cover these other guys' routes. But it's going to be on a trial basis, maybe for a couple of months, and then we'll decide whether or not we're going to hire you." It was a sales job and the customers were 99 percent Puerto Rican.

Within the first week he was working there, a route that normally sold $7,000 brought in $14,000. Within two years, he was the first person in the history of the company to sell $1,000,000—and he still could barely speak English. After that, he started making really good money. Within five years of leaving Cuba, he was making over $100,000. He bought a condominium in Miami Beach and opened a grocery store on Jerome Avenue and 181st Street in the Bronx.

During my senior year of high school we bought a house in Bergenfield, New Jersey, across the Hudson River from New York. I thought, "I just got here from Cuba, I've made some friends, and now they're asking me to move out to the suburbs—to a neighborhood that is 99.9 percent Italian and Irish." By that time, I had made some friends in Washington Heights, mostly Ecuadorians. I had also gotten into soccer, and that did a lot for me because I really liked the sport and it sort of kept me away from trouble. I had also met and become friends with a guy from Spain who was from a town in Asturias near where my grandparents were from.

Since my friends were in New York, I wanted to go see them every weekend after we moved to New Jersey. My parents would fight with me about that. They would ask, "Why do you want to go back to Washington Heights?" I would say, "Because that's where all my friends are." When I started going back to visit, I saw that some of my old friends were falling by the wayside. These guys had been pretty straight, and all of a sudden they were offering me stuff. I suddenly realized that I could have been one of them. I saw how lucky I was that my parents had gotten me out of there.

It was culture shock when we moved to New Jersey. Bergenfield was a small town and the people there knew each other their whole lives. School was tough for me, since I was like one of ten Hispanic kids in the whole place. I made very few friends. While I was there, I realized that my teachers back in Washington Heights had actually been pretty good; they had had a sense of empathy, maybe because they were used to immigrants and they would help you out. In the middle-class white neighborhood, it was almost like, "What are you doing here?" and that sense of empathy wasn't there from the teachers. But I passed all my courses and did OK academically. I eventually came to accept that nothing was going to change in Cuba and that I wasn't going to return. I saw that I just needed to concentrate on moving forward. I think that's when I started coming out of my shell. My English started getting better, too.

My mom had a Ph.D. from the University of Havana and she always told me, "You have to go to college." So I went to Bergen Community College for a year and then transferred to Montclair, where I majored in political science. When I started attending Bergen Community College, I also got a job at the Grand Union supermarket. I worked there for eight years and that's how I paid for my college education, both at Bergen and at Montclair. I made a combination of friends during that time. I had some Cuban friends, but I had more American friends— American meaning Irish and Italian. Grand Union was a gathering place, and I had become friends with them there. I also made friends at Montclair with Americans of all different backgrounds. Anyhow, by my second year at Montclair I was feeling pretty confident and at ease with my surroundings. New York City became a different chapter of my life.

When I was almost in my senior year at Montclair, I took some courses for my Spanish requirement. One of my professors said, "I like some of the papers you've written. I like what you're doing. Why don't you get a minor in Spanish?" I had never thought of that. Although I was considering going to law school, I applied for a graduate school teaching assistantship in Latin American literature at the University of Arizona. I didn't think they would accept me because I hadn't taken that many Spanish literature courses. Anyhow, they told me to take three graduate level courses to see how I would do. I did that, and ultimately received a scholarship to the University of Arizona. I received my master's degree and my Ph.D. there in Latin American literature. I also met my wife there. Then I got the job teaching at Florida Southern College in the fall of 1999.

Andrés Reynaldo, Journalist

I arrived in Key West on May 20. The next day they put us aboard a bus and took us to the Orange Bowl in Miami. There were tents all over the stadium and I was placed in one in the field area. While we were there, they gave us food, water, clothes, everything. Of course, the first question they asked you was whether or not you had a sponsor. Those who had none were taken to the camps out of state. Around May 23 or 24, early in the morning, they took me from the Orange Bowl to Opa-locka for processing. I spent half a day there. The transactions were brief: in one place they'd interview you and give you your Social Security, in another they'd give you your parole, and in another you were received by the people with the assistance agencies. That afternoon, my friends [the ones who had paid for his voyage and sponsored him] picked me up and the first thing they did was to take me to eat at La Carreta [a Cuban restaurant]. I hadn't showered or changed clothes since May 17.

I stayed with one of my friends for several days. Another friend worked the front desk at the Nautilus Hotel in Miami Beach, and she told me that they had a job available there as a bellhop. Of course, I didn't have a car and the public transportation here in Miami is horrible. My uncle who had left Cuba right after the Revolution lived in New York, but his ex-wife, who was like family to me, lived in Miami Beach with a child she had from another marriage. So I went to live with her and her son for a couple of months until I found a place to live. I worked at the hotel as a bellhop until December 1980, and then went to the home of an aunt in West New York, New Jersey. I was there for two years working different jobs. Then in 1982 I went to Puerto Rico and stayed until 1987 working in newspaper advertising.

After that I came back to Miami to work for the *Miami Herald* as assistant editor for local news at the *Nuevo Herald*. In 1998 I went to New York to work for Time Warner as editor-in-chief for *People* Magazine in Spanish. I was there for two years, and I would have stayed but I got divorced and my ex-wife decided to come back to Miami with the children. After six months I didn't want to be away from the children any longer and returned to the *Miami Herald*. I spent ten more years there. In 2012 I went to Channel 41 and I am now editorial director there.

Michellee Cabrera León, Attorney

Michellee Cabrera León appeared previously in chapter 1, when she related her experience at the Peruvian Embassy. Even before she left Cuba, she had dreamed of becoming an attorney.

They took us to a place [Tamiami Fairgrounds] and there I saw my grandfather, whom I had met just a year earlier. From there, we went to my grandparents' house on Southwest 34th Street and 107th Avenue in Westchester and lived there for around six months.[25] My parents later rented an apartment nearby, on Southwest 102nd Avenue and 40th Street. By then my paternal grandmother had come from Cuba on the Mariel Boatlift. We had a one-bedroom apartment and I would sleep on the sofa bed. We later moved to a two-bedroom apartment in the same complex.

I started second grade in the school year that started after I arrived. There was an ESOL program at Rockway Elementary for second, third, and fourth graders, and I was there for about a year because I was still at my grandfather's house. When we moved I attended Olympia Heights Elementary. When my parents purchased their first home— a townhouse—on Miller Drive and 129th Avenue, I attended Royal Green Elementary. I took ESOL in second grade. In third grade, I was in regular English classes. By fifth grade, I was in advanced classes. I remember that my fourth grade teachers were amazed that I had only been here for two years and that I could read and write better than the kids who were born here. After elementary school I went to McMillan Junior High School. My parents purchased their first house on Sunset Drive and 134th Court and I attended Sunset Senior High School and graduated from there in 1991.

After high school I went to Florida International University on a scholarship and graduated in three years. I then attended the University of Miami School of Law and graduated in 1997. I'm now a practicing attorney and currently work as in-house counsel for an insurance company defending their workers' compensation claims. I handle cases in Miami-Dade County, Broward County, West Palm Beach, Fort Myers, and other places.

So, yes, I finally became an attorney. But when we first got here, my father and mother each worked two jobs. When I would get home from school, my mother would feed me and then we would all leave and I would do my homework at Tamiami Airport—my mother worked there during the day and she and my father cleaned the offices in the evenings. So those were my evenings during the weekdays. Then my brother was born and my mom cleaned houses for almost eighteen years before going back into the regular work force. My dad always worked as an airplane mechanic and retired a couple of years ago. I wrote my college essay on that: on the struggle to leave your country and going to a new country. Now that I'm older, I realize what it meant, how important it was to be able to leave.

Isis Gottlieb, School Counselor

As related in chapter 2, Isis Gottlieb had not been told by her family that their journey to the United States was for the purpose of emigration. She was told, instead, that they were simply going on vacation to visit relatives in the United States.

We got here on May 25, and I was told that we were in the United States to stay when I started school after Memorial Day, around a week later.

After coming from Key West, we went to stay at my mom's aunt's home on Southwest 14th Street. They had left Cuba in 1962, and had prepared a little efficiency on the side of the house for us to live in. They had two girls my age who were sleeping when we arrived. I was so excited. When they woke up, we started playing; they had Barbie dolls and all these really amazing toys.

I started school the following week at Auburndale Elementary. A bus came to pick me up—that was something new for me because I used to walk to school. When I first got to the school, they put me in the second grade although I was supposed to be in kindergarten. I remember the kids in my class were so much bigger than I was. My teacher didn't speak any Spanish, so it was very hard for me. I was crying so much and my parents couldn't understand why because I used to love school. Two weeks later, they went down to the school and figured out what was going on. They told them I was five, not seven, and I was put into kindergarten.

When we first arrived from Cuba it was difficult for us financially. My mom worked at a factory in Hialeah and she was unemployed every two or three months. It was pretty tough. My dad scrubbed swimming pools for about a month, then worked pumping gas at a gas station. After that he installed carpeting and vinyl flooring. On Saturdays and Sundays, I would barely see him because he did his own thing, doing little odd jobs for people. Then he worked as a plumber. He was having a hard time because he wasn't making enough money, so he asked the owner of the company to give him a raise. The owner said, "I can't give you a raise because you don't speak English." My dad said, "Listen, the shovel doesn't speak English, OK?" He might have given him a little bit of a raise. He later went off and worked as a plumber on his own. In the meantime, he was saving money and he now owns thirteen different rental properties. And he owns an auto mechanic shop.

I graduated from Miami Senior High School in 1993. I had applied to the University of Florida and got accepted, but my parents really did not want me to go away. They told me that what they offered here in Miami was exactly what was going to be offered in Gainesville. And, unfortunately, that was right after all those murders in Gainesville and they really scared me with that.[26] I was an only child and felt really guilty about putting my parents through that—plus, I really was scared. I had a scholarship to go to Miami-Dade Community College for two years for free, and so I did. After Miami-Dade, I went to FIU [Florida International University] where I majored in psychology. Then I started studying for my master's degree in mental health counseling, also at FIU. I received my master's degree and took six extra courses to become a school counselor.

I started working as a school counselor in 2000. At first I was with alternative education in Liberty City, working with troubled youth at different schools. I did that for six years, and then the state started cutting budgets. I guess because I was one of the youngest working in the program, I was told, "We're going to have to cut the budget and you're probably going to have to leave." So before that actually happened, I left on my own terms. I heard about Young Women's Preparatory Academy [all-girls magnet school, Miami-Dade County Public Schools] opening up and I went over there and applied. I got the job the first year the school opened. I am now the school counselor there. The bulk of what I do is to get students into college.

And I'm still living here. I'm still on vacation.

[After her interview Isis Gottlieb accepted a position as a counselor at Miami Senior High School.]

Almost all of the other interviewees in the present work, at the time of their interviews, had all long ago achieved stability in the United States, and some had gained impressive career success. Most voluntarily expressed deep gratitude during the interviews for the lives they've lived since leaving Cuba. Ivonne Cuesta became a lawyer and, after having worked as a public defender for several years, was elected as a Miami-Dade County judge in 2012, just days before being interviewed for this work. Marino Mederos Jr. became a master electrician and owned his own company. Javier Delgado graduated from law school in 2001 and worked as an attorney for a major law firm. Lourdes Campbell was a twenty-four-year employee at Florida Power and Light, where she worked as an administrative assistant in the regulatory department. After working at a window factory after his arrival from Cuba, Manuel Vega became a mechanical engineer in Florida's sugar industry. Emilio Izquierdo owned his own limousine company in Miami and had become a pro-democracy activist. Ramón Dueñas began working as a busboy as a teenager and later became a chef at various high-end restaurants and eateries. He was praised in a 2014 *Miami Herald* article for his culinary skills and was working as a chef at Joanna's Marketplace in Miami at the time of his interview. Jacqueline Capo graduated from college as a teacher and then became a proud full-time mother. Gustavo Ulloa started out working in a medical warehouse and eventually became a banker. His wife, Bertha, worked in finance for Burdines Department Store for twenty-five years before retiring. Andrés Valerio emerged as a major force in the art world and worked from his studio off Miracle Mile in Coral Gables. His work has hung in top galleries in South Florida and in foreign countries.

After working different jobs, Carlos Cabrera made a successful living as an airplane mechanic. Raúl Inda, denied exit from Cuba in 1980, eventually made it to the United States and established a medical equipment business. Ronald Díaz spent two years living and working in New York City and then settled in Union City, New Jersey. In 1997 he relocated to Orlando, Florida, and later to West Palm Beach, where he made his living as a shuttle bus driver for a rental car company and then as a city bus driver. Braulio Saenz became a science teacher at Miami's La Salle High School and, after five years at La Salle, joined the full-time faculty at Miami-Dade Community College. Manuel Nieves worked in auto body shops, coached at a baseball academy, and eventually purchased a truck with which he made an independent living. Andrés Pazos began working on a bus line that operated between Miami and New Jersey and soon afterward entered the world of social services. He eventually became vice president of finance for the Cuban American National Council and CNC Management, nonprofit human services agencies in Miami.

Epilogue

WHILE IT MERITS REPEATING that most Mariel immigrants adapted successfully to life in the United States, it is obvious that the preceding stories do not necessarily represent the trajectory taken by all who left Cuba during the 1980 exodus. As explained in the preface, it was my intention from the start to focus primarily on those Mariel refugees who came to be reunited with family and who, like most of the refugees, ultimately had a successful adjustment. Yet as noted throughout the work, a percentage of refugees were indeed criminals, mental patients, and the like, who had been deliberately mixed into the Boatlift by Cuban authorities and whose assimilation to American society was not successful. There were also those who never quite got over the trauma of transition. And there were thousands, like Bartolo Díaz, who experienced long-term difficulties after suffering what most people would consider a series of injustices both in Cuba and in the United States.

What the interviewees' stories and the overall record do clearly attest to is that the stereotype of Mariel refugees as criminals, parasites, or the dregs of society was patently false. Still, for many years it was commonplace for people to hold such notions and, consequently, to view most if not all who came via Mariel in a negative light. It is lamentable that the well-intentioned majority of Mariel refugees, who had already endured so much violence, humiliation, and calumny upon leaving their country of birth, were burdened by an unjust stigma in their adopted land. The seeds of the negative stereotype, of course, were planted well before most of them debarked on the docks at Key West. And while time has all but done away with the stigma, one must bear in mind always the motives of those responsible for creating and disseminating it: a dictatorship willing to inflict harm on entire families and imperil innocent lives in order to make a political point with its "enemies," while simultaneously using the opportunity to project its own failures onto a group of individuals whose only crime was to express a desire to emigrate; certain individuals in the news media unable to restrain themselves from emphasizing and grossly exaggerating the more sordid aspects of the migration; and certain public officials and other interest groups, motivated by a series of factors, adding fuel to the fire by reinforcing the view that Mariel refugees overall were somehow "dangerous" people.

The stories also symbolize an oft-repeated pattern. People from a radically foreign place arrive in the United States, settle in, and experience a degree of marginalization. Established citizens are dismayed by the newcomers' foreignness and believe that, unlike previous groups, they are so far out of the cultural mainstream that they cannot possibly assimilate to the American way of life. Ever. It is beyond the imagination of casual observers that this latest group, or their offspring for that matter, could ever become "one of us." Then, almost imperceptibly, the new group quietly assimilates, scratches out a place for itself, is accepted, and becomes part of the social fabric. Those who once doubted them concede defeat, either implicitly or explicitly, to the unrelenting ability of United States society to assimilate people of nearly all backgrounds into its culture.

The testimonies likewise demonstrate that despite certain unique challenges encountered by Mariel refugees, the opportunities provided by the United States to those fortunate enough to reach its shores remain unmatched. Although some might view terms like the "American Dream" with skepticism and even cynicism, the lives of most of the interviewees provide a powerful and convincing response to those doubters. In the end, after nearly forty years, one can only bow in admiration to the resilience, tenacity, mettle, spirit, courage, and enterprise of the Mariel refugees.

"Give me your tired, your poor,
Your huddled masses yearning to breathe free,
The wretched refuse of your teeming shore.
Send these, the homeless, tempest-tost to me,
I lift my lamp beside the golden door!"

Perhaps it is time for the American people to tell the Cuban government that much of what its Communist leaders once derided as "*escoria*" has been transmuted into America's gold.

Acknowledgments

As in all my works, I am indebted to a long list of individuals. I would like to thank especially my friends Joseph Childs, Judy Mérida, Fernando Andrade, Tony Varona, and Roberto Allen for reading early versions of the manuscript and offering their valued critiques. I would also like to express my gratitude to my wife, Emilia, and my mother-in-law, Migdalia, who, as eyewitnesses of the events in Cuba in 1980, provided key insights. Likewise deserving my gratitude are the people who provided referrals for the interviews, especially Roberto Allen, Wilfredo Allen, Siro del Castillo, Lourdes Triay, Concepción Martínez, Carmen Valdivia, Carmen Romañach, James "Mike" Denham, Beatriz Godoy, Michelle Niemeyer, Maurice Ferré, Emilio Izquierdo, Daniel Serrano, Margarita Fuentes, Clara Moreno, Berta Bauchman, Juan Clark, and Daniel Mérida.

I would also like to thank my parents, Andrés and María Elena, for their undying support in all my literary efforts and throughout my career. Without their assistance, support, and encouragement, neither this work nor any of my previous ones would have been possible. Whatever good I have achieved in my life and whatever positive attributes I may have as a human being are completely and exclusively attributable to them. I would also like to thank them for the two greatest gifts parents could give a child: my faith and my education. My wife, Emilia, and my children—Victor Andres Jr., Gabriela Elena, and Francisco Xavier—as always, have demonstrated the patience of Job and provided the encouragement of a championship coach. My cousin Ralph Serrano, as he has done for many years, made his home and office available to me at all hours during my research visits to

Miami—whether it was for actual logistical support or a much-needed Cuban coffee break.

Deserving my profound thanks is also my extended family at Middlesex Community College in Middletown, Connecticut. For over twenty-seven years the college's administration and my colleagues have been unwavering in their support of my literary and research projects. I would especially like to thank Campus CEO Steven Minkler, former president Anna Wasescha, and the entire staff at the Jean Burr Smith Library for their assistance, encouragement, and patience.

A note of gratitude also goes out to the Capuchin Franciscan friars at St. Pius X parish in Middletown, Connecticut. Their selfless devotion to their flock has provided me, along with many others, a supportive community and a place of worship, reflection, meditation, and prayer in good times and bad.

Lastly, I would like to thank Dr. William Rogers (1929–2017), my former major professor at Florida State University. His guidance while I was a graduate student and his mentorship for more than two subsequent decades have proved invaluable in my career. Dr. Rogers, thank you, and may you rest in eternal peace.

Notes

Preface

1. In fact, it was not until years later that I learned that a few of my childhood classmates had been born in Cuba and had migrated as infants and toddlers.

2. Juan M. Clark, Jose I. Lasaga, and Rose S. Reque, *The 1980 Mariel Exodus: An Assessment and Prospect* (Washington, D.C.: Council for Inter-American Security, 1981), 4.

3. Most of Emilia's relatives had left Cuba in the 1960s, but the drawn-out terminal illness of a grandparent, and later the Cuban government's restrictions on the emigration of certain university-trained professionals (her father had a degree in chemical engineering), had prevented her parents from joining them. A relative hired a boat to get her family at Mariel in 1980. Although her father was again denied permission to emigrate for the same reason as before, Emilia was sent with her younger brother and a few older relatives.

4. Gastón A. Fernández, *The Mariel Exodus: Twenty Years Later* (Miami: Ediciones Universal, 2002), 20.

5. Ibid., 29–34.

6. A fellow Mariel researcher (and a Mariel refugee himself) who encountered the same problem in finding Afro-Cuban interviewees, although emphasizing that his view was merely anecdotal and not an officially measured phenomenon, attributed the difficulty to the fact that the trauma Afro-Cuban refugees experienced was so much more severe, and the stigma they bore so much worse than for non-Afro-Cuban Mariel refugees, that many prefer not to discuss or even recall the experience—much less grant an interview about it to a researcher they had never met. Also, according to Heike C. Alberts, in "Changes in Ethnic Solidarity in Cuban Miami" (cited in note 7 to the introduction) many Mariel-era Afro-Cubans did not settle in the same residential areas as white Cubans and blended with other groups of African heritage in the United States. In addition, many had no relatives in Miami and were

resettled in other parts of the country. The aforementioned Mariel researcher made this same point. The plight of Afro-Cubans is discussed in the historical narrative later in the present work.

7. Clark, Lasaga, and Reque, *The 1980 Mariel Exodus*, 7.

Introduction

1. Juan M. Clark, *Cuba: Mito y Realidad* (Miami: Saeta Ediciones, 1992), 25, 26; Alex Larzelere, *Castro's Ploy—America's Dilemma: The 1980 Cuban Boatlift* (Washington, D.C.: National Defense University Press, 1988), 45.

2. Clark, *Cuba: Mito y Realidad*, 24–28.

3. Ibid., 28–29.

4. Lowry Nelson, *Cuba: The Measure of a Revolution* (Minneapolis: University of Minnesota Press, 1972), 18.

5. Thomas D. Boswell and James R. Curtis, *The Cuban American Experience: Culture, Images, and Perspectives* (Totowa, N.J.: Rowman and Allanheld, 1983), 43.

6. Miguel González-Pando, *The Cuban Americans* (Westport, Conn.: Greenwood Press, 1998), 33.

7. Heike C. Alberts, "Changes in Ethnic Solidarity in Cuban Miami," *Geographical Review* 95, no. 2 (April 2005), http://go.galegroup.com/ps/i.do?id=GALE%7CA144298763&v=2.1&u=20300&it=r&p=AONE&sw=w&asid=330bbb124535257334b9827dc57d804c; Boswell and Curtis, *The Cuban American Experience*, 45.

8. David Engstrom, *Presidential Decision Making Adrift: The Carter Administration and the Mariel Boatlift* (Lanham, Md.: Rowman and Littlefield, 1997), 16.

9. Ibid., 16, 17.

10. Ibid.

11. Victor Triay, *Fleeing Castro: Operation Pedro Pan and the Cuban Children's Program* (Gainesville: University Press of Florida, 1998).

12. González-Pando, *The Cuban Americans*, 34.

13. Ibid., 28, 29, 38.

14. Ibid., 33, 34.

15. Engstrom, *Presidential Decision Making Adrift*, 18.

16. Ibid., 19, 20.

17. Ibid., 20.

18. Ibid., 19.

19. Clark, Lasaga, and Reque, *The 1980 Mariel Exodus*, 3.

20. Engstrom, *Presidential Decision Making Adrift*, 21, 22, 23.

21. Ibid., 24, 25.

22. Ibid., 25, 26.

23. Ibid., 26.

24. Ibid., 27.

25. Clark, Lasaga, and Reque, *The 1980 Mariel Exodus*, 3.

26. González-Pando, *The Cuban Americans*, 44.

27. Boswell and Curtis, *The Cuban American Experience*, 48.

28. Engstrom, *Presidential Decision Making Adrift*, 43.

29. González-Pando, *The Cuban Americans*, 51.

30. Alberts, "Changes in Ethnic Solidarity"; González-Pando, *The Cuban Americans*, 51.

31. González-Pando, *The Cuban Americans*, 55, 56.

32. Ibid., 58, 59.

33. Ibid., 58.

34. Ibid., 59–61; Elena Carrión, interview by author, September 14, 1994.

35. Carmelo Mesa-Lago, *Cuba in the 1970s: Pragmatism and Institutionalization* (Albuquerque: University of New Mexico Press, 1978), 5.

36. Ibid., 6–8.

37. Ibid., 6

38. Ibid., 8.

39. Richard Gott, *Cuba: A New History* (New Haven: Yale University Press, 2004), 236; Clark, Lasaga, and Reque, *The 1980 Mariel Exodus*, 2.

40. Gott, *Cuba: A New History*, 236; Clark, Lasaga, and Reque, *The 1980 Mariel Exodus*, 2.

41. Larzelere, *Castro's Ploy—America's Dilemma*, 91.

42. Ibid.

43. Ibid.

44. Mesa-Lago, *Cuba in the 1970s*, 113–15.

45. Clark, *Cuba: Mito y Realidad*, 208, 209.

46. Ibid., 209.

47. Anonymous, interview by author, n.d.; Emilia Ferrer-Triay, interview by author, July 25, 2012.

48. Migdalia Garí, interview by author, July 25, 2012.

49. Mesa-Lago, *Cuba in the 1970s*, 105.

50. Ibid., 108.

51. Ibid., 109.

52. Clark, *Cuba: Mito y Realidad*, 164, 166, 167.

53. Ibid., 203, 204.

54. Mesa-Lago, *Cuba in the 1970s*, 105.

Chapter 1. The Road to Mariel

1. Gott, *Cuba*, 262.

2. Mirta Ojito, *Finding Mañana: A Memoir of a Cuban Exodus* (New York: Penguin Books, 2005), 47; Felix Roberto Masud-Piloto, *From Welcomed Exiles to Illegal Immigrants: Cuban Migration to the U.S., 1959–1995* (Lanham, Md.: Rowman and Littlefield, 1996), 72, 73.

3. Engstrom, *Presidential Decision Making Adrift*, 43–44.

4. Ojito, *Finding Mañana*, 38.

5. Gott, *Cuba*, 265; Ojito, *Finding Mañana*, 45, 48–52.

6. Wayne Smith, *The Closest of Enemies: A Personal and Diplomatic Account of U.S.-Cuban Relations since 1957* (New York: W. W. Norton, 1987), 147, 159, 160.

7. Gott, *Cuba*, 265.

8. Smith, *The Closest of Enemies*, 160.

9. Larzelere, *Castro's Ploy—America's Dilemma*, 112; Smith, *The Closest of Enemies*, 160–163.

10. Smith, *The Closest of Enemies*, 171, 197.

11. Migdalia Garí, interview, July 25, 2012.

12. Smith, *The Closest of Enemies*, 198; Migdalia Garí, interview, July 25, 2012.

13. Larzelere, *Castro's Ploy—America's Dilemma*, 113; José Llanes, *Cuban Americans: Masters of Survival* (Cambridge, Mass.: Abt Books, 1982), 142–43; Smith, *The Closest of Enemies*, 198; Migdalia Garí, interview, July 25, 2012.

14. Engstrom, *Presidential Decision Making Adrift*, 47.

15. Engstrom, *Presidential Decision Making Adrift*, 47; Ronald Díaz, interview, August 19, 2012.

16. Clark, Lasaga, and Reque, *The 1980 Mariel Exodus*, 9.

17. Larzelere, *Castro's Ploy—America's Dilemma*, 107.

18. Mesa-Lago, *Cuba in the 1970s*, 101–6, 114–15.

19. Smith, *The Closest of Enemies*, 193–94.

20. "Cuba: Fleeing from Fidel's Rule," *Time*, April 21, 1980, http://content.time.com/time/magazine/article/0,9171,924008,00.html.

21. Engstrom, *Presidential Decision Making Adrift*, 47; Clark, Lasaga, and Reque, *The 1980 Mariel Exodus*, 2.

22. Larzelere, *Castro's Ploy—America's Dilemma*, 217.

23. Engstrom, *Presidential Decision Making Adrift*, 46.

24. Clark, Lasaga, and Reque, *The 1980 Mariel Exodus*, 2; Larzelere, *Castro's Ploy—America's Dilemma*, 93.

25. Engstrom, *Presidential Decision Making Adrift*, 47.

26. Larzelere, *Castro's Ploy—America's Dilemma*, 4, 5.

27. Leycester Coltman, *The Real Fidel Castro* (New Haven, Conn.: Yale University Press, 2003), 251.

28. Engstrom, *Presidential Decision Making Adrift*, 49.

29. Ibid., 53.

30. Larzelere, *Castro's Ploy—America's Dilemma*, 115, 218.

31. Smith, *The Closest of Enemies*, 203; Engstrom, *Presidential Decision Making Adrift*, 49.

32. Engstrom, *Presidential Decision Making Adrift*, 50.

33. Fidel Castro, "Castro Stresses Women's Equal Rights at FMC Congress," March 8, 1980, Latin American Network Information Center, Castro Speech Data Base, http://lanic.utexas.edu/project/castro/db/1980/19800308.html.

34. Ojito, *Finding Mañana*, 85–93.

35. Ojito, *Finding Mañana*, 104; Larzelere, *Castro's Ploy—America's Dilemma*, 6.

36. "Havana Removes Guard from Embassy," *New York Times*, April 5, 1980, ProQuest Historical Newspapers: New York Times.

37. Smith, *The Closest of Enemies*, 207.

38. Larzelere, *Castro's Ploy—America's Dilemma*, 8.

39. Smith, *The Closest of Enemies*, 208; Larzelere, *Castro's Ploy—America's Dilemma*, 10.

40. Larzelere, *Castro's Ploy—America's Dilemma*, 14; Ojito, *Finding Mañana*, 106.

41. Larzelere, *Castro's Ploy—America's Dilemma*, 14, 18.

42. Ojito, *Finding Mañana*, 116, 117; Larzelere, *Castro's Ploy—America's Dilemma*, 15–18.

43. Ojito, *Finding Mañana*, 116, 117.

44. Larzelere, *Castro's Ploy—America's Dilemma*, 27.

45. Ibid., 14, 15; Ojito, *Finding Mañana*, 116, 117.

46. Georgie Anne Geyer, *Guerrilla Prince: The Untold Story of Fidel Castro* (Boston: Little, Brown and Company, 1991), 368.

47. Jo Thomas, "Marchers Rally Round Cuba, Castro, Communism," *New York Times*, April 20, 1980, ProQuest Historical Newspapers: New York Times.

48. Ojito, *Finding Mañana*, 140.

49. Engstrom, *Presidential Decision Making Adrift*, 61, 62; Larzelere, *Castro's Ploy—America's Dilemma*, 122.

50. A. Luis Varona Jr., interview, January 8, 2015; Llanes, *Cuban Americans*, 150, 151.

51. "Cuba: Fleeing from Fidel's Rule," *Time*, April 21, 1980; Larzelere, *Castro's Ploy—America's Dilemma*, 19.

52. Larzelere, *Castro's Ploy—America's Dilemma*, 19, 29.

53. Ojito, *Finding Mañana*, 117, 118; Larzelere, *Castro's Ploy—America's Dilemma*, 19, 20; Anonymous, interview; Manuel Nieves, interview, July 5, 2014.

54. The Andean Pact was a group of South American nations, including Peru, that, bound by the Cartagena agreement of 1969, sought to work together to bring about industrialization and regional trade.

55. Larzelere, *Castro's Ploy—America's Dilemma*, 28.

56. Ibid., 31, 32.

57. Ibid., 32, 33; "Cuba: Start of a Mass Exodus," *Time*, April 28, 1980, http://content.time.com/time/magazine/article/0,9171,924055,00.html.

58. Clark, Lasaga, and Reque, *The 1980 Mariel Exodus*, 3; "Cuba: Start of a Mass Exodus," *Time*, April 28, 1980.

59. "Cuba Bars Refugee Flights to Costa Rican Staging Area," *New York Times*, April 19, 1980, ProQuest Historical Newspapers: New York Times; Llanes, *Cuban Americans*, 152; Larzelere, *Castro's Ploy—America's Dilemma*, 34–36.

60. Ojito, *Finding Mañana*, 139, 152.

61. Ibid., 139.

62. Ibid., 153.

63. Ibid., 156.

64. Smith, *The Closest of Enemies*, 211.

65. Larzelere, *Castro's Ploy—America's Dilemma*, 37, 38; Llanes, *Cuban Americans*, 152; Thomas, "Marchers Rally Round Cuba, Castro, Communism."

66. Larzelere, *Castro's Ploy—America's Dilemma*, 37, 38.

67. Thomas, "Marchers Rally Round Cuba, Castro, Communism."

68. John M. Crewdson, "Hundreds in Boats, Defying U.S., Sail for Cuba to Pick Up Refugees," *New York Times*, April 25, 1980, ProQuest Historical Newspapers: New York Times.

69. "Refugees: Voyage from Cuba," *Time*, May 5, 1980, http://content.time.com/time/magazine/article/0,9171,948846,00.html.

70. Engstrom, *Presidential Decision Making Adrift*, 62.

71. Larzelere, *Castro's Ploy—America's Dilemma*, 124.

72. Engstrom, *Presidential Decision Making Adrift*, 62.

73. Ibid., 51.

74. Ojito, *Finding Mañana*, 199.

75. Engstrom, *Presidential Decision Making Adrift*, 50.

76. Main daily newspaper in Cuba; published by the Central Committee of the Communist Party and named after the yacht Fidel Castro used to transport his troops from Mexico to Cuba to launch his war against Batista in 1956.

Chapter 2. The Odyssey Begins

1. Larzelere, *Castro's Ploy—America's Dilemma*, 329; Janet Battaile, "Cuban Exiles' Boats Pick Up 40 Refugees," *New York Times*, April 22, 1980, ProQuest Historical Newspapers: New York Times.

2. Engstrom, *Presidential Decision Making Adrift*, 67; "Refugees: Voyage from Cuba," *Time*, May 5, 1980.

3. "Cuba's Boat People—Dilemma for Carter," *U.S. News and World Report*, May 5, 1980.

4. Ojito, *Finding Mañana*, 199.

5. Engstrom, *Presidential Decision Making Adrift*, 73, 74.

6. Ojito, *Finding Mañana*, 201.

7. Kate Dupes Hawk, Ron Villella, and Adolfo Leyva de Varona, *Florida and the Mariel Boatlift of 1980* (Tuscaloosa: University of Alabama Press, 2014), 71; Engstrom, *Presidential Decision Making Adrift*, 73.

8. Ojito, *Finding Mañana*, 200.

9. Engstrom, *Presidential Decision Making Adrift*, 74.

10. Ibid., 73.

11. Larzelere, *Castro's Ploy—America's Dilemma*, 236; Engstrom, *Presidential Decision Making Adrift*, 79, 80.

12. Fidel Castro, "Castro Delivers Speech at May Day Rally," May 1, 1980, Latin American Network Information Center, Castro Speech Data Base, http://lanic.utexas.edu/project/castro/db/1980/19800501-1.html.

13. Smith, *The Closest of Enemies*, 217–234; Larzelere, *Castro's Ploy—America's Dilemma*, 259–61.

14. Emilio Izquierdo, interview, August 16, 2012.

15. Ojito, *Finding Mañana*, 206.

16. Engstrom, *Presidential Decision Making Adrift*, 87.

17. Ojito, *Finding Mañana*, 206.

18. Larzelere, *Castro's Ploy—America's Dilemma*, 248.

19. Ibid., 262, 263; Masud-Piloto, *From Welcomed Exiles to Illegal Immigrants*, 85.

20. Engstrom, *Presidential Decision Making Adrift*, 115.

21. Larzelere, *Castro's Ploy—America's Dilemma*, 274; Engstrom, *Presidential Decision Making Adrift*, 105–7.

22. Larzelere, *Castro's Ploy—America's Dilemma*, 276, 277; Ojito, *Finding Mañana*, 239.

23. Larzelere, *Castro's Ploy—America's Dilemma*, 277–78; Ojito, *Finding Mañana*, 239–40.

24. Larzelere, *Castro's Ploy—America's Dilemma*, 279–80.

25. Ojito, *Finding Mañana*, 244.

26. Engstrom, *Presidential Decision Making Adrift*, 112–13; David M. Alpern, with Jerry Buckley, Vern Smith, Kim Willenson, and Stryker McGuire, "Carter and the Cuban Influx," *Newsweek*, May 26, 1980, 22.

27. Larzelere, *Castro's Ploy—America's Dilemma*, 300–2, 355–57.

28. Engstrom, *Presidential Decision Making Adrift*, 113–14.

29. Clark, Lasaga, and Reque, *The 1980 Mariel Exodus*, 5.

30. "Cuba's Boat People—Dilemma for Carter," *U.S. News and World Report*, May 5, 1980.

31. Fernandez, *The Mariel Exodus*, 24–26.

32. Smith, *The Closest of Enemies*, 212; Migdalia Garí, interview, July 25, 2012; Emilia Ferrer-Triay, interview, July 25, 2012.

33. Jo Thomas, "Behind Barred Doors in Havana," *New York Times*, May 2, 1980, ProQuest Historical Newspapers: New York Times.

34. Migdalia Garí, interview, July 25, 2012; José García, interview, August 13, 2012; Emilia Ferrer-Triay, interview, July 25, 2012.

35. Thomas, "Behind Barred Doors in Havana"; Smith, *The Closest of Enemies*, 212–13; Migdalia Garí, interview, July 25, 2012; Emilia Ferrer-Triay, interview, July 25, 2012.

36. Smith, *The Closest of Enemies*, 212.

37. Migdalia Garí, interview, July 25, 2012.

38. Clark, Lasaga, and Reque, *The 1980 Mariel Exodus*, 4; Smith, *The Closest of Enemies*, 212.

39. Migdalia Garí, interview, April 5, 2015.

40. Smith, *The Closest of Enemies*, 213.

41. José García, interview, August 13, 2012; Emilia Ferrer-Triay, interview, April 3, 2015; Ojito, *Finding Mañana*, 173.

42. Emilia Ferrer-Triay, interview, April 3, 2015.

43. Andres Reynaldo, interview, July 10, 2014.

44. Fernandez, *The Mariel Exodus*, 20.

45. Larzelere, *Castro's Ploy—America's Dilemma*, 227.

46. Silvia Pedraza, *Political Disaffection in Cuba's Revolution and Exodus* (Cambridge: Cambridge University Press, 2007), 154.

47. B. E. Aguirre, Rogelio Sáenz, and Brian Sinclair James, "Marielitos Ten Years Later: The Scarface Legacy," *Social Science Quarterly* 78, no. 2 (June 1997): 492.

48. Ojito, *Finding Mañana*, 211–12.

49. Ojito, *Finding Mañana*, 212; Aguirre, Sáenz, and James, "Marielitos Ten Years Later," 492.

50. Larzelere, *Castro's Ploy—America's Dilemma*, 227; Fernandez, *The Mariel Exodus*, 26, 27.

51. Larzelere, *Castro's Ploy—America's Dilemma*, 227.

52. Aguirre, Sáenz, and James, "Marielitos Ten Years Later," 491.

53. A Marxist term referring to the lowest level of society, the "scum," such as criminals and prostitutes (as opposed to the "worker"), incapable of developing a revolutionary consciousness and easily used as tools by counterrevolutionaries and class enemies.

54. Clark, Lasaga, and Reque, *The 1980 Mariel Exodus*, 6.

55. Ibid.

56. Ibid.

57. Larzelere, *Castro's Ploy—America's Dilemma*, 217; Clark, Lasaga, and Reque, *The 1980 Mariel Exodus*, 6.

58. Pedraza, *Political Disaffection in Cuba's Revolution and Exodus*, 154.

59. Hotel in Havana, reserved by the Cuban government, for use by those arriving in Mariel via boat from the United States. See chapter 4.

60. Ibid.

61. This loosely translates as, "Pin pon out! Down with the worm bed!" but rhymes in Spanish.

Chapter 3. Herded into the Abreu Fontán and the "Mosquito"

1. Ojito, *Finding Mañana*, 177.

2. Enrique Morató, "El Sueño de la Calabaza," *El Balsero Suicida*, https://gilbertogutierrez.wordpress.com/cuentos-y-estampas/el-sueno-de-la-calabaza/; Andrés Reynaldo, interview, July 10, 2014; Lourdes Campbell, interview, August 15, 2012; Michellee Cabrera, interview, July 7, 2014; Isis Gottlieb, interview, July 4, 2014; Manuel Nieves, interview, July 5, 2014.

3. Manuel Vega, interview, August 14, 2012.

4. Anonymous, interview; Braulio Saenz, interview, August 17, 2012; Andrés Reynaldo, interview, July 10, 2014.

5. Ojito, *Finding Mañana*, 177.

6. Manuel Vega, interview, August 14, 2012.

7. Isis Gottlieb, interview, July 4, 2014.

8. Andrés Reynaldo, interview, July 10, 2014; Emilia Ferrer-Triay, interview, July 25, 2012; Andres Valerio, interview, August 21, 2012; Morató, "El Sueño de la Calabaza."

9. Raúl Inda, interview, July 8, 2014; Anonymous, interview; Ojito, *Finding Mañana*, 179; Morató, "El Sueño de la Calabaza."

10. Marino Mederos Jr., interview, August 16, 2012; Braulio Saenz, interview, August 17, 2012; Morató, "El Sueño de la Calabaza."

11. Ojito, *Finding Mañana*, 179.

12. Morató, "El Sueño de la Calabaza"; Manuel Vega, interview, August 14, 2012; Emilia Ferrer-Triay, interview, July 25, 2012.

13. Bertha Ulloa, interview, August 17, 2012; Andres Valerio, interview, August 21, 2012; Morató, "El Sueño de la Calabaza"; Andrés Reynaldo, interview, July 10, 2014; Larzelere, *Castro's Ploy—America's Dilemma*, 127.

14. Lourdes Campbell, interview, August 15, 2012; Emilio Izquierdo, interview, August 16, 2012; Ojito, *Finding Mañana*, 180.

15. Emilia Ferrer-Triay, interview, July 25, 2012; Ojito, *Finding Mañana*, 182.

16. Anonymous, interview. In Cuba a distinction is made between "political" prisoners, incarcerated for dissent or political offenses, and what Cubans refer to as "common" prisoners, meaning they were in prison for crimes of a nonpolitical nature.

17. Larzelere, *Castro's Ploy—America's Dilemma*, 129; Morató, "El Sueño de la Calabaza."

18. Larzelere, *Castro's Ploy—America's Dilemma*, 128, 131.

19. Ibid., 131.

20. Ojito, *Finding Mañana*, 182.

21. Anonymous, interview; Emilia Ferrer-Triay, interview, July 25, 2012; Emilio Izquierdo, interview, August 16, 2012.

22. Afro-Cuban religious sect based on Yoruba spiritualism that frequently incorporated aspects of Roman Catholic beliefs. It often syncretized African gods with Catholic saints.

Chapter 4. A Perilous Voyage at Sea and Arrival in Key West

1. "Refugees: Voyage from Cuba," *Time,* May 5, 1980.

2. Ibid.

3. Llanes, *Cuban Americans,* 162.

4. Vern E. Smith, "In the Flotilla at Mariel," *Newsweek,* May 12, 1980, 63.

5. Smith, "In the Flotilla at Mariel," 63; Larzelere, *Castro's Ploy—America's Dilemma*, 133.

6. Larzelere, *Castro's Ploy—America's Dilemma*, 133.

7. Smith, "In the Flotilla at Mariel"; Larzelere, *Castro's Ploy—America's Dilemma*, 137.

8. Ron Laytner, "Timeless Feature—The Mariel Boatlift," *Edit International,* 1980.

9. Ibid.

10. Larzelere, *Castro's Ploy—America's Dilemma*, 134.

11. Anonymous, interview; Laytner, "Timeless Feature—The Mariel Boatlift."

12. "In the Flotilla at Mariel"; Laytner, "Timeless Feature—The Mariel Boatlift."

13. Ojito, "Finding Mañana," 205.

14. Laytner, "Timeless Feature—The Mariel Boatlift"; Smith, "In the Flotilla at Mariel."

15. Clark, Lasaga, and Reque, *The 1980 Mariel Exodus*, 4.

16. Hawk, Villella, and Leyva, *Florida and the Mariel Boatlift of 1980*, 113–14; Laytner, "Timeless Feature—The Mariel Boatlift."

17. Edward Schumacher, "Misery and Merriment Are Filling Nights in Havana for the U.S. Kin," *New York Times*, May 9, 1980, ProQuest Historical Newspapers: New York Times.

18. Ojito, "Finding Mañana," 203.

19. Schumacher, "Misery and Merriment"; Laytner, "Timeless Feature—The Mariel Boatlift."

20. Schumacher, "Misery and Merriment."

21. Schumacher, "Misery and Merriment"; Laytner, "Timeless Feature—The Mariel Boatlift."

22. Hawk, Villella, and Leyva, *Florida and the Mariel Boatlift of 1980*, 113–14; Larzelere, *Castro's Ploy—America's Dilemma*, 133.

23. Ojito, *Finding Mañana*, 212.

24. Smith, *The Closest of Enemies*, 213.

25. Anonymous, interview.

26. Laytner, "Timeless Feature—The Mariel Boatlift."

27. Ojito, "Finding Mañana," 249.

28. Clark, Lasaga, and Reque, *The 1980 Mariel Exodus*, 14; Anonymous, interview.

29. Clark, Lasaga, and Reque, *The 1980 Mariel Exodus*, 14; Larzelere, *Castro's Ploy—America's Dilemma*, 376.

30. Larzelere, *Castro's Ploy—America's Dilemma*, 329–35.

31. Hawk, Villella, and Leyva, *Florida and the Mariel Boatlift of 1980*, 93.

32. Larzelere, *Castro's Ploy—America's Dilemma*, 333–38.

33. Engstrom, *Presidential Decision Making Adrift*, 141.

34. Larzelere, *Castro's Ploy—America's Dilemma*, 342, 343, 347.

35. Ibid., 357.

36. Ibid., 330–31.

37. Ibid., 349.

38. Ibid., 349–52.

39. Ojito, *Finding Mañana*, 225.

40. Clark, Lasaga, and Reque, *The 1980 Mariel Exodus*, 7; Hawk, Villella, and Leyva, *Florida and the Mariel Boatlift of 1980*, 56.

41. Hawk, Villella, and Leyva, *Florida and the Mariel Boatlift of 1980*, 56.

42. Ibid., 214.

Chapter 5. Reception and Resettlement

1. Engstrom, *Presidential Decision Making Adrift*, 139.

2. Mario Antonio Rivera, *Decision and Structure: U.S. Refugee Policy in the Mariel Crisis* (Lanham, Md.: University Press of America, 1991), 13; Engstrom, *Presidential Decision Making Adrift*, 140.

3. Rivera, *Decision and Structure*, 13, 14; Larzelere, *Castro's Ploy—America's Dilemma*, 283–84; Dennis A. Williams, with Jerry Buckley, Vern E. Smith, and Jane Whitmore, "Cuban Tide Is a Flood," *Newsweek*, May 19, 1980, 28.

4. Clark, Lasaga, and Reque, *The 1980 Mariel Exodus*, 13; Engstrom, *Presidential Decision Making Adrift*, 147, 148, 152–53; Larzelere, *Castro's Ploy—America's Dilemma*, 285–87.

5. Engstrom, *Presidential Decision Making Adrift*, 139.

6. Ibid., 161; Larzelere, *Castro's Ploy—America's Dilemma*, 285–86; Rivera, *Decision and Structure*, 13–14.

7. Rivera, *Decision and Structure*, 13.

8. Engstrom, *Presidential Decision Making Adrift*, 161–63.

9. Philip A. Holman, "Refugee Resettlement in the United States," in *Refugees in America in the 1990s: A Reference Handbook*, edited by David W. Haines, 3–27 (Westport, Conn.: Greenwood Press, 1996), 15; Jorge Domín-guez, "Cooperating with the Enemy? U.S. Immigration Policies toward Cuba," in *Western Hemisphere Immigration and United States Foreign Policy*, edited by Christopher Mitchell, 31–88 (University Park: Penn State University Press, 1992), 76, 77; Engstrom, *Presidential Decision Making Adrift*, 164–68.

10. Domínguez, "Cooperating with the Enemy?" 76, 77; Rivera, *Decision and Structure*, 15; Engstrom, *Presidential Decision Making Adrift*, 164–68.

11. María Cristina García, *Havana USA: Cuban Exiles and Cuban Americans in South Florida, 1959–1994* (Berkeley: University of California Press, 1996), 146; Engstrom, *Presidential Decision Making Adrift*, 186–87.

12. Engstrom, *Presidential Decision Making Adrift*, 186–88.

13. César Odio, interview, July 8, 2014.

14. Sergio Pereira, interview, July 3, 2014.

15. Silvia M. Unzueta, *The Mariel Exodus: A Year in Retrospect* (Miami: Metropolitan Dade County Government Office of the County Manager, 1981), Cuban Information Archives, Document 0033, http://cuban-exile.com/doc_026-050/doc0033.html.

16. Unzueta, *The Mariel Exodus*; Siro del Castillo, interview, August 15, 2012.

17. Siro del Castillo, interview, August 15, 2012; Hawk, Villella, and Leyva, *Florida and the Mariel Boatlift of 1980*, 173, 199; "Open Heart, Open Arms," *Time*, May 19, 1980, http://content.time.com/time/magazine/article/0,9171, 924093,00.html.

18. Unzueta, *The Mariel Exodus*; Siro del Castillo, interview, August 15, 2012.

19. César Odio, interview, July 8, 2014; Maurice Ferré, interview, July 2, 2014.

20. César Odio, interview, July 8, 2014.

21. Siro del Castillo, interview, August 15, 2012.

22. Clark, Lasaga, and Reque, *The 1980 Mariel Exodus*, 11.

23. George J. Church, "The Welcome Wears Thin," *Time*, September 1, 1980, http://content.time.com/time/magazine/article/0,9171,922111,00.html.

24. Larzelere, *Castro's Ploy—America's Dilemma*, 377, 379, 357.

25. Clark, Lasaga, and Reque, *The 1980 Mariel Exodus*, 15; "Impatient for Freedom," *Time*, June 16, 1980, http://content.time.com/time/magazine/article/ 0,9171,924198,00.html.

26. Clark, Lasaga, and Reque, *The 1980 Mariel Exodus*, 15.

27. Ibid.

28. Fernández, *The Mariel Exodus: Twenty Years Later*, 72, 73; Clark, Lasaga, and Reque, *The 1980 Mariel Exodus*, 15.

29. Fernández, *The Mariel Exodus: Twenty Years Later*, 48–50; Church, "The Welcome Wears Thin"; Dennis A. Williams, with Frank Maier, Susan Agrest, Ronald Henkoff, and Mary Lord, "The Cuban Conundrum," *Newsweek*, September 29, 1980, 30.

30. "Impatient for Freedom," *Time*, June 16, 1980.

31. Clark, Lasaga, and Reque, *The 1980 Mariel Exodus*, 15.

32. Larzelere, *Castro's Ploy—America's Dilemma*, 227.

33. Ibid.; Rivera, *Decision and Structure*, 120; Gastón Fernandez, "The Flotilla Entrants: Are They Different?" *Cuban Studies* 12 (January 1982): 50.

34. Rivera, *Decision and Structure*, 120.

35. Clark, Lasaga, and Reque, *The 1980 Mariel Exodus*, 15; Rivera, *Decision and Structure*, 120.

36. Rivera, *Decision and Structure*, 120; Wilfredo Allen, interview, July 3, 2014.

37. Rivera, *Decision and Structure*, 119–27.

38. Clark, Lasaga, and Reque, *The 1980 Mariel Exodus*, 14, 15.

39. Hawk, Villella, and Leyva, *Florida and the Mariel Boatlift of 1980*, 182, 183.

40. Fernández, *The Mariel Exodus: Twenty Years Later*, 45–48.

41. Ibid., 47–50.

42. Clark, Lasaga, and Reque, *The 1980 Mariel Exodus*, 16.

43. Ibid.

44. Ibid., 14; Williams, "Cuban Tide a Flood," *Newsweek*, May 19, 1980.

45. Fernández, *The Mariel Exodus*, 42–43, 74–77.

46. Mark S. Hamm, *The Abandoned Ones: The Imprisonment and Uprising of the Mariel Boat People* (Boston: Northeastern University Press, 1995), 58–67.

47. Ojito, *Finding Mañana*, 264; Hamm, *The Abandoned Ones*, 67.

48. Masud-Piloto, *From Welcomed Exiles to Illegal Immigrants*, 100; Aguirre, Sáenz, and James, "Marielitos Ten Years Later: The Scarface Legacy," 496.

49. Hamm, *The Abandoned Ones*, 88.

50. Masud-Piloto, *From Welcomed Exiles to Illegal Immigrants*, 101–2.

51. William E. Schmidt, "Judge Reasserts Right of Cubans to Get Hearing," *New York Times*, January 1, 1985.

52. Larzelere, *Castro's Ploy—America's Dilemma*, 386–89.

53. Hamm, *The Abandoned Ones*, 95, 96, 100, 101.

54. Engstrom, *Presidential Decision Making Adrift*, 185; Larzelere, *Castro's Ploy—America's Dilemma*, 429, 430.

55. Hamm, *The Abandoned Ones*, 156, 161, 162.

56. Ibid., 18, 176.

57. Engstrom, *Presidential Decision Making Adrift*, 186; Hamm, *The Abandoned Ones*, 23–29.

58. Hamm, *The Abandoned Ones*, 24–29.

59. Ibid., 176.

60. Mirta Ojito, "The Long Voyage from Mariel Ends," *New York Times*, January 16, 2005, https://www.nytimes.com/2005/01/16/weekinreview/the-long-voyage-from-mariel-ends.html.

61. The interviewee seemed to say Worcester. Because of his pronunciation and heavy accent, however, this is not 100 percent certain.

Chapter 6. In the Land of Opportunity

1. Hamm, *The Abandoned Ones,* 77; Ojito, "The Long Voyage from Mariel Ends."

2. Clark, Lasaga, and Reque, *The 1980 Mariel Exodus*, 7; Larzelere, *Castro's Ploy—America's Dilemma*, 221, 222.

3. Clark, Lasaga, and Reque, *The 1980 Mariel Exodus*, 16; Ojito, *Finding Mañana,* 240, 241; Mike Clary, "They Seized the Moment and Came to America," *Los Angeles Times*, May 29, 1990, http://search.proquest.com/docview/281062556?accountid=41655.

4. Engstrom, *Presidential Decision Making Adrift,* 75, 76.

5. Ibid.

6. Fernández, *The Mariel Exodus*, 29–36; Hamm, *The Abandoned Ones*, 74–82.

7. Aguirre, Sáenz, and James, "Marielitos Ten Years Later," 492.

8. John S. Lang with Joseph L. Galloway, Linda K. Lanier, and Gordon M. Bock, "Castro's 'Crime Bomb' Inside U.S.," *U.S. News and World Report,* January 16, 1984.

9. Aguirre, Saenz, and James, "Marielitos Ten Years Later," 499–505.

10. For a more detailed discussion on the possible reasons and motives for exaggerating the threat posed by Mariel refugees, see Aguirre, Sáenz, and James's discussion on "moral epidemics" in "Marielitos Ten Years Later" and Hamm's discussion on the "Moral Crusade" in *The Abandoned Ones*.

11. Fernandez, "The Flotilla Entrants: Are They Different?" 50–51; Clark, Lasaga, and Reque, *The 1980 Mariel Exodus*, 7.

12. Clark, Lasaga, and Reque, *The 1980 Mariel Exodus*, 7.

13. Ibid.

14. Ibid., 12.

15. Ojito, *Finding Mañana,* 256.

16. Clark, Lasaga, and Reque, *The 1980 Mariel Exodus*, 12.

17. Alberts, *Changes in Ethnic Solidarity*; Clary, "They Seized the Moment."

18. Clark, Lasaga, and Reque, *The 1980 Mariel Exodus*, 12; Church, "The Welcome Wears Thin."

19. Fernandez, "The Flotilla Entrants: Are They Different?" 52, 53.

20. Ojito, *Finding Mañana,* 241.

21. Larzelere, *Castro's Ploy—America's Dilemma*, 224.

22. Eduardo Padrón, interview, August 16, 2012.

23. Gonzalez-Pando, *The Cuban Americans*, 70.

24. Fabiola Santiago, "Flowing from Mariel," *Miami Herald,* April 17, 2005, Cubanet.org, http://www.cubanet.org/htdocs/CNews/y05/apr05/19e7.htm.

25. A suburban neighborhood in Miami that contains a substantial Cuban American population.

26. The interviewee is referring to a 1990 episode when a serial killer murdered five students—one from Santa Fe College and four from the University of Florida—in Gainesville, Florida.

Bibliography

Interviews

All interviews were by the author. Three interviewees preferred to remain anonymous, and Luis A. Varona Jr. was interviewed by telephone.

Allen, Wilfredo. Miami, Fla., July 3, 2014.

Anonymous 1. No date.

Anonymous 2. No date.

Anonymous 3. No date.

Cabrera, Carlos. Miami, Fla., July 7, 2014.

Cabrera León, Michellee. Miami, Fla., July 7, 2014.

Campbell, Lourdes. Miami, Fla., August 15, 2012.

Capo, Jaqueline. Miami Beach, Fla., July 5, 2014.

Carrión, Elena. Middletown, Conn., September 14, 1994.

Carro, Laida. Coral Gables, Fla., August 22, 2013.

Clark, Juan. Miami, Fla., August 9, 2012.

Cuesta, Ivonne. Miami, Fla., August 16, 2012.

del Castillo, Siro. Coral Gables, Fla., August 15, 2012.

Delgado, Javier. Coral Gables, Fla., August 20, 2012.

Díaz, Ronald. Miami, Fla., August 19, 2012.

Díaz García, Bartolo. Miami, Fla., August 3, 2016.

Dueñas, Ramón. Pinecrest, Fla., July 9, 2014.

Ferré, Maurice. Coral Gables, Fla., July 2, 2014.

Ferrer-Triay, Emilia. Clewiston, Fla., July 25, 2012; April 3, 2015.

García, José. Orlando, Fla., August 13, 2012.

Garí, Migdalia. Clewiston, Fla., July 25, 2012; April 5, 2015.

Gottlieb, Isis. Doral, Fla., July 4, 2014.

Inda, Raúl. Hialeah, Fla., July 8, 2014.

Izquierdo, Emilio. Miami, Fla., August 16, 2012.

Manso, Andrés. Miami, Fla., August 8, 2016.

Mederos, Marino Jr. Miami, Fla., August 16, 2012.

Mederos, Marino Sr. Miami, Fla., August 16, 2012.
Nieves, Manuel. Miami Beach, Fla., July 5, 2014.
Odio, César. Key Biscayne, Fla., July 8, 2014.
Padrón, Eduardo J. Miami, Fla., August 16, 2012.
Pazos, Andrés. Miami, Fla., July 9, 2014.
Pereira, Sergio. Miami, Fla., July 3, 2014.
Pérez, Ernesto. Miami Lakes, Fla., July 4, 2014.
Reynaldo, Andrés. Miami, Fla., July 10, 2014.
Saenz, Braulio. Miami, Fla., August 17, 2012.
Ulloa, Bertha. Miami, Fla., August 17, 2012.
Ulloa, Francisco Gustavo. Miami, Fla., August 17, 2012.
Valerio, Andrés. Coral Gables, Fla., August 21, 2012.
Varona, Luis A. Jr. January 8, 2015.
Vega, Manuel. Clewiston, Fla., August 14, 2012.
Vilariño, Miriam. Doral, Fla., July 3, 2014.

Secondary Sources

Aguirre, B. E., Rogelio Sáenz, and Brian Sinclair James. "Marielitos Ten Years Later: The Scarface Legacy." *Social Science Quarterly* 78, no. 2 (June 1997): 487–507.

Alberts, Heike C. "Changes in Ethnic Solidarity in Cuban Miami." *Geographical Review* 95, no. 2 (April 2005): 231–48. doi: https://doi.org/10.1111/j.1931-0846.2005.tb00364.x

Alpern, David M., with Jerry Buckley, Vern E. Smith, Kim Willenson, and Stryker McGuire. "Carter and the Cuban Influx." *Newsweek*, May 26, 1980, 22.

Battaile, Janet. "Cuban Exiles' Boats Pick Up 40 Refugees." *New York Times*, April 22, 1980. ProQuest Historical Newspapers: New York Times.

Boswell, Thomas D., and James R. Curtis. *The Cuban American Experience: Culture, Images, and Perspectives*. Totowa, N.J.: Rowman and Allanheld, 1983.

Castro, Fidel. "Castro Delivers Speech at May Day Rally." May 1, 1980. Latin American Network Information Center. Castro Speech Data Base. http://lanic.utexas.edu/project/castro/db/1980/19800501-1.html.

———. "Castro Stresses Women's Equal Rights at FMC Congress." March 8, 1980. Latin American Network Information Center. Castro Speech Data Base. http://lanic.utexas.edu/project/castro/db/1980/19800308.html.

Church, George J. "The Welcome Wears Thin." *Time*, September 1, 1980. http://content.time.com/time/magazine/article/0,9171,922111,00.html.

Clark, Juan M. *Cuba: Mito y Realidad*. Miami: Saeta Ediciones, 1992.

Clark, Juan M., Jose I. Lasaga, and Rose S. Reque, with the collaboration of Beatriz Reed and Eduardo Dieppa. *The 1980 Mariel Exodus: An Assessment and Prospect.* Washington, D.C.: Council for Inter-American Security, 1981.

Clary, Mike. "They Seized the Moment and Came to America." *Los Angeles Times,* May 29, 1990. http://search.proquest.com/docview/281062556?acc ountid=41655.

Coltman, Leycester. *The Real Fidel Castro.* New Haven, Conn.: Yale University Press, 2003.

Crewdson, John M. "Hundreds in Boats, Defying U.S., Sail for Cuba to Pick Up Refugees." *New York Times,* April 25, 1980. ProQuest Historical Newspapers: New York Times.

"Cuba Bars Refugee Flights to Costa Rican Staging Area." *New York Times,* April 19, 1980. ProQuest Historical Newspapers: New York Times.

"Cuba: Fleeing From Fidel's Rule." *Time,* April 21, 1980. http://content.time. com/time/magazine/article/0,9171,924008,00.html.

"Cuba's Boat People—Dilemma for Carter." *U.S. News and World Report,* May 5, 1980.

"Cuba: Start of a Mass Exodus." *Time,* April 28, 1980. http://content.time.com/ time/magazine/article/0,9171,924055,00.html.

Domínguez, Jorge. "Cooperating with the Enemy? U.S. Immigration Policies toward Cuba." In *Western Hemisphere Immigration and United States Foreign Policy,* edited by Christopher Mitchell, 31–88. University Park: Penn State University Press, 1992.

"Exodus Goes On." *Time,* June 2, 1980. http://content.time.com/time/magazine/article/0,9171,924147,00.html.

Engstrom, David W. *Presidential Decision Making Adrift: The Carter Administration and the Mariel Boatlift.* Lanham, Md.: Rowman and Littlefield, 1997.

Fernandez, Gaston A. "The Flotilla Entrants: Are They Different?" *Cuban Studies* 12 (January 1982): 49–54.

———. *The Mariel Exodus: Twenty Years Later.* Miami: Ediciones Universal, 2002.

García, José M. *Voices from Mariel.* DVD. Directed by Jim Carleton. Lakeland and Tampa: NFocus Pictures, 2011.

García, María Cristina. *Havana USA: Cuban Exiles and Cuban Americans in South Florida, 1959–1994.* Berkeley: University of California Press, 1996.

Geyer, Georgie Anne. *Guerrilla Prince: The Untold Story of Fidel Castro.* Boston: Little, Brown and Company, 1991.

González-Pando, Miguel. *The Cuban Americans.* The New Americans Series. Westport, Conn.: Greenwood Press, 1998.

Gott, Richard. *Cuba: A New History.* New Haven: Yale University Press, 2004.

Hamm, Mark S. *The Abandoned Ones: The Imprisonment and Uprising of the Mariel Boat People.* Boston: Northeastern University Press, 1995.

"Havana Removes Guard from Peruvian Embassy." *New York Times,* April 5, 1980. ProQuest Historical Newspapers: New York Times.

Hawk, Kate Dupes, Ron Villella, and Adolfo Leyva de Varona. *Florida and the Mariel Boatlift of 1980: The First Twenty Days.* Tuscaloosa: University of Alabama Press, 2014.

Holman, Philip A. "Refugee Resettlement in the United States." In *Refugees in America in the 1990s: A Reference Handbook,* edited by David W. Haines, 3–27. Westport, Conn.: Greenwood Press, 1996.

"Impatient for Freedom." *Time,* June 16, 1980. http://content.time.com/time/magazine/article/0,9171,924198,00.html.

Lang, John S., with Joseph L. Galloway, Linda K. Lanier, and Gordon M. Bock. "Castro's 'Crime Bomb' Inside U.S." *U.S. News and World Report,* January 16, 1984.

Larzelere, Alex. *Castro's Ploy—America's Dilemma: The 1980 Cuban Boatlift.* Washington, D.C.: National Defense University Press, 1988.

Laytner, Ron. "Timeless Feature—The Mariel Boatlift." *Edit International,* 1980, copy in author's possession.

Llanes, José. *Cuban Americans: Masters of Survival.* Cambridge, Mass.: Abt Books, 1982.

Masud-Piloto, Felix Roberto. *From Welcomed Exiles to Illegal Immigrants: Cuban Migration to the U.S., 1959–1995.* Lanham, Md.: Rowman and Littlefield, 1996.

Mesa-Lago, Carmelo. *Cuba in the 1970s: Pragmatism and Institutionalization.* Albuquerque: University of New Mexico Press, 1978.

Morató, Enrique G. "El Sueño de la Calabaza: 30 años del Mariel." *El Balsero Suicida,* May–June, 1996. https://gilbertogutierrez.wordpress.com/cuentos-y-estampas/el-sueno-de-la-calabaza/.

Nelson, Lowry. *Cuba: The Measure of a Revolution.* Minneapolis: University of Minnesota Press, 1972.

O'Connor, Colleen, with Ginny Carroll. "Men without a Country." *Newsweek,* June 9, 1986, 28.

Ojito, Mirta. *Finding Mañana: A Memoir of a Cuban Exodus.* New York: Penguin Books, 2005.

———. "The Long Voyage from Mariel Ends." *New York Times,* January 16, 2005. http://www.nytimes.com/2005/01/16/weekinreview/the-long-voyage-from-mariel-ends.html.

"Open Heart, Open Arms." *Time,* May 19, 1980. http://content.time.com/time/magazine/article/0,9171,924093,00.html.

Pedraza, Silvia. *Political Disaffection in Cuba's Revolution and Exodus.* Cambridge: Cambridge University Press, 2007.

"Refugees: Voyage from Cuba." *Time,* May 5, 1980.

Rivera, Mario Antonio. *Decision and Structure: U.S. Refugee Policy in the Mariel Crisis.* Lanham, Md.: University Press of America, 1991.

Santiago, Fabiola. "Flowing from Mariel." *Miami Herald,* April 17, 2005. Cubanet.org, http://www.cubanet.org/htdocs/CNews/y05/apr05/19e7.htm.

Schmidt, William E. "Judge Reasserts Right of Cubans to Get Hearing." *New York Times,* January 1, 1985.

Schumacher, Edward. "Misery and Merriment Are Filling Nights in Havana for the U.S. Kin." *New York Times,* May 9, 1980. ProQuest Historical Newspapers: New York Times.

Smith, Vern E. "In the Flotilla at Mariel." *Newsweek,* May 12, 1980, 63.

Smith, Wayne S. *The Closest of Enemies: A Personal and Diplomatic Account of U.S.-Cuban Relations since 1957.* New York: W. W. Norton, 1987.

Thomas, Hugh. *Cuba: The Pursuit of Freedom.* New York: Harper and Row Publishers, 1971.

Thomas, Jo. "Behind Barred Doors in Havana, Would-Be Emigrés Wait in Fear." *New York Times,* May 2, 1980. ProQuest Historical Newspapers: New York Times.

———. "Marchers Rally Round Cuba, Castro, Communism." *New York Times,* April 20, 1980. ProQuest Historical Newspapers: New York Times.

Triay, Victor. *Bay of Pigs: An Oral History of Brigade 2506.* Gainesville: University Press of Florida, 2001.

———. *Fleeing Castro: Operation Pedro Pan and the Cuban Children's Program.* Gainesville: University Press of Florida, 1998.

Unzueta, Silvia M. *The Mariel Exodus: A Year in Retrospect.* Miami: Metropolitan Dade County Government Office of the County Manager, 1981. From: Cuban Information Archives, Document 0033. http://cuban-exile.com/doc_026-050/doc0033.html.

Williams, Dennis A., with Jerry Buckley, Vern E. Smith, and Jane Whitmore. "Cuban Tide Is a Flood." *Newsweek,* May 19, 1980, 28.

Williams, Dennis A., with Frank Maier, Susan Agrest, Ronald Henkoff, and Mary Lord. "The Cuban Conundrum." *Newsweek,* September 29, 1980, 30.

Index

VICTOR ANDRES TRIAY, professor of history at Middlesex Community College in Middletown, Connecticut, is the author of *Fleeing Castro: Operation Pedro Pan and the Cuban Children's Program*; *Bay of Pigs: An Oral History of Brigade 2506*; *La Patria Nos Espera: La Invasión de Bahía de Cochinos Relatada en las Palabras de la Brigada de Asalto 2506* (Spanish version of *Bay of Pigs: An Oral History of Brigade 2506*); *The Cuban Revolution: Years of Promise*; and the historical fiction trilogy *The Unbroken Circle*. He was the lead researcher for Florida International University's Brigade 2506 oral history project in 2016 and 2017. Triay, whose parents left Cuba in 1960, was born and raised in Miami, Florida.